Tribal Development Since Independence

About the Editor

S.N. Chaudhary, Professor of Sociology, is currently Rajiv Gandhi Chair Professor at Barkatullah University, Bhopal. He is a former fellow of A.N. Sinha Institute, Patna, Indian Institute of Advanced Study, Shimla and SMH, Paris. He has conducted fieldwork among Red Indians in Canada. He has completed and edited 23 books and published 50 research articles. He has produced 23 Ph. Ds. Currently he is working on Tribal Development, Tribal Indebtedness, Primitive Tribe and Impact of Technology on Society.

Tribal Development Since Independence

S.N. Chaudhary

CONCEPT PUBLISHING COMPANY, NEW DELHI-110059

ISBN : 13-978-81-8069-622-0 **ISBN : 10-81-8069-622-7**

First Published 2009

Published and Printed by

Since 1974

Concept Publishing Company

Regd. Office:

A/15-16, Commercial Block, Mohan Garden
New Delhi-110059 (India)
Phones : 25351460, 25351794, *Fax* : 091-11-25357109
Email : publishing@conceptpub.com,
website: www.conceptpub.com

Editorial Office:

H-13, Bali Nagar, New Delhi-110 015, India.

Cataloging in Publication Data--*Courtesy:* D.K. Agencies (P) Ltd. <docinfo@dkagencies.com>

National Seminar on Tribal Development (2008 : Bhopal, India)
Tribal development since independence / [edited by] S.N. Chaudhary.
p. cm.
Papers presented at the National Seminar on Tribal Development, held at Bhopal in March 2008.
Includes bibliographical references and index.
ISBN 13: 9788180696220 ISBN 10: 8180696227

1. India--Scheduled tribes--Social conditions--Congresses. 2. India Scheduled tribes--Economic conditions--Congresses. 3. India-Scheduled tribes--Government policy--Congresses. I. Chaudhary, S. N. (Shyam Nandan), 1954- II. Title.

DDC 305.5680954 22

Foreword

Since times immemorial Scheduled Tribes have been an integral part of Indian society. Unarguably they are one of the earliest inhabitants of our country. As we know, they are spread all over the expanse of India in several varied groups, each displaying a distinct socio-cultural identity. The scholars place them under 250 tribal groups speaking more than 300 fascinating intermix of languages and dialects. Though seemingly diverse and different, a stream of similarity runs through this diverse conglomeration of differing life styles. What brings them into a composite one is the thought that they remind how all this began. All this which we call civilization.

Times have moved on. So have societies and countries. The Schedule Tribes, wherever they are, have remained where they were. In fact they and their lives continue to be untouched and unconcerned by all the overwhelming forces of change that are making everything into new. This changelessness is indisputably the one characteristic that all these groups have. A trait that gains strength and meaning from their ecological and soeio-cultural environment.

We have compelled ourselves to believe that these tribal societies need to get into the mainstream. The mainstream is what we have defined as per our perception of social change and development. In the light of this, scholars and government generally think that the tribal societies should not remain away from the mainstream of development. Development is like the blind men's elephant. It means different things to different people. In this nebulous territory of development; it needs to be carefully articulated what development means for these enduring tribal societies. Should it turn them around into carbon copies of the non-tribal groups or should it be a process in which their pristine elements of life are carefully preserved and continued along with the new. All this is a very complex process—a complex process for an inordinately simple people.

This process has inherent contradictions and multi-dimensional opening for churning of ideas, opinions, interpretations, differences and disputes. The two days National Seminar on Tribal Development organized by the Rajiv Gandhi Chair in Contemporary Studies, Barkatullah University, Bhopal towards the end of March 2008 followed this pattern of an exciting churning of ideas. Present volume is an outcome of this precious process. As was natural, the Seminar reflected the variety of vision that dominates all discussions on Tribal Development. Purpose of publication of this volume is to disseminate the deliberations of the Seminar. I hope this volume will be useful for students of tribal studies, government and civil societies working for the cause of tribal development.

I congratulate, Prof. S.N. Chaudhary for editing this volume in a short span of time.

BHUPAL SINGH
Vice Chancellor
Barkatullah University
Bhopal

Preface

Issues, dimensions and strategies pertaining to tribal development have drawn attention of different stakeholders. State is one among these. And it is most powerful instrument of change among them. Nature of change whether caused by state or other intervention is both positive and negative or sociologically speaking functional and dysfunctional from the point of view of fulfilment of their basic needs, storation or restoration of their human rights and attainment of the state of empowerment. In other words, if we examine tribal development in relation to these three objectives the picture is mixed, i.e. rosy as well as alarming. While it is rosy and selective in some cases and areas, it is frustating and alarming in many other areas.

This volume is an outcome of two days National Seminars on Tribal Development organized by Rajiv Gandhi Chair is Contemporary Studies. Purpose of the seminar was to examine tribals socio-economic status today. It also aimed to examine functioning of tribal development projects, search and suggest mechanisms, under the existing framework, to translate their alarming state of affairs into joy and development. In course of organising the seminar we have received support and cooperation from different corners.

At the outset we are thankful to Shri Bhupal Singh, Vice-chancellor, Barkatullah University, Bhopal for his guidance and cooperation in the organization of this seminar. He was also kind enough to write foreword of this volume.

Porf. Yogesh Atal, Professor Sachchidananda and Prof. Samrendra Saraf delivered keynote address, First Rajiv Gandhi Memorial Lecture and Valedictory speech respectively. I am obliged and indebted to them.

Scholars from different parts of the country participated and presented papers in the seminar. Many of the resubmitted revised version of papers. I am thankful to all of them. I am sorry that due to one or another resesons several important papers were not included in this volume. Last but not the least I am thankful to the faculty of Sociology, Registrar Dr. Sanjay P. Tiwari and Deputy Registrar (Deve.) Shri Anand Kamble of the University and the fellows and staffs working under Rajiv Gandhi Chair for their cooperation in successful conduction of the seminar.

Bhopal **S.N. Chaudhary**

Contents

About the Contributors

Prof. Yogesh Atal

Distinguished Professor of Sociology and Social Anthropology. Currently he is settled at Gurgaon (Haryana)

Prof. Sachchidanand

Well known sociologist and social anthropologist. He is based at Patna (Bihar)

Prof. D.C. Sah

Professor of Economic and Director, Madhya Pradesh Institute of Social Science Research, Ujjain (M.P.)

Prof. S.N. Tripathy

Professor of Economics at Gokhale Institute of Politics and Economics, Pune (Maharashtra)

Prof.Permananda Panda

Professor of Anthropology, Sambalpur University, Sambalpur, (Orissa)

Dr. H. Samanataraya

Faculty member, associated with Sambalpur University (Orissa)

Prof. Jitendra Prasad

Professor of Sociology at M.D. University, Rohtak (Haryana)

Prof. J.J. Roy Burman

Professor of Sociology and Social Anthropology at Tata Institute of Social Sciences, Mumbai (Maharashtra)

Prof. Y.G. Joshi

Former Dean (Academics), Dr. Babasaheb Ambedkar National Institute of Social Science, Mhow (M.P.)

Prof. D.K. Verma

Head, Division of SC, ST and OBC Development, Dr. Babasaheb Ambedkar National Institute of Social Science, Mhow (M.P.)

A. Sohrot

Research Associate, Dr. B.R. Ambedkar National Institute of Social Science, Mhow (M.P.)

Dr. Debasis Debnath

Associate Professor, Indian Institute of Forest Management, Bhopal (M.P.)

Dr. Yatindra Singh Sisodia

Senior Fellow, Madhya Pradesh Institute of Social Science Research, Ujjain (M.P.)

R.S. Shrivastava

Additional Director (Retd.) Tribal and SC Welfare Department, Government of M.P., Bhopal (M.P.)

Tapas Kumar Dalapati

Fellow at Madhya Pradesh Institute of Social Science Research, Ujjain (M.P.)

Prof. Gaya Pandey

P.G. Department of Anthropology, Ranchi University, Ranchi (Jharkhand)

V.K. Srivastava

Director (Retd.) SC and ST Commission, Government of India, Bhopal (M.P.)

Shailendra Prasad Sinha

P.G. Department of Anthropology, Ranchi University, Ranchi (Jharkhand)

Vishal Massey

Research Scholar, Department of Sociology, Barkatullah University, Bhopal (M.P.)

Asha Shukla

Director, Women's Studies Centre, Barkatullah University, Bhopal (M.P.)

Jaya Phookan

Research Officer, Women's Studies Centre, Barkatullah University, Bhopal (M.P.)

Tripti Singhai

JRF, SAH Bangalore (Karnataka)

1 Introduction

S.N. Chaudhary

I

Broadly speaking there are two perspectives to comprehend conceptual dimensions of tribe. These are the constitutional perspective and social scientists perspective. According to former all those categories and clusters of population, no matter at what level of development they are, where do they reside and to what extent they carry tribal culture and ways of life, but whose name have been listed under Article 342 and the list is always increasing, they all are called scheduled tribes. In contrary to this a significant number of social scientists have conceptualized tribe on the basis of its structural and cultural features. According to them the ideal type attributes of tribe is that it is a group of families with having a distinct name, language or dialect, common territory, common taboos, common occupation, common culture and reciprocal relationship. In other words, although there is no agreement on the features of tribe but most of the social scientists agree that there is relative communality among them in terms of occupation, language, reciprocal relations and territory (Beteille, 1986; Singh, 1991; Xaxa, 1999). Conceptual dimensions of tribes in the current context was also discussed in the seminar.

If we see the tribal situation today especially from

attributional point of view the picture is radically different. Many of their attributes are now the thing of the past. Actually there is now wide gap between the "field view" and the "book view". There are large number of tribal population who are the victims of civilization. Many of them have significantly lost their religion and languages or dialects. Some of the broad factors which have either in isolation or in combination with other factors brought assimilative or degenerative variety of change in their both material and non-material culture are culture contact, impact of Hinduism and Christianity, Forest Acts of 1865 onwards, industrialization and urbanization, erosion of forests and migration, development projects, Constitution of India, social movements, NGO intervention, individualism and expansion of consumer culture including globalization and so on. Seminar examined tribes in relation to these causative factors.

From development point of view especially from the view point of improvement in their physical and social quality of life how and to what extent these interventions and exposure to outside world have impacted tribals is a matter of debate because in terms of economic development neither all are hunter and gatherer nor all are employed in secondary sector. The reality is that some of them are even today called as "primitive tribe" but some tribes have state and national level leadership. Significant number of elites among Santhal and Oraon tribes of Jharkand and Chhattisgarh and lack of elites among Bharia, Baiga and Saharia primitive tribes of Madhya Pradesh is an example (Chaudhary and Singh, 2006). But it is beyond doubt that now many of the tribal groups are the victim of cultural degeneration. And because of being the victim of cultural degeneration and encroachment they have paid price in social, economic, health and environmental terms. The degeneration of forests, which is primarily led by the state and the lopsided process of modernization, have forced many of them to move towards insecurity and dependence zone resulting thereby negative impact on health and education and *vice versa*. Industrialization have contributed to national development but land alienation, environmental degradation and social disorganization among them. Sachchidananda and Mandal (1985) with reference to a section of tribes of Chhotanagpur rightly observed that industrialization has led to landlessness, alcoholism, beggary and so on among them. Hardly few of the tribals who were already relatively betterly placed in socio-economic ladder have gained out of industrialization process.

If we examine their status from both empowerment and human rights point of view here also the picture seems significantly frustrating. Besides being the victim of land alienation since the British days they are the victims of poverty and indebtedness, bonded labour, housing, quality education, alcoholism, communication, unemployment, disease and illness, malnutrition, migration and decreasing condition of local resources and their access to these resources and mega development projects.

If we examine roots of poverty among tribals it seems that not by accident they are poor. They have been systematically deprived of their lands, homes and livelihood by the state since the British days. Following two observations made by Hutton (1931) and Ghurya (1999) support the above argument.

According to Hutton (op.cit.): "Far from being of immediate benefit to the primitive tribes, the establishment of British Rule in India did most of them much more harm than good.... It may be said that the early days of British Administration did very great detriment to the economic position of tribes through ignorance and neglect of their rights and customs .... many changes have been caused incidentally by the penetration of the tribal country, the opening up of communications, the protection of forests and the establishment of schools, to say nothing of the openings given in this way to Christian Missions. Many of the results of these changes have caused acute discomfort to the tribes."

According to Ghuriya (op.cit.) : "The acuteness of discomfort was very aften so great that it led to apathy, indifference, moral deterioration and even a decline in population."

In order to address these and many other problems number of efforts have been made. Constitution of India has reformulated different laws to protect and promote their concerns. Such provisions are broadly of four types. These are : (1) *Protective Provisions* (Articles 15, 16, 19, 23, 29, 46, 164, 330, 332, 335, 338, 339, 342, and 371). (2) *Developmental* (Articles 15, 16, 19, 46, 275, and 399). (3) *Administrative* (Article 344 for fifth scheduled areas. It covers 2.5 million tribes of different states and 6th schedule for north-east states under Articles 338 and 339). (4) *Reservation* (Articles 330, 332, 334, 335, 340, for reservation in Parliament/state assemblies/government jobs and admission).

To actualize these provisions and Articles of Constitution of India number of development projects are in progress among tribes across the nation. Important among these are IRDP, NREP, NRLEGP, TRYSEM, JRY, SHG, IAY, JY, DPAP, IWLDP, NRY, SEEUY, SJGSY, AY, National Old Age Pension Scheme, ICDS, INHP, Literacy Mission, Watershed Mission, Sarva Shiksha Abhiyan, Pre- and Post-Matric Scholarship, Ashram School, Tendu Patta Policy, Employment Guarantee Scheme and so on. The role of tribal culture and heritage, *Jhola Chap* doctor, Primary Health Centres, NGOs dealing with health issues all needs critical assessment not only to know its functioning but also to restructure these schemes in the light of the ongoing socio-economic scenario (Fernandes, Menon and Viegas, 1988; Upadhyay and Pandey, 2003; Sharma, 1976;

Vidyarthi, 1980; Shukla, 1998; Singh, Pandey and Singh, 1998; Sah and Bhatt, 2004; Chaudhary, 2004). Focus of the seminar was to discuss structure and functioning of these schemes and its problems from the point of view of empowerment of tribes and to search mechanisms for the effective functioning of these schemes under the given socio-political context which is partly democratic and partly not. Also, there are number of NGOs engaged in capacity building and overall development of tribes. Philanthropic intervention is also active in some areas. Further, number of tribal social movements are going on for the protection of their human rights particularly from the local money lenders, globalization forces and trauma of state run major development projects (Sengupta, 1988). Narmada Bachao Andolan is an example. Naxalite movement is also active in some tribal areas in Jharkhand, Orissa, M.P., A.P and Chhattisgarh. The role of tribal culture, particularly their indigenous knowledge and other crisis and dispute management techniques are historically very effective in this context. But how and to what extent these century old practices are effective and functional today? What is the perception of tribal youth about these issues today? How emerging tribal elites perceive and react to the challenges experienced by tribal masses? These issues were also discussed in the seminar.

Also, today one can see the impact of globalization process. However, in most of the studies negative impact of globalization especially on tribes have drawn attention. The positive impact of globalization if any, especially in sociological terms is yet to be traced and documented. Seminar discussed interface between globalization and cross section of tribes from the point of view of gains and pains of the latter (Chaudhary, 2005). There is need to examine, from the point of view of empowerment of tribes, their participation in Panchayats and impact of Panchayat on their socio-economic and political development (Chaudhary, 2004, 2005).

These were some of the broad issues which were debated in different technical sessions in the seminar.

Broad objective of the seminar was:

- To examine socio-economic, educational and health status of Scheduled Tribes today in relation to the intervention of state, civil societies, globalization, decentralization process and the local initiatives,
- To identify factors and conditions, both historical and contextual, which contribute to/hinder the development process, and
- To search and suggest possibilities of effective functioning of these and similar other interventions which may suit to the changing socio-economic context in the tribal society.

Themes and Sub-themes of the seminar were as under:

- Social, economic and health status of tribes: Post-independence scenario;
- Impact of Constitution of India, State run development projects, civil society organizations and social movements on cross-section of tribes;
- Participation of cross-section of tribes in these interventions;
- Impact of outmigration and indigenous knowledge on socio-economic status of tribes;
- Impact of globalization, consumer culture and new panchayati raj on quality of life of tribes;
- Tribal situation tomorrow: Agenda for Action for all the change agents.

II

Many articles were presented in the seminar. It was not possible for us to include all the papers in this volume. Gist of the papers covered in this volume are as under :

> Yogesh Atal, in his inaugural address, dealt with the old debate of isolation *versus* integration strategy of tribal development, attributes of tribes, Gurjar controvercy for its inclusion in the category of ST in Rajasthan, constitutional dimension of tribe and views of different commissions on tribes and their status. Finally, Atal remarked that beside formulating geographical area specific development schemes and prioritising development agenda which may address poverty and illiteracy among them, the development policy should also promote connectivity, both social and technical, for development of tribes in a sustainable manner.

Sachchidananda in his first Rajiv Gandhi Memorial Lecture, explained miseries of tribal development schemes over the time. He discussed constitutional provisions and state run development schemes. But he accused all these interventions for being imposed from above. These interventions lack spirit and participation from the below. He also explained 73rd constitutional measure as a corrective mechanism. He highlighted dysfunctional or non-functional dimensions of tribal development schemes. Finally, he explained some specific challenges and suggested mechanisms to deal with these challenges in the wider interest of tribals. He also advised formation of a commission for tribal development under the Chair of a tall and socially legitimate tribal leader.

D.C. Sah discussed politics of development. He explained

the role of culture, institutional forces, social capital formation among non-influentials, the local influential etc; in the ongoing process of tribal and rural development which is destruction-ridden and which promote protest. Finally, he argued in favour of translation of social and cultural capital into political capital for inclusive, holistic and sustainable development of tribals. To him once tribals are politically capacitated and articulated their problems will occupy front seat for its management.

S.N. Tripathy dealt with socio-economic impact of watershed project in a region of Orissa. To him water scarcity in the area under study is primarily due to mining and industrialisation. It has adversely affected tribals economically, socially and ecologically. Hence, to address these problems he pleads for an integrated management of land, water and other resources looking into dynamic concerns of locals. He strongly warned that management of water in isolation cannot deal with water problem. Holistic approach is the need of the hour.

Permananda Panda and H. Samanataraya explained the process of involuntary displacement of tribals from their domain in favour of mega and nation centric development project. They also explained the role of protest of different stakeholders in this context. Finally, the paper offers a sustainable alternative using the transactional model in this era of politics of imbalance.

Jitendra Prasad expressed that the structure of exploitation which existed during colonial period among santhals of erstwhile Santhal Pargana has acquired a new form today. The process of globalisation has contributed to the ongoing process of exploitation. National Rural Employment Guarantee Scheme (NREGS) as an example is the victim of corruption. The emergence of tribal elites and apathy among them, especially while dealing with tribal problems, have also adversely affected the process of mass mobilisation and protest for which Santhals are historically known. To him there is no difference between the old and the new leadership in dealing with problems of tribals.

Paper of J.J. Roy Burman deals with the formulation and functioning of Autonomous District Councils (ADCs) in the mitigation of the problem of alienation and marginalisation among the people of North East India. As per the paper ADC is not effective and functional enough to stop the process of alienation. The paper also question the logic of population size in the determination of parliamentary constituency. To him geographical area and its size should also be a determinant of constituency. Finally, as a coping mechanism, the paper pleads for introduction of sixth schedule throughout the NE states as it is functioning in Manipur.

Paper of Y.G. Joshi examined the ongoing socio-economic transformation among Bhil tribe of Jhabua. According to him Bhils are rapidly experiencing change due to multiple causative factors like increasing income, increasing amount of awareness due to different factors, decreasing crime, increasing process of assimilation and creation of separate identities. This process has its impact on socio-economic status of tribals.

D.K. Verma examined the question of food security among tribals. He dealt with different dimensions involved in food security. Finally, the paper suggest livelihood options for tribals. To him it is possible provided tribal development policy is reoriented ensuring expanded livelihood resource base as an alternative option for food and enchanced capability of food *absorption*?

Paper of D. Debnath explained features of Forest Right Act, 2006 in realation to the forest dwellers especially tribals. The paper dealt with 5 specific promises of the Act. Debnath apprehends that under the given context when there is mass encroachment of forest land coupled with number of historical constraints how the act will be effective and functional is a matter of concern.

Paper of Y.S. Sisodia dealt with functioning of *Panchayati Raj* at the grassroots in the tribal belt of Western Madhya Pradesh. He examined M.P. *Panchayat Raj Adhiniyam,* 1993, Panchayat (Extension to the scheduled Areas) Act, 1996 and M.P. Panchayat Raj (*Devitiya Sansodhan)* Adhiniyam, 1997. To author the Panchayat of Scheduled areas in M.P., on the one hand, have the first taste of democratic decentralisation and on the other hand theoretically it is able to protect and safeguard their cultural identity, tradition and customs.

Paper of R.S. Shrivastava explored dysfunctional consequences of globalisation and consumer culture on tribes. New Panchayati Raj System was a ray of hope to mitigate many of their problems, including problems created by globalisation but it is totally failed to deal with such problems. The net result of such intervention is continuation of their exploitation and marginalisation. The paper also provide some suggestions to deal with these challenges.

T.K. Dalpati outlined problems of scheduled tribes in the historical perspective. To him after prolonged injustice by introducing the Scheduled Tribes and other Traditional Forest Dwellers (Reorganisation of Forest Rights) Rules, 2007, the government is trying to deal with tribal's problems. He also explained the process of tribal's exploitation by providing case study of Kondh tribe of Kalahandi district of Orissa.

According to Gaya Pandey today layers among STs are more obvious incomparison to the past. There is inequality among them. This shows that development initiatives have reached to them disproportionately. It reflects that for development purpose putting all tribal population together under one category has proved wrong. As per his suggestion today there is need to rethink over the package of development and safeguard. There is need to think and act for the left out tribal population independently.

V.K. Srivastava's paper examined tribal situation in the historical perspective. To him there are large number of development measures meant for tribals. But the output is selective. Tribal masses are failed to avail benefits of development. He lamented that of course literacy rate among them have increased but gap between them and the general population is also widening. Persistence of indebtedness among them reflect both poverty and wider economic malaise.

Asha Shukla, Jaya Phooken and Tripti Singhai examined functioning and achievement of Kasturba Gandhi Balika Vidyalaya in the promotion of literacy and education among tribal girls residing in certain areas of tribal dominated Jhabua district of M.P. Authors have specifically examined status and functioning of residential facilities, infrastructure and other initiatives in the attainment of main objective of the scheme.

On the basis of these field and data based empirical articles it seems that fruits of development have reached to tribals differently depending upon their socio-economic status, exposure to the outside world and area of their habitation. This calls for, besides honest implementation of the existing development schemes, formulation of tribewise specific scheme. Globalisation process is dysfunctional for them. New initiatives like 73rd Consitutional Amendment, Forest Right Bill etc. are still to show its impact. Under the given situation when the model of development is capitalistic it is different to achieve socialistic goal like tribal development. How is it possible? Present volume is an attempt to search answer of this historical question.

REFERENCES

Beteille, A. (1986) : "The Concept of Tribe with Special reference to India;" *Arch. Europ Social.* Vol. XXVII.

Chaudhary, S. N. and R. P. Singh (2006) : *Tribes of Pachmarhi Biosphere*

Reserve and Their Indigenous Knowledge, Bhopal : Indira Gandhi National Museum of Men.

Fernandes W., G. Menon and P. Viegas (1988) : *Forest Environment and Tribal Economy : Deforestation, Impoverishment and Marginalisation in Orissa,* New Delhi : Indian Social Institute.

Ghurya, G. S. (1999): *The Scheduled Tribes,* Bombay: Papular, (Second edition).

Hutton, J.H. (1931): *Census of India,* Delhi: Gian.

Sachchidananda and B. B. Mandal (1985) : *Industrialization and Social Disorganization : A Study of Tribes in Bihar*; Delhi : Concept.

Sah, D. C. and A. Bhatt (2004) : "Health and Education in Remote Tribal Areas : Evidence from Southwestern Tribals of M.P.," *Madhya Pradesh Journal of Social Sciences*; Vol. 9, No. 2.

Sengupta, N. (1988) : "Reappearing Tribal Movement," *EPW*, 6th May.

Sharma, B. D. (1976) : *Tribal Development : Conceptual Frame,* Bhopal : TRI.

Shukla, R. K. (1998) : *Forestry for Tribal Development,* New Delhi.

Singh, K. S. (1991) : "Trbial Perspectives-1969-1990," *Continuity and Change in Tribal Society,* (ed.) Mrinal Miri, Shimla : IIAS.

Singh, A. K., Gaya Pandey and P.K. Singh (1998) : *Forest and Tribals,* New Delhi : Classical Publishing House.

Upadhyay, V. S. and G. Pandey (2003) : *Tribal Development in India,* Ranchi, Crown.

Vidyarthi, L.P. (1980) : *Tribal Development and Its Administration,* Delhi : Concept.

Xaxa, V. (1999) : "Transformation of Tribes in India : Terms of Discourse," *EPW,* pp. 1519-1524.

2 Inaugural Address

Yogesh Atal

More than sixty years after independence, and with a history of major development efforts at the state level carried out to change the socio-economic profile of the country, it is perhaps useful to look back and take stock of our achievements and failures. Our country being predominantly rural – both in terms of our population residing in rural areas and our economy being mainly agricultural – it was natural that our planners and policy makers gave priority to rural and tribal development. While important strides have been made towards urbanization and industrialization, India still continues to be primarily rural, and population projections suggest that more than half of our population is going to be rural even after crossing the first-half of the 21st century.

I believe it is this context that gives significance to this Seminar. I am hopeful that the deliberations here would not just be the rehash of what we already know about our development experience – the inadequacies and the frustrations – but would help develop guidelines for a new blueprint for future action.

I have carefully studied the guidelines prepared for this Seminar. It appears from the Note that the organisers are interested in (i) the clarification of some basic conceptual categories, (ii) highlighting the great damage that has been done to our tribal cultures, and (iii) assessing their present socio-economic and health status. This is the order in which the concerns have been expressed in the Guidelines. However, the under current in the entire Note is that of dissatisfaction with the development strategy which, according to the organizers, has done a good deal of damage to the tribals.

Despite this, I detect some sort of ambivalence regarding development in the Note : it seems that while the need for development is not denied the organizers appear to be unhappy with the consequences that development has caused.

I wish to pick up this thread to elaborate my point. The conceptual issue that the organizers have raised relates to the definition of the word "Tribe", but the concerns that are expressed in the subsequent paragraphs relate to the word "Development". I shall dwell upon both the conceptual categories, but reverse the order. First, let me talk about the concept of "Development". The Outline supplied by the organizers for this Seminar does not suggest a definition of this concept, nor does it refute any of the prevailing definitions. It has provided a long list of adverse consequences of development which are summed up in one phrase : *Cultural Degeneration*. The tribals are described as "victims of civilization" who have lost their religion and their dialects; who now suffer from landlessness and alcoholism which has forced them to beggary. And all this has been caused by culture contact, impact of Hinduism and Christianity, Forest Acts of 1865, migration, industrialization and urbanization, development projects, NGO intervention, consumer culture, and advancing globalization. It gives an impression that development has done nothing positive. As if the development efforts have further worsened the life of the tribals. Implicit in it seems to be the plea that the process needs to be halted almost instantly.

Such a characterization makes an interesting copy for a political statement, but makes one wonder as to what kind of future do we envisage for our tribal brethren.

What do we mean by development? The very fact that the development exercise is an *exogenous effort* to bring about culture change, and what we are doing here is also an *outsider review*, can we talk of insulation from culture contact? Or, are we advocating complete stoppage of any outside influence and a return for the primitive to his pristine purity? If we are concerned about his health, his poverty, and his limited worldview and wish to provide him with better nutrition and Medicare, improved means of earning a livelihood, and widened cognitive horizons, how do we do it? Do we still wish to keep him in the proverbial "Anthropological Zoo"? Is the tribal leading an idyllic life style worthy of our emulation? Or do we intend to bring him out of poverty, and of isolated existence? Should the tribal be deprived of the fruits of modern civilization, of advancements in science and technology? Should he remain where he has remained all through, or need we help him develop empathy to relate himself with the wider world?

When one turns to the other concern – namely their current status – one finds that the backward condition of the tribals is the worrying factor. Perhaps here one finds the hidden allegation that development has not reached its target audience. Taken seriously, this complaint signifies a demand for development. It says that despite so many years of development, there are still pockets of underdevelopment. And the Seminar is invited to suggest mechanisms through which such a deficit can be corrected.

Clearly, there is ambivalence regarding development. We detest development and we demand development. There will be no one in this audience who will not wish a better life for the tribals living in remote areas and pursuing a primitive way of life. And yet there will be many amongst us who would also wish to eulogise tribal cultures and the traditional stock of knowledge they possess, advocating not only its preservation but also its promotion.

Some time back I had the opportunity of addressing a similar Seminar held in this very city and the University on Indigenous Knowledge. In that Seminar also I raised a somewhat uncomfortable question as to the purpose of gathering data on Indigenous Knowledge.

The Anthropological Survey of India is now engaged in a massive project on what it calls Traditional Knowledge – TK for short. Since I am also associated with that project let me share the questions that I have posed before the research team in order to have a clear direction.

Any such exercise, to my mind, can be prompted by several considerations.

First, in the 1960s, for example, there was a movement in favour of what was named as *Urgent Anthropology*. The supporters of that movement had argued that we are living in an era of rapid social change under the influence of which there is a real danger of disappearance of not only several cultural traits, but also of many small primitive communities – that may not survive or get submerged into larger entities losing their own identity. The movement, therefore, focused on the "dying" cultural traits and cultural communities and wanted them to be studied and recorded for posterity, and for the professional interest, before it was too late. Not studying them now, they argued, would mean never studying them as they would disappear from the world scene. This genuine concern for recording important aspects of human civilization is understandable. It was motivated by sheer academic interest, and not by any ideology that celebrates the past and the primitive. Work on TK or IK can, thus, be a fulfilment of the objective of Urgent Anthropology.

There can be, secondly, a set of people who sincerely feel that the primitive way of life is ideal and deserves to be preserved. This is what the proponents of Anthropological zoos in fact intended; of course, some alleged that they were more eager to save the subject matter of their study rather than the welfare of the people they studied. This charge was countered by the likes of Verrier Elwin who thought that uncontrolled contacts with the outside world have led to the unfortunate exploitation of the tribals, who were rendered homeless in their own homes. The worry over cultural degeneration expressed in the Seminar outline clearly follows this line of argumentation.

Third, there are others who think that the vast canvas of Human Civilization has been enriched, in a variety of ways, by the multitude of cultures. There is a need, according to them, to give due credit to each society and culture for its contribution, and that learning should not be a one-way process where the tribals are at the receiving end and the so-called modern societies at the giving end. There is much good in the traditional knowledge that can be used for the general good of human society as a whole and should not be neglected simply because of its origin. This may relate to, for example, tribal pharmacopoeia, and even treatment of some ailments. In the general field of agriculture and horticulture, such knowledge may be immense and vastly scattered which needs to be collected and catalogued. It would, however, be wrong to plead that such TK can replace all other modern knowledge, or that modern knowledge has no place in the tribal setting. Acknowledgement of the multiplicity of cultures and, therefore, plurality of the Traditional Knowledge bases should disallow cultural chauvinism. Anthropology's strength has been the emphasis on *cultural relativity*.

We need to come out of the either-or kind of dichotomy.

Let me now turn to the concept of Tribe by briefly alluding to the recent crisis in Rajasthan where one of the castes raised hell to be reclassified as a Tribe. I am referring to the case of the Gujars. In the year 2007, a caste that has been rising upward in the Hindu hierarchy chose to go downhill to be counted amongst the backward groups as it found that the benefits of development are accruing to the tribals, and they have special privileges in the Indian polity which are denied to it because of its "alleged" high status. This incidence refutes to a certain extent the allegation that the benefits of development had not reached the tribals. The Gujar leadership spared no effort to prove that the powerful tribal group of the Meenas in Rajasthan have captured all major positions of power in the government machinery as was indicated by their number in IAS, IPS, and the State public services, in which the number of the Gujars was nearly nil.

Since I had the onerous task of serving on the High-Powered Committee—popularly known as Chopra Committee—appointed by the Government of Rajasthan to examine the claim of the Gujars for a Scheduled Tribe Status I had scanned all official records relative to the definition of the word tribe in the Indian context.

Even anthropologists, for whom tribes had been, a subject matter of study, have not developed a universally acceptable definition of tribe. When societies were classified into civilized and uncivilized – as savage or barbaric – the task was simpler. All uncivilized societies were *preliterate*, meaning thereby the absence of writing. That meant that the transmission of culture was through oral tradition, and the history of the society went as far back as human memory could take it; beyond this was prehistory. With absence of history, oral transmission of society's knowledge pool to the younger generation, elementary technology, and greater dependence on nature for survival, and faith in the supernatural described their way of life. Living in small hordes, and unaware of the world outside the narrow confines of the community, the geographically and socially isolated communities defined themselves as residents of a given territory, and as belonging to a specific racial stock. Such groups became the subject matter of study of the anthropologists who came to these societies as a consequence of colonization. In this sense, tribals were also described as non-Western cultures.

Initially these students of "Other cultures" came to the Non-

Western societies and studied those small groups that were remotely located as "Little Communities", cut-off from civilizational societies and pursuing primitive economic activities in settlements that were cradle-to-the-grave arrangements.[1]

Problems arose when countries like India were colonised. Described as an indigenous civilization, India got divided into the civilized and uncivilized sections, but belonging to the non-Western part of Human Civilization. In India, the original inhabitants got pushed into the remote tribal tracts by the groups that migrated from abroad at different phases of its history – as nomads and pastoralists, as invaders who became conquerors of parts of the vast territory of India. Many such groups who came from the Middle East, Eastern Europe and Mongolia came as adventurers or nomads and gradually got assimilated with the local populace; this involved initial confrontation, accommodation, and finally, integration into the main stream. Historians of the Nineteenth century – mostly foreign, and primarily administrators or military officers of the Raj – called all such migrating groups as tribes – because of their common origin and a distinct identity. But they also acknowledged the process of their gradual assimilation into the Hindu fold.

It is important to note that there is no indigenous word for tribe in any of the Indian languages. In Sanskrit, there is a word *Atavika Jana,* which was used to denote agglomeration of individuals with specific territorial, kinship and cultural pattern. Prior to the colonial period, they were also commonly referred to as a *Jati* – caste. But the Colonial administration began calling them as tribes, and differentiated them from the other groups as animists. In this category, some food gathering groups and shifting cultivators were also included, though they lived closer to the villages. In the censuses they were first called "forest tribes". In the 1931 Census, they were named as "primitive tribes". In 1935, the British began calling them as "backward tribes".

Without questioning the nomenclature, the anthropologists, both foreign and natives, took those groups as subject matter of their study which were officially designated as tribes. It is interesting that in the 1931 Census, which had recorded castes for the last time, had given the listing of the tribes. But even in this Census, the groups that were identified by a distinct tribal name were classified in terms of their religion. Only those that were not converted to any religion – Christianity, Islam, Hinduism, or Jainism – were called Tribals. Let me quote as an instance the Bhils and Minas of Rajasthan. The Bhils were classified into Christian, Hindus, Jains, Muslims and Tribals; similarly, Grassia and Mina were classified into Hindu, Muslim and Tribals. Classified this way, the Tribal Bhils constituted only 23.62 per cent of the total Bhil population in 1931. Among the Minas, the conversion rate was so high that only 3.35 per cent of them remained tribals despite the fact that the total population of both the Bhils and the Minas was more than 6 lakhs. See the following table:

Table 2.1 : Percentage tribals among Bhils, Minas and Grassias

Ethnic group	*Total Population*	*Tribal Segment*	*Per cent Tribal*
Bhil	655,647	198,005	23.62
Grassia	29,231	8,258	24.10
Mina/ Meena	607,369	20,336	3.35

Source: 1931 Census.

The 1931 Census suggests that only 19 per cent of the Bhils were reported as Hindus in the previous Census, conducted in 1921; that percentage rose within 10 years to 70. In case of the Minas the conversion rate was much higher. Both these groups are acknowledged by the Census as "original inhabitants" and yet they were taken out of the tribal category on the basis of their religious affiliation.

Regarding the 1931 Census as the basis for identification of castes and tribes, the Indian government named them in 1948 as *Adivasis*, ignoring the religious distinction of the 1931 Census, and thus increasing their size. When the new Constitution of India was promulgated in 1950, all the Adivasi groups considered as backward tribes were included in the Schedule for special privileges, and thus all groups included in the Schedule were named as Scheduled Tribes.

It must, however, be said that the Constitution of India nowhere defines the word Tribe. Article 342 of the Constitution says just the following:

> The President may with respect to any State or Union territory, and where it is a State, after consultation with the Governor, thereof, by public notification, specify the tribes or tribal communities or part or groups within tribes or tribal communities which shall for the purposes of this Constitution be deemed to be Scheduled Tribes in relation to that State or Union territory, as the case may be.

Article 366(25) defines the Scheduled Tribes as follows :

> "Scheduled Tribe" means such Tribes or Tribal communities or parts of groups within such Tribes or Tribal communities as are deemed under article 342 to be Scheduled Tribe for the purposes of this Constitution.

When the two articles are read in tandem, one discovers the tautological nature of these definitions. Left with such a situation, the Government of India prepared the list of those groups that were identified as tribes in the previous censuses. The 1951 Census listed a total of 212 Scheduled Tribes in India.

But the moment the lists were made public, there were demands from the concerned groups to be included either in the category of Scheduled Tribes or Scheduled Castes. And those who could not be accommodated in either of the categories were provided with a separate category of "Other Backward Classes"; for the later, a separate Commission – Backward Classes Commission was set up under the Chairmanship of Kaka Kalelkar.

Responding to these demands, the lists have been significantly enlarged, and demands continue for additional inclusion. The recent case of the Gujars is a good example of this trend.

As was said before, the Constitution is silent about the definition, but is quite clear on one front, namely the eligibility for entry in the tribal fold. While in case of Scheduled Castes it says that "*the castes, races or tribes, or parts of, or groups within castes, races or tribes*" could be notified for inclusion in the category of scheduled castes, the scope for eligibility in the category of scheduled tribes is limited only to "*the tribes or tribal communities, or part or groups within tribes or tribal communities*". Implicit in the formulation is the point that *only* those groups that were included in the category of tribes in the Census of 1931, and in the following decennial censuses, qualify for inclusion in the category of Scheduled Tribes; no caste can be reclassified as a tribe and yet we find that today the number of Scheduled Tribes in India has crossed the figure of 700, a big jump of over 500 from the 1951 Census. But this number has not increased because of conversion of castes into tribes. It has increased because each state in the Union of India has a right to declare particular groups as tribes. So the subgroups within a major group have now established themselves as separate entities.

Let me quote one instance from Rajasthan. In the 1951 list, only one category of Minas – namely Chowkidar Minas— was included who hailed from southern Rajasthan. As I said earlier, only 3 per cent of the Minas (out of a total of more than 6 lakhs) even in the year 1931 were classified as tribals. But the Meenas raised their demand for inclusion of all categories of Meenas and succeeded in getting the demand fulfilled. It is now alleged that the real tribals amongst this group continue to remain disadvantaged and all benefits have been cornered by the advanced sections of this community that had long been converted to other religions and thus raised its political and social status.

The point I am making is that the 1951 list of Scheduled Tribes created several anomalies. For example, Bakarwal Gujars were studied, prior to 1991, as a nomadic Muslim caste in Jammu and Kashmir; but now it is given a tribal status. A similar thing has happened among Muslim Gujjars in the State of Himachal Pradesh. The Rabari are a Scheduled Tribe in Gujarat, but in Rajasthan they are included in the category of "Other Backward Classes". The old State of Hyderabad (Nizam) did not recognise Yenadis, Yerukulas, Sugalis as tribes, but the Andhra State has given them the recognition. Similarly, Gaddis are treated as a ST in Himachal Pradesh, but in Punjab, they enjoy this status only in the scheduled areas where they do not live. For a number of years, the State of Uttar Pradesh did not acknowledge tribal status for the Khasas of Jaunsar-Bawar and the Gonds and Cheros of the Mirzapur district, now they are included in the tribal category.

In 1967, a Joint Parliamentary Committee under the Chairmanship of Shri Anil K. Chanda was constituted to consider the claims of various communities for inclusion in the category of Scheduled Tribes. This Committee adopted the following five criteria for judging the eligibility of any group as a tribe:

1. Indication of Primitive Traits

2. Distinctive culture
3. Geographical Isolation
4. Shyness of contact with the larger community
5. Backwardness

The official documents nowhere provide any indicators for each of these variables to develop an objective index. Different people have interpreted each of these variables differently.

The Lokur Committee which was set up earlier in 1965, also used more or less the same criteria. However, it was firm in stating that : " care was necessary in drawing up the schedule in order to ensure that communities which had been assimilated in the general population were not at this stage invested with an artificial distinctiveness as tribes, and that communities which might be regarded as tribes by reason of their social organization and general way of life but which were really not primitive should not now be treated as primitive". The Lokur Committee categorically stated (page 7) that "...in 1931 and 1935, as well as in 1950 and 1956, it was acknowledged that every tribe need not be regarded as requiring special treatment; the list of 1931 was of "primitive tribes" while the list of 1935 was of "backward tribes". It further said: "...we have considered that tribes whose members have by and large mixed up with the general population are not eligible to be in the list of Scheduled Tribes".

Let us now look at the five criteria that the Government of India still uses in judging the eligibility of a group for the tribal status. Objectively speaking, the first criterion — namely indication of primitive traits— is broad enough to cover all the other criteria: the primitives are those that have a distinct culture of their own, live in relative isolation, and therefore, fight shy of contacts with the outsiders, and as a consequence of their isolation, they have remained backward. What, then, are the additional "Primitive" characteristics to be included in the first criterion?

It appears that the basic distinction, as is made in the context of USA, Australia, and New Zealand, between the tribals and the non-tribals is the criterion of "indigeneity". The tribals are the indigenous people, also known as "autochthonous". During the debates of the Constituent Assembly – drafting the Constitution of the Republic of India – a tribal leader, Jaipal Singh asked President Rajendra Prasad :

> I wish that you would issue instructions to your Translation Committee that the translation of Scheduled Tribes should be *Adivasi* (meaning original inhabitants or indigenous peoples). The word *Adivasi* has a grace... Why this old abusive epithet of *Banjati* (forest dwellers) being used....

Even the SC&ST Commission, in its 1961 Report, stated that Scheduled Tribes are known as indigenous peoples under international law. There are people who believe that the word "primitive" is antithetical to the universally recognised principles of dignity for, and equality of all human beings. These problems notwithstanding, Anthropological Survey of India prepared an initial list of 6,748 communities in India. Of these, 461 were tribal, having 172 segments, comprising 8.1 per cent of the total population of the country. This number is much larger than the original figure of 212 given in 1951 Census when the Tribal Population constituted around 6 per cent of the Indian population.

The new Tribal Policy document, issued by the Government of India in July 2006 acknowledges the redundancy of the five criteria. It boldly asserts: "...all these broad criteria are not applicable to Scheduled Tribes today. Some of the terms used (e.g. primitive traits, backwardness) are also, in today's context, pejorative and need to be replaced with terms that are not derogatory" (para 1.2). In para 20.4, it says that "Other more accurate criteria need to be fixed". It is significant that the Tribal Policy acknowledged the need for a process of "descheduling" so as "to exclude those communities who have by and large caught up with the general population. Exclusion of the creamy layer among the Scheduled Tribes from the benefits of reservation has never been seriously considered. As we move towards, and try to ensure, greater social justice, it would be necessary to give this matter more attention and work out an acceptable system" (para 20.6)

The Chopra Committee, of which I was a member, expressed its inability to employ these criteria and pass a judgement on the candidature of Gujars for the Scheduled Tribe status. In fact, it strongly advocated for a national debate on the issue to halt this process of what some people have begun calling "reverse Sanskritization".

The various references to the Commissions and Committees that I have made is to bring home the point that the social situation in India has drastically changed over the years with several forces of change – planned or unplanned, endogenous or exogenous, and there is no point of return. And the change has touched all sections of our society be the urban, rural or even tribal. If we stuck to our old definitions then we should be prepared to take out those groups which earlier matched the definition but are now metamorphosed. To invent new definitions to suit the vested interests of the concerned groups is an exercise of little value. If the intentions of our Constitution makers were to include only the backward among the tribes in the Schedule and make specific provisions for them so that their backwardness is removed then we should develop objective criteria for descheduling the groups that have shown improvement; and at the same time disallow entry of fresh groups on false pretexts. To insist on retention of the primitive traits is nothing more than conspiring to keep certain groups backward for all times. In today's context, tribal areas of the past can also easily be classified into urban, rural, and even tribal. In many groups the claim of being tribal is of historical significance only. Many individuals or families who belonged to these groups but who have changed their personal and social profile by acquiring good education, a better employment, or a political stature should voluntarily opt out rather than wait for their ouster as a "creamy layer".

Today, it is more relevant to identify the geographical areas that are suffering from development deficit and develop suitable strategies to reach development to all those who inhabit that region rather than be partial to certain groups in such areas. Poverty or illiteracy is the attribute that needs to be evaluated at the level of the family or the individual and not at the higher category of ascribed status – be it caste or tribe. Time has come when we need to reprioritise our actions and direct them to those specific areas that have suffered from neglect. The connectivity slogan befits that strategy which would create India as a country of interlinkages, of grids, and of communication highways.

3 Tribal Development in India

Sachchidananda

I

We have gathered here once again to discuss the problems and challenges of tribal development in India. During the last fifty years there have been hundreds of meets on this issue in different parts of India attended by administrators, policy makers and academics. I have participated in several of these seminars and conferences. Every time we have to grapple with the same problems and solutions are recommended. We have to ponder over this issue as it is not a trivial matter. The tribals account for eight crores of our population and they are a grave concern of the nation. We have to analyse where we went wrong, what are our omissions and commissions at the policy level and the implementation level. We have to search our souls as to why the tribals in middle India are seething with discontent.

Our Constitution provided for a social order, free from all forms of discrimination and also a comprehensive frame for the protection and advancement of the tribal people. The policy of reservation ensured representation of tribals in legislatures, services and educational institutions. Provision was also made for special funds for the speedy progress of tribals in social and economic sectors. The constitution devised an ideal, holistic and legal frame that reflected the deep concern of the Constitution makers about tribal communities.

However, the present scenario in tribal areas has belied their hopes. The government remained complacent with the formal compliance of the constitutional mandate. It did not worry about the outcomes reflected in its performance. It was satisfied with the expenditure made according to the outlay provided.

There is no doubt that with the spread of education and impact of reservation policy, a small middle class emerged in tribal communities. It interacts with the regional economy and society. The overall economic status of the bulk of the tribals, particularly in middle India, has gone down. There has been huge influx of outsiders, destruction of natural resources, displacement and destitution. Land alienation has not stopped in spite of various steps taken by the government. Landlessness is rising and the literacy rates are extremely law and malnutrition is widespread. Under the circumstances, the entire tribal belt in middle India, is gripped by unrest, which has reached the boiling point.

Sharma has attributed it to the policy vacuum in regard to tribal affairs after the adoption of Constitution. Pandit Nehru in his own way, provided a vision to the government and administrators for the development of the tribals. The vision enshrined the principles upheld by anthropogists for the speedy development of tribals. The five principles were that the tribal people should be allowed to develop according to the own genius, their rights over land and forest, which provided livelihood for them, should be protected, their social institutions should be utilized for their development and emergence of their own leadership, over administration was to be avoided and the advancement in tribals areas was to be measured not by statistics but by improvement in the quality of life. In some areas, particularly in NEFA these guidelines were followed but in middle India they were neither appreciated nor translated into action. The idea of the genius of the tribals was a matter of ridicule among the administrators.

The exercise of the task of scheduling of communities was

faulted. There were cases of omission, prejudice and favour in this regards. The blunders of early days are haunting the government even to this day. The state failed as protector of tribal people. They were left to the mercy of market forces. It was not only a socio-economic crisis but also led to psychological trauma. The unrest escalated in the tribal areas in the late sixties. In order to meet this challenges, the Tribal Sub Plan (TSP) emerged. This holistic policy, comprised elimination of exploitation and empowerment of the community. But gradually these elements disappeared from the tribal development agenda and the tribal Sub Plan became a routinised activity resulting in severe backlash of development without protection.

One of blunders in tribal development planning in India has been clubbing together of all scheduled tribes. They were perceived as a monolithic and homogenous group. Nothing can be farther for truth, as the tribes of India reflect a whole spectrum of socio-cultural evolution, from foragers through shifting cultivation and pastoralists to marginal farmers. They do not have identical problems and therefore a uniform development plan will not suit them. This was realized only in the seventies and 74 tribal groups were identified as primitive. These groups comprised small pre-agricultural tribes. These were threatened groups and were kept outside the Tribal Sub-Plan. Special financial support from the Government of India was made available for the preparation and execution of projects for them. This innovative step largely remained a non starter for one reason or another and it became dysfunctional.

II

In 1961 Verrier Elvin published a book entitled *A New Deal for Tribal India*. It was an abridged version of the report submitted by the first tribal commissions under the chairmanship of Shri

U.N. Dhebar. More than fifty years have elapsed and we need another new deal for tribals. The new deal should have a large and lofty vision which should embody the present day aspirations and ensure better quality of life for them. It should carry a clear message delineating the future of the Tribals in every respect. Its programmes should meet both the short-term and long-term needs of the Tribals.

The two immediate concerns of the tribals are poverty eradication and the preservation of their identity. For poverty alleviation, the tribal economy needs complete revamping. At present tribal economy has been vitiated by continuous expropriation in many ways. The community feeling has been almost destroyed. To build up a healthy economy, efforts should be made for sustainable development with equity for tribal groups having different patterns of sustenance. Plans should be drawn up for optimizing the resource endowment of the area concerned. Such planning should keep the interests of the tribals as the top most priority.

The association of the tribes with its habitat and its traditional local resources should be guaranteed. This should create confidence among the people which has been badly shattered by displacement. The injustice implicit in the industrial development in tribal areas should be undone. This was recommended by the Bhuria Committee. Any industrialist operating in the scheduled area should be bound to induct the tribal people as equal partners. Minor forest produce in most tribal areas constitute an important source of livelihood for them. The collection of minor forest produce is regarded as a concession. In 1976 a policy decision was taken conceding community ownership but this was not made operational in areas outside Madhya Pradesh and Chhattisgarh. This principle has been accepted in the new Forest Right Act. It is necessary that it should be immediately translated into action and the primary collector of the non-timber forest produce is given full value of their collection without levy of any kind.

The commercial vending of liquor was prohibited in 1975 under the Tribal Sub-Plan but the practice was reintroduced in many states for enhancing their excise revenue. There are examples in Jharkand where tribal women organized a movement against this practice but the vendors came back with the support of the administration.

Employment is a concept that comes with development. In the traditional set up in the village, no body is unemployed. The term unemployed refers to a person who is unable to get the job he wants. With the growth of education, many tribal youths are unemployed because the traditional economy does not provide a job commensurate with his educational level. By linking traditional economy with market oriented economy and by creating degree linked employment opportunity, we have created the problem of unemployment in tribal societies. Every degree holder thinks in terms of government service or employment outside the village. This nexus between degree and job needs to be broken if unemployment in tribal society is to be removed. It can be done with specific vocational training and adoption of appropriate technology for the area concerned. Training could be given in such crafts as wood carving, carpentry, agriculture, bamboo handicrafts, lac cultivation, fruit packaging, vegetable growing, etc.

To ensure development it is necessary to deal with tribal indebtedness. Step must be taken to liquidate all doubtful and iniquitous liabilities of tribal people. The debt burden is increasing as unregistered money lenders carry out their activities and extort money from the tribal debtor many times the amount given as the loan. All existing debt liabilities should stand liquidated on an appointed day. All liabilities arising from any transaction in which the beneficiary did not receive the stipulated benefits should also be liquidated. All money lending by private agencies should be stopped. Arrangements should be made for meeting credit needs for tribals for productive as well as consumption purposes should be met through co-operative societies or Self Help Groups. The system of bonded labour is still operating in many areas, although the Bonded Labour Act came into operation in 1976. Sometimes liberated bonded labourers have gone back to their old masters as they could not find alternative employment in their habitat. Efforts have not been made to rehabilitate such labourers. An effective campaign has got to be launched in scheduled areas for the complete eradication of bonded labour.

The other most important issue plaguing tribal mind is his identity. A resource less tribal has no identity. A man without his 'des' or traditional habitat is a rootless person. It is also necessary that he should have a command over resources of his traditional habitat. The life of a wage labourer or slum dweller is ignominious for a tribal. With the loss of commutarian values and dignity of labour, there is a visible decline in the quality of life in which he lived, moved and had his being. It is essential that every tribal in scheduled areas should be enabled to create a resource base for his living.

In the colonial period and even after independence, tribals in middle India have suffered from exploitation, injustice and oppression. They have lost faith in promises of the government. It is, therefore, necessary to establish credibility about the steps to be taken for their development. The most sensitive aspect at tribal life is self-governance. For the Schedule V areas, the Government of India enacted PESA Act in 1996. A great deal of labour, goodwill and empathy went into the making of this legislation. In many states, it has not been made functional. In those where it is in operation the Gram Sabha as envisaged in the Act has not been functioning properly. Once the Gram Sabha became effective, people will have feeling of participative democracy. It is necessary for the Schedule V states to prepare guidelines for the functioning of Gram Sabha so as to enable the people to deal with the system with confidence and authority. A regulation has also to be made to the effect that all formal and informal transaction of any kind between a tribal and any other person shall have no effect unless it is authenticated by the Gram Sabha.

In the social sector like education and health more effective steps have to be taken so that the fruits of development in those areas are visible. Special effort is necessary to ensure that education is made socially relevant for the children. The curriculum and the text books should be related to the local environment. The special handicaps arising from the location in hill and forest areas have to be overcome so that all children in the school going age, go to school which is not far away from their habitation. Their cultural heritage has to be used as the foundation of education. A time bound programme should be evolved for universal enrolment at the elementary stage. At the primary level, as far as possible, the medium of instruction should be the mother tongue, but at higher level, the regional language should be the medium. Suitable bridge courses should be designed so that the transition from the mother tongue to regional language is smooth. The school on the village should be the centre not only for education but also for citizenship. Non-formal education may also be introduced from the primary to the secondary level for such students who cannot afford to join regular schools as full time students.

Health services in most tribal areas are extremely weak. The primary health centre and sub-centres are largely non-functional. Neither the doctors nor the medicine or other necessary infrastructure are available. On account of malnutrition, tribals have poor resistance to diseases. They have to depend largely on herbal remedies and traditional healers. Mother and child care health programmes should be made more effective. All traditional healers and birth attendants should be integrated with state health services with some training. For each Panchayat fully equipped health centres should be set-up for comprehensive health coverage.

III

It has been hinted above that besides faulted policies, the major failure is in the implementation of development plans. Mistakes made in the past should be mended and fresh initiatives have to be taken so that the level of governance is upgraded to meet the challenges thrown up in tribal development.

Under the Constitution the Schedule V provides measures for the peace and good governance of the tribal areas. It endows the Governor of the state with power to frame regulations for this purpose. But it has been used only for transfer and allotment of land. In fact the Governor is the 'legislature' for the scheduled areas. Regulations can be made in consultation with the Tribes Advisory Council and sent the President of the Union for his assent. The Tribes Advisory Council comprises not more than 20 members out of which not less than two-third shall be tribal MLAs. The TAC has been constituted to advise the Governor on any matter concerning the welfare and development of the tribals of that state. In actual practice, however, Governors have not used the power given to them. Thus the Union Government does not have the advantage of reviewing the state of administration in the Scheduled areas as the Governor's report is the report prepared by the state government. The Governor's report should present an overall assessment of the tribal situation and indicate the deficiencies in the system and recommend remedial action.

There is a National Commission for Scheduled Tribes. It

has been appointed under Article 338A to investigate and monitor all matters relating to safeguards provided for the Scheduled Tribes. The government has to present before the parliament a report on the tribal situation based on the commission's report and detail the action taken thereon.

Under Article 339A there is provision for the appointment of a Scheduled Areas and Scheduled Tribes Commission for high level review of the administration of Scheduled area and the welfare of Scheduled Tribes. There is no fixed periodicity for such a review. The first commission was appointed in 1960 under the chairmanship of Shri U.N. Dhebar. No commission has been appointed after that.

In spite of holistic constitutional frame the new challenges faced by the tribal people have not been appreciated tackled by political leaders, administrators and social activities. The failures on the tribal front have been largely administrative. Supporting laws, regulations and rules not made for the constitutional provisions. *Ad hoc* decisions were made as and when required in the field situation. In the fifties of the last century all the laws, central as well as the state, were extended to tribal areas. The tradition of tribal self-governance was lost sight of. This was accompanied by the loss of community's command over resources. All these made the tribal people resource less, powerless and defenceless. This constituted gross injustice for the tribals. The simple tribal is bewildered by the numerous departments and agencies working for their development in various sectors. A single line administration should be established at the level of ITDP with clear chain of command and wide functional powers. While Panchayat Raj institutions at different levels should have the decision making power in the respective areas, implementation should be the task of the administration. At the village level, administration should play a supportive role.

The bane of administration has been planning from the

above. In fact planning should be from the village level. Competent micro planning units should be established at the state and at the ITDO level. There should be a single window organization for credit, marketing and supply. The best organization for this should be the large size multipurpose society (LAMPS).

Administrative and development personnel should be selected from persons who have knowledge and empathy for tribal people. In many cases, posting in tribal areas is regarded as a punishment. As such, the bulk of the staff are disinterested in carrying out their responsibilities. At one point of time, it was assumed that only tribals should be posted in tribal areas as they would be keen for the development of the own people. However, this was not true in most cases. Willing people should be posted in tribal areas with tenure of not less than five years. In larger states sub-cadres may be established for tribal areas in the bigger departments. Provision should also be made for incentives and rewards for staff posted in tribal areas.

At the Government of India level and in Schedule V States all development departments should set up a tribal unit in consultation with the nodal Ministry of Tribal Affairs for consultation in respect of the departmental programmes for tribal areas. The Ministry of Tribal Affairs at the Centre should be the nodal department to ensure coordination in the preparation of sectoral plans in order to give it a holistic look. It should also provide supplemental inputs at the planning stage and monitor and oversee implementation of development programmes. It should not take up any line functions. Its officers should visit the field to have realistic feel of the situation, quality of administration, deficiencies in the system and also devise remedial measures in crisis situations.

There is great need of independent, systematic and regular appraisal of the tribal situation. This can be done by the Tribal

Research Institutes. They should also evaluate development programmes and garner the outcomes. In many states the Tribal Research Institutes are in a state of decay and neglect. The research faculty had been depleted. They should be made fully functional and vibrant. A Central Tribal Research Institute should be established under the Ministry of Tribal Affairs, where tribal development oriented research can be started at the national level. It can take up national level surveys and appraisals. It should define its future tasks in the light of past experience and future vision.

IV

During the past two years things are beginning to look up in the context of Tribal development. A National Tribal policy has been made by the Government of India and it is hoped that it will act as a lighthouse for tribal development in the country. The need for it had been felt all along. There was no single policy which looks at the issue of protection and development of the STs in an integrated and holistic manner.

The policy has been guided by the principles enshrined in the Constitution of India for social, political and economical empowerment of the STs including extension of the 73rd and 74th amendment through the PESA Act and the Nehruvian "Panchsheel". The main objectives of NTP are regulatory protection of tribal communities and their socio-economic empowerment, stepping up their participation in national affairs at all levels, promotion and development of tribal handicrafts, creation of awareness about elimination of an anti-social practices such as addiction to alcohol, witchcraft etc. It also aims at rationalizing the process of scheduling and development of vulnerable tribal groups so as to bring them at par with other STs. The conservation and protection of the intellectual property regime of the STs and its proper utilization on a commercial basis is also envisaged.

These objectives have to be achieved by the adoption of certain strategies such as re-orienting the administrative machinery in tribal areas to improve governance and delivery of goods and services. It includes the construction of tribal development index on the basis of certain agreed indicators, preparation of separate tribal centric units in all development departments, strengthening of ITDP, MADA as effective administrative units of administration so that they can become focal points for all development and regulatory functions, adoption of area planning approach and Tribal Sub-Plan strategy, in letter and spirit, to ensure flow funds and convergence of resources for development of needy areas.

Special efforts have to be made to prevent alienation of tribal lands and ensure tenurial security; the tribal forest interface has also to be changed to foster better relationships. The recent legislation giving right to tribal in the forest is a move in this direction. Special attention has to be paid to see that tribal interests are protected in the collection and marketing of minor forest produce since these contribute about the 70 per cent of the income of tribal families. The policy recognizes that *Jhum* cultivation is a farming system that protects collective ownership of natural resources and is the only source of livelihood in those areas. The policy recognizes that displacement of tribals on account of development induced, projects produce a multi-dimensional trauma which cannot be easily compensated. It deprecates the acquisition of land in access of the requirement for mining and industrial activities. The people of displacement, rehabilitation and resettlement does not take into account the project affected families. It is therefore necessary to take into account the suffering they have to under go in account of industrial activity.

The policy has kept in focus the human development

parameters such as education, health, employment, income, etc. In all these aspects there is a gulf of difference between tribals and non-tribals. Tribal areas are marked by low literacy, heavy drop-outs, absence of teachers and lack of schools in the convenient locations. The infant mortality, child mortality and mal-nutrition are high in tribal areas. Sanitation and drinking water supply needs a great deal of attention.

Livelihood opportunities are extremely limited in tribal areas. Agriculture and horticulture need a great deal of effort for improvement. The creation of critical infrastructure and speedy development of communication facility is extremely essential to improve their quality of life. In the absence of the long neglect of tribal areas, there has been the growth of a deep sense of exclusion and alienation; large parts of tribal areas in middle India are swept by Naxalite violence. The state has been regarded as an exploiter, an enemy and perpetrators of violent action are being welcomed as protectors and friends. The National Tribal Policy believes in the promotion of an inclusive society in which tribal communities are given command over natural and financial resources for the elimination of their economic and psychological deprivation in a time bound manner.

In the last enlisting the support of NGOs is necessary. The NGOs will be encouraged to reduce the dependence of tribals on government. Special attention has to be paid to preservation of tribal culture and traditional knowledge. This is necessary for the pride and identity of tribal community. The wisdom embodied in the traditional knowledge is reflected in water harvesting techniques, construction of cane bridges, utilization of forest species like herbs and plants.

The problems of the tribals have to be viewed in a dynamic perspective one time solution will not hold to with the passage of time. New problems will emerge as the present problems are resolved. There has also been a revolution of rising expectation in tribal societies in account of various socio-economic changes and the impact of education. The policy needs to be updated every few years in the light of the fast changing scenario.

We have attempted to identify the challenges in tribal development. The first challenge before the government is to regain the confidence of the tribal people. The PESA Act and the new Forest Act have the potential of reviving the confidence in the government as the trustee of the legitimate interest and the possibility of revitalizing communities to end the long standing confrontation between the state and the tribal people. Once this confidence is regained tribal people may be helped to prepare their own people vision to lighten the path of socio-economic and political advancement.

The second sets of challenges are centred around restoring resources, rebuilding livelihood and reaffirming tribal dignity.

The third challenge is for the administration. It should develop a system of continuous information flow in the form of administration reports and the annual reports of the Governor. The National Commission of STs has to be depoliticized and empowered to act as the tribune of the tribal people. The National Development Council should also review the tribal situation in its meetings. The time has also come for the setting up of a new Tribal Commission as required under the Article 339. It should be headed by a tribal leader who enjoys the confidence of the community.

4 Social Exclusion and Marginalisation

Poor among Tribals in Village Democracy

D.C. Sah

Introduction

Rapid agricultural growth — despite a falling share of agriculture in the GDP — still fascinates imagination of researchers and the policy-makers in India[1]. The agricultural growth, along with some other measures, reduced the rural poverty[2] from over 57 per cent in early 1970s to less than 26 per cent in 1999-2000. The growth strategy in the last half a decade has revolved around high farm-gate prices to producers and low prices to consumers, high subsidy to farmers for fertilisers, irrigation, power, and market controls in the form of levies on sugar and rice and controls on storage, transport and credit. As tribals have remained untouched by this growth strategy, poverty in these areas is still very high; it is about 50 per cent (Sah, 2007a). The important question is whether state withdrawal, due to liberalisation, shall have any impact on the tribals. It is argued that exclusion of tribals from agricultural technology, markets, and social sector investment is absolute. This, along with growing dissent against their marginalisation, would result in a process where decision making in village democracy will be controlled by a small elite group.

After independence, three important processes have brought

considerable change in constitutive ideas and behavioural expectations of tribals of South-western Madhya Pradesh. Factors like development interventions by state, political decentralisation and seasonal migration have influenced the tribals social and economic outlook. In order to appreciate the struggles between continuity and change, each of these processes have to be located within the cultural construct that tribals employ to interpret them. Development for tribals brings, in its train, images of large projects, displacement and associated hardship[3]. Otherwise, large sections of the tribals have missed the fruits of post-independence development interventions, which have been poor in terms of both coverage and quality. Except elementary education and Public Distribution System, other amenities like access to electricity, all weather roads, health services, drinking water and sanitation, irrigation, agricultural extension, rural co-operatives etc. are poor. In fact, their remoteness to administration and civil society institutions is overriding enough to allow these facilities to reach the needy area. What has, however, reached them is the fear of displacement due to development projects and the administrative insensitivity that accompanies with them. Presence of administration — in the form of police, forest and revenue officials — is synonymous with corruption, repression and exploitation[4]. The experiences of development in tribal's consciousness leaves behind a trail of mistrust towards non-tribals, caution and apathy towards state interventions, and loss of land and natural resources for tribals.

The change in the form of technologically driven agriculture, though restricted to a small subset of area, is not entirely an outcome of state intervention either. It happened because of seasonal migration. Seasonal migration for Tribals is not coping with scarcity alone[5]; it is experiencing development that has by-passed them[6]. What a migrating tribal learns during his stay as a labourer either on irrigated farms of Nimar plains or on the farms of irrigated HB cotton growers of Khandesh or on the fields of irrigated paddy and sugarcane growers in south Gujarat is a main source of agriculture technology transfer. How to energise the well and distribute water, how to grow irrigated fertiliser-responsive cotton, soybean and wheat, and utilisation of post-harvest technology of these market-oriented crops *etc.* is learnt during seasonal migration. No matter how much the Adivasi Mukti Sangathan discredits it, this process of production of knowledge is creating space for non-tribal institutions that is inducing conversion of subsistence way of agriculture to a market driven agriculture[7]. This process is internalised without any state support. In irrigated areas, the *bania* is providing agricultural credit without any security. The tribals are also able to repay the loans promptly at least during good agricultural years. But in the process, tribals have started attaching a high degree of dependence on non-tribal institution they loathed the most, the market. This is an ideological contradiction that is the handiwork of modernity. This emerging consciousness about technological change, along with conditions of larger tracks of poor quality of land, produced a feeling in which *bania* finds that land as a source of exploitation is not as remunerative for their money-lending business as it used to be during pre-independence years.

The third important process that is imprinting the tribal consciousness is the process of decentralised governance. The logic of decentralised governance is to bring decision-making nearer to the masses. In the last eight years of its working in the region, decentralisation has brought about considerable transformation. Traditional leadership and its social dominance have given way to elected leadership; many a role that Patel used to play has become redundant when identity of Patel is subsumed in the position of *Sarpanch*. But when Patels are unable to establish themselves as elected leaders, especially in multi-village Panchayats, decentralisation has become a ground where traditional ideology would assert to re-establish itself. This has resulted in divide and fractions in village polity. Social interests that used to be supreme are giving way to economic interests. Generation divide has sharpened with older people being sceptical of all economic changes, whereas the younger generation is receptive and adaptive to interventions and economic changes. Both sides with their experiences — marginalisation and exploitation versus modernity and economic affluence — have stood to their ideological stand. But the divide is apparent[8]. Both the agents, the *Patels* with their social power as well as the elected representatives with their political influence and reach-up to high echelons of administration, are playing their respective roles. Changes are accepted slowly in tribal society with caution.

The above discussion clearly reveals that tribal society is as stratified on political and economic lines as non-tribal society. It becomes pertinent to explore whether a group among tribals is systemically excluded from state policies, programmes and economic and political institutions. If so, it would be worth understanding the implications of marginalisation and exclusion in the decision-making for development. The paper argues that the lack of formal institutional structure and lack of development have not discouraged formation of social capital[9] in this region. The recently acquired awareness — with the help of the civil society — has strengthened the social network's capabilities in terms of associational activities, trust among the social groups and individuals, and collective actions for shared goals. The social capital in this tribal region manifests itself through social hierarchy and moves to political domain, though with varying intensity. In relatively less remote areas, the stratifications created by political and economic processes have displaced the social hierarchy. But, in remote rural areas, where economic hierarchy is fragile and reshuffles itself within a short span[10], the social elites get an upper hand even in non-social affairs. In so far as the bonding social capital is necessary to meet crisis, the bridging social capital between community and outsiders brings economic opportunities. In remote tribal areas, the well-to-do are able to develop these bridges and control development decision-making at the grassroots level.

The study is based on both qualitative and quantitative data from three predominantly tribal villages of Badwani district of Madhya Pradesh. The qualitative data[11] is collected from villages Kirchali and Pospur whereas the quantitative data is generated from Kirchali and Chikalkuan[12]. The paper is divided into four sections, including this introduction. The second section reviews the tribal marginalisation, exclusion and dissent that helped the dormant social capital to manifest. The third section presents the creation and manifestation of social capital in this tribal belt as well as the role played by bridging social capital in village development and decision-making. The last section presents conclusions based on the major issues discussed in the paper.

Marginalisation, Exclusion and Dissent

Tribal marginalisation is not a new phenomenon; historically, British and their interest in the forests of their areas started it. In the process, tribals were increasingly excluded from the forest and their customary use rights were restricted. Even after independence, tribal situation did not improve. The pattern of development adopted is responsible for fundamentally altering three crucial bases of tribal livelihood: water, land and forest. Development, environmental sustainability and governance have different meanings for the tribals and the state. This mismatch in the definition is contested by everyday practices; violent sometimes but in more sublime way bring out the contradictions of state actions relating to access to natural resources. State, as the authority of development, rationalises its action through projects of national interest and through interventions that rest on obsolete mode of land acquisition, which makes the tribals all the more powerless. The struggles against the state are placed within the discourse of ecology and development as is the case with Narmada Bachao Andolan (NBA) or are located against state's force and repression as in the case of Adivasi Mukti Sangathan (AMS). These struggles are able to mobilise tribals of the region. The success of these initiatives is, however, mixed in weakening of the state repression and bringing transparency in development initiatives.

A critical analysis of tribal mobilisation by NBA and AMS (Sah, 2007) reveals that these movements were able to create awareness about the state repression among the tribals of south-western Madhya Pradesh. The effect of the two agencies within the tribal community of Nimar has been binding. The campaigns helped in intensification of the dormant social capital in the form of closer ties between the communities, despite serious economic differences within the community. Within this scenario, it will be worth to appreciate the extent of stratifications in the society and social exclusion within the tribal community. For, the economic and political hierarchies are crucial agency in the political economy of decentralised governance. Although both the study villages (Pospur and Kirchali) are independent parts of group panchayats, political leadership in both locations is highly corrupt. What really differs between the two is the nature of economic stratification: while the remote Pospur is economically homogenous, less remote Kirchali is highly stratified on economic lines.

Economic and Political Hierarchies

Economic stratification in Kirchali is well-developed and visible when one moves in the village during early rabi season. The two hundred plus household village looks deserted and unmanned, except for about thirty households that are engaged in wheat and gram cultivation; pre-sowing irrigation and sowing of the crops are the major activities that engages some of the family members. These households have perennial source of irrigation, obtained at a very high cost and risk. Kirchali is an unelectrified village enclosed from two sides by Ramkula and Surana villages that have electric connections. Individual initiatives have resulted in intensive investment in irrigation and energising the farms in order to reap economic gains. Two families — of the Patels and the Bhagats — took the early initiatives in investment in agriculture in Kirchali. They have strong political clout and could get cheap institutional credit for a risky agricultural investment in digging well and energising it. Demonstration of economic gains attracted others to come forward for such investment; a substantial investment is involved in such transfer of agricultural technology that includes digging well in rocky terrain, drawing electricity line from some distance, investment in new seed varieties and yield increasing fertilisers. All the money needed for this has to be borrowed at a high interest and sizeable risk[13]. The risk involved in digging of a well in Kirchali is high. But, economic incentives in the form of cropping pattern changes and increase in yields keep the desire alive to invest. Half of the wells in Kirchali provide water only up to November. The perceptions on size and certainty of economic gains of investment attract new entrepreneurs; as such, there are individual attempts to draw electricity even from a distribution point that lies two km away. The community in Kirchali is stratified on economic lines; there are about 25 wealthy families with perennial irrigation while 100 poor households have less land and no irrigation facility. The middle group constitutes of farmers of average size of land. Each group has its own agenda; the rich want cheap labour, modern yield increasing inputs and investment so that their agricultural income is protected. The poor, on the other hand, want employment and labour opportunities nearby so that they need not have to migrate. Such economic stratification has not yet developed in Pospur. The failure of irrigation well is very high in Pospur, and its implications — repayment of loan to *bania* at an exorbitant interest rate — are disastrous. Consequently, there are only a few irrigated farms in Pospur; largely, the economic homogeneity of the community is undisturbed.

Poverty and Social Exclusion

In a community like tribals of south-western Madhya Pradesh, where a sizeable population lives in poverty, it becomes important to recognize that movements in and out of poverty are associated with access to economic opportunities. But, chronic nature of poverty[14] may be associated with social exclusion of poor, as a group, from public services and economic and political institutions. Investigating social exclusion, in its analytical form, assumes significance because it makes disparities visible. This not only ensures possibility to reach the excluded groups but also may curb tendencies of violent dissents.

Despite all-round claims of the state, a significant proportion of the poor in south-western tribal Madhya Pradesh continues to experience exclusion from necessities. Chronic poor are three times more likely to be excluded from literacy drive than others are. As a result, the opportunities for education have been seized by the non-poor (Table 4.1). Also, the poor ignore their sickness and are able to bear only a third of expenses for healthcare compared to the non-poor. Their exclusion from healthcare services is indicative of meagre accessibility to these services to poor households. Access failure to land and labour market forces a sizeable proportion of labour remaining surplus among poor than non-poor. Consequently, chronic poor are twice more likely to be migrants compared to other households; in this process, they remain disconnected with bulk of social, economic and political institutions. Access to public distribution system for poor is dismally low, and an insignificant proportion of cereal consumption of poor is supported by PDS supplies. Nor the benefits from state programme and schemes like SGRY, SJGSY, drought relief etc reach the poor equitably (Table 4.1).

The above evidences show that poor and chronic poor, as a group are excluded from various state interventions. However, their exclusion from political decision-making in Gram Panchayats is worrisome. The poor among tribals have lost faith in village democracy as a process of development and change. The decision-making, of late, has become highly centralised, where the poor, as a group, have no role to play. The poor as a group do monitor as how the governance is neglecting them. However, it does not get enough opportunity to register its protest about such mal-governance. Moreover, the poor have no freedom in the process of planning programmes they need. The blame for this unfreedom to decide what and how the local development should take place falls at various levels (Sah, 2007; Sah and Bhatt, 2004): First, the process of centralisation at the Panchayat level is too overpowering for community to exert pressures for participatory process to begin. Secondly, the quantum of financial allocation is too meagre to meet the demands of the community. Third, the desire of the bureaucracy and the elected representatives at higher echelons to control the activities and finance of the Gram Panchayat, does not allow needed independence to the Panchayat. Lastly, existing laws that govern the natural resources obstruct the process of giving control to the community.

Table 4.1: Poverty and Social Exclusion among Tribals

Factor	*Income Poverty*		*Chronic Poverty*		*Interaction with Remoteness*	*Nature of the role of remoteness in explaining chronic poverty*
	c²	*Odd ratio*	*c²*	*Odd ratio*		
Asset	6.5*	2.8	5.1**	3.3	Significant	Higher assets in less-remote areas reduces significantly chronic poverty than remote areas
GCA	6.5**	2.5	NS	1	NS	—
Irrigation	6.8**	3.0	6.8**	5.0	Significant	No irrigation in remote areas significantly increases chronic poverty than in less-remote areas
Agricultural production	7.7*	2.5	5.6*	2.5	Significant	Production growth in remote areas significantly reduces chronic poverty than less-remote areas
Labour in village	NS	1	NS	1	NS	—
Family size	45*	.41	NS	1	NS	—
Years of existence	NS	1	NS	1	NS	—
Literacy	9.2**	3.0	4.7*	3.3	Puro relation	Higher literacy rates in both remote and less-remote areas reduce chronic poverty
Agricultural debt	NS	1	6.8**	.07	Significant	Higher debt in remote areas increases chronic poverty significantly more as compared to less remote areas
Other debt	NS	1	NS	1	NS	—
migration	4.25*	0.5	4.9*	0.5	Significant	Chronic poor in remote areas is more likely to migrate than not as compared to less-remote areas
Panchayat benefits	NS	1	NS	1	NS	—
PDS dependence	NS	1	NS	1	NS	—

(Contd...)

Table 4.1 : *(Contd...)*

Organisation membership	1 NS	NS	1	NS	—		
Sickness Expenses	12 **	.3	NS	1	NS	—	—
Remoteness	NS	1	4.8 **	.3.3	See next column		

1. Odd ratio of being economically poor rather not.
2. Odd ratio of being chronic poor rather not.

Note: NS not significant. Significance level— *: 10% , **: 5% and ***: 1%

Source: Sah and Bhatt (2004).

Poverty, Culture and Development

This brief recapitulation reveals that social exclusion is multidimensional and is a process that keeps poor out from public goods and services on the one hand and denies their access to social, economic and political institutions on the other. This being an institutionalised process may also have implications for social relations. It can be argued that this may not be detrimental in the case of relations within the community, but this exclusion would certainly have implications so far as the relations with outside world are concerned. Interpreting social exclusion in this manner allows us to ponder over the notion of social capital that allows bonding within community as well as building bridges with outside world. Sah (2007) has shown that pattern of settlement in tribal villages is one of the important supports for development of social capital[15]. This apart, three other processes are instrumental in awakening the dormant social capital: First, presence of left-oriented civil society that helped easing economic repression; second, dependence on informal community legal structure that binds together people. Lastly, lack of development of the region and livelihood struggles gave space to social elites to oversee emerging political and economic leadership.

The civil society organisations, namely Narmada Bachao

Andolan and Adivasi Mukti Sangathan took advantage of development-induced displacement, depletion of natural resources and repression of tribal rights by the state[16] to mobilise tribals. The presence of NBA and AMS not only made the community aware about its rights[17] but also sceptical to outsiders in their villages[18]. Notwithstanding the catalytic role of civil society in creating social capital, the relationship between civil society and governance, as would be discussed, could be vicious as well as virtuous. The question is under what conditions the social capital manifests itself in the political domain in a virtuous pattern. The remoteness of the region with respect to legal, constitutional and administrative structures[19] helped the community to create its own informal institutions. These institutions exercised their power through social hierarchy and further strengthened social bonds within community. At times, there is an extension of formal structures with the informal institutions[20]. However, in locations where economic stratification has set in, owing to economic compulsions, economic hierarchy dominates the social hierarchy,[21] otherwise the social hierarchy dominates.

The state and market failures have influenced differently life and livelihood of the tribals in tribal region. Where agriculture is unsustainable, a sizeable section of the community is engaged in livelihood struggles that force them to seasonally migrate for seven to eight months in a year[22]. In order to optimise their family labour, agricultural land is pushed in short-term arrangements like leasing, renting or mortgage[23]. Land under such arrangements [24] engenders a symbolic presence of migrant in the village. In the process, land in exchange engenders a symbolic presence of the migrant household in the village[25] and his representation in social hierarchy without his being physically present[26].

The social capital in relatively remote tribal villages seems to be developing and providing dominant support to traditional social hierarchy to exert its power on political hierarchy. In the process, programmes that could have positive economic implications for well being of the community are resisted. This is something to admire as well as to criticise. Does it not mean that the social capital, in its negative aspect, puts people aloof from outside world and development? This seems to be keeping the community frozen in time and deny the social capital a space in development. This criticism seems to be partially true. Inasmuch as the state repression and access failure to common resources are the basic constraints in well-being, the importance of emerging social capital cannot be overemphasised as an important force behind their united struggle. But, the desire for change is also present. This has resulted in diverting the social trust and solidarity in the community in the form of emerging organisations that take advantage of non-tribal ways: technology, markets and development initiatives.

The increasing popularity of self-help groups in relatively remote areas is an indication of parallel leadership that is emerging in society. The first is the traditional social leadership that helps the social capital preserve natural resources by blocking explorative non-tribal entry in the village. Another is organising tribals to take advantage of existing government programmes through self-help group[27], that too against the wishes of the traditional social elites. Though both processes have extended social base, the latter is not the legitimate successor of the former. Despite the fact that both forms of social leaderships are exploring new dimensions of social relations, the latter does not directly contest the supremacy of traditional social elites and their ways of employing the social capital. It is unlikely that various forms of leaderships would come together in near future. But there is a possibility that the traditional leadership may be influential only in social processes; the economic processes may be governed by newly emerging leadership. It shall, however, be difficult to define operation of self-help groups as an indicator of social capital formation because these groups do surrogate the interests of individuals. This, in fact, is seen as a process that erodes homogeneity that is a prerequisite for social capital to manifest[28].

The social capital as it manifests in Pospur may not be operationalised by indicators like community engagements with various organisations and associations. It has to be observed in day-to-day involvement of community in the affairs of the village. The social hierarchy has a potential to create space for community involvement in politicising a debate. But it does not ensure participation in the decision-making. For, a vibrant social structure is present in these areas but it is only in relatively remote villages that one witnesses the manifestations of social capital. Moreover, the way the social capital is employed, strengthen the fact that (a) social capital may not necessarily manifest in virtuous imperatives; (b) all associations may not likely create trust and cooperation in the society while some, like SHGs with economic interests in-built, may even stratify the society.

These findings are at variations with what Pai (2001) has tried to establish. She observes that social segmentation emerges as a significant context determining development of trust and social capital between groups. Findings of this study reveal that trust and social capital within tribal context are omnipresent. Economic segregation and its intensity play a dominant role in manifestation of social capital. It remains unutilised under some conditions, is used in virtuous pattern in some and vicious in others. These findings, however, corroborate observations of Rudolph (2000) that not all associations are likely to create trust and cooperation with positive implications.

As seen in above analysis, social capital in the form of trust and bond within tribal context is omnipresent. Its utilisation in development decision-making and, more importantly, its pattern of manifestation would be contextual to the milieu where it is operational. Our analysis also reveals that (i) factors like the pattern of settlement, importance of social norms, and failure of state have helped perpetuate trust and cooperation in the community, (ii) civil society has played a significant role in making this capital available for wider use, and (iii) complexities of economic stratification and efficiency of decentralised governance are contextual to social capital to manifest. Three different types of elites have emerged in this tribal society: the traditional, the emerging economic elites and the political elites. All the three have created their own spaces in the community. But their relevance is contextual to their ability to deliver. The efficiency and working of political decentralisation is not different in different tribal areas and the political leadership is unable to use social capital for the betterment of conditions of the people. Not so much because of the nature of the leadership but because of the policy and programmes it has introduced that are inappropriate and ineffective. What, however, is different across villages is the individual economic efforts in some areas (less-remote villages) that have created sizeable benefits as compared to remote villages. The dormant social capital in development decision-making in former areas is significantly influenced by intense economic segregation that has given a strong message to community that well-being is a function of individual efforts. In contrast, in economically homogenous remote villages, the social capital is much more vibrant.

But the trust and concerns for fellow members in both the villages are in perpetual conflict with political hierarchy that is self-serving. In remote villages, this conflict has expressed itself in a vicious as well as virtuous pattern of social capital. On the other hand, in relatively less remote areas the social capital has remained uninvested and dormant. Despite the fact that the social capital has positively influenced non-social events since early 1990s, its manifestations in governance have been marginal. One wonders as to why the social capital could not be transferred in the sphere of governance. Answer to this question could be found in an analysis of (a) the nature of benefits that decentralised governance could potentially give to the community, and (b) is it worthwhile to put so much faith in a process that can never address the livelihood problems of the marginalised. Community at large finds the benefits not worth wasting their days' labour[29].

Economic stratification also affects trust in institutions, agencies and individuals. By and large, trust and faith in relatives, tribals, and people from Gram Panchayat or belonging to Jati Panchayat is still high. On the other hand, a large proportion of respondents do not trust Panchayati Raj institutions. Teachers and health workers are trustworthy but government officers like forester, police and outsiders like MLA, MPs have failed to gain trust of tribals. If we try to establish association between chronic poverty profile and level of trust (Table 4.2), we find that there is no significant difference in the level of trust between chronic poverty groups when it comes to trust within the community. This bond[30] within the community does not vary owing to social, political and economic stratification. But the trust on outsiders like police, forester or Janpad CEO is significantly high (revealed by significant and positive correlation coefficient) in the case of always non-poor whereas chronic poor do not trust the outsiders. It can be argued that well-off (socially, economically and politically) are trying to reach significantly more to outsiders. Their increasing trust on these agencies is a product of their desire to economically benefit from the newfound association. On the basis of such bridges, the always non-poor and transitory non-poor receive benefits of government schemes. But, the chronic poor, owing to their inability to bridge, have failed to get economic benefits. It will now be easy to understand why it was that the always non-poor and the transitory non-poor were receiving significantly more proportion in the resource redistribution in the area than what they actually deserved[31].

Table 4.2 : Correlation between Trust[1] on Agency and Chronic Poverty Profile[2]

Agency	*Correlation Coefficient*
Bonds within the community [3]	Strong and not significantly different across poverty profile
Bridges Outside Community[4]:	
Police	+ 0.28 ***
Forest Officials	+ 0.26 **
Janpad CEO	+ 0.26 ***
Teacher, *bania*, Health worker, MLA, MP, Civil society like NBA, AMS	Weak and Not significantly different across poverty profile

1. Trust is operationalised in 4 point scale with 1 never trust to 4 always trust
2. Chronic poverty profile is as follows:
   1: chronic poor; 2: poor; 3: transitory poor and 4: always non-poor.
3. Relatives, Jati panchayat, Gram Panchayat, Gramwasi, Panchayatwasi, Adiwasi, Sarpanch, Panch.
   Significance level — **: 5%; ***: 1%

Source: Sah (2007).

These evidences indicate that social relations are central to governance outcome. They also reject the idea of *cultural determinism*, which rationalises that some communities are encumbered with cultures that restrict them from progressing. Culture in our construct is, thus, a form of relationship that influences and is being influenced by socio-political and economic features. Two important issues in this context need some elaboration. First, despite dissent within the community against repressions and strong bond within, there are relational forces in the form of bridges outside community that lead towards a fractured conformity. This conformity redefines the power relationship within the community. Secondly, some people use social relations to enhance their position and also reproduce the processes that influence governance outcome. In a sense, the bridging social capital of the groups engenders ability to exert and fulfil their aspirations, disregarding all the dissents. These two contesting forces coexist and help in redistributing the opportunities created by development. Those who are influential in exploring bridging relations could fulfil their aspirations whereas those who are less fortunate remain in square one despite having strong bonds within. The ray of hope for equity lies in the capability of bonding social capital's capability to dissent. A conferment between the two may result in bonding social capital to dominate the bridging social capital.

Then why does not confrontation between the two is taking place? We need to answer if there is a sort of modality between bonding and bridging social capital that indicates if one type of trust increases, the other shall reduce. Findings of Table 4.2 reveal that it is not necessary that bond within members of one's own community reduces trust in people from outside. On the contrary, the always non-poor provide clear evidence that it is possible to trust outsiders without losing or reducing trust within the community. Trust within, in the form of bond, is important to cope with the remoteness. But bridging the distance with outsiders provides economic opportunities; those who are well off, benefit from governance by dictating development decision-making, disregarding all the equity norms. What it, however, denote that participation is subordinate to bridging relational outcome. Unless these social realities are recognised, community participation in decentralised governance may remain a distant dream.

Conclusions

Central to the debate on impact of culture on development is a much misunderstood and deterministic notion that some societies are encumbered with cultures that hinder them from participating efficiently in the non-traditional market-driven institutions. In other words, cultures of these societies are stumbling block in their assimilation with non-traditional economic and political institutions and processes. In the final analysis, their cultures force them to remain underdeveloped. Evidences indicate that social relations are central to governance outcomes. Rejecting the idea of *cultural determinism*, it is argued that culture needs to be located in socio-political domain as a form of relationship that is influencing and at the same time gets influenced by economic transformation the community is experiencing.

Despite difference of opinion within the community[32] and also exclusion of poor, there are relational forces (bridges constructed by some well-to-do in the community with outsiders like Forester, Police, taluka officials and Janpad CEO *etc.*) that lead to an apparent symmetry of opinions. Below the surface, there is a feeling of anger because, in the process, the well-to-do are able to corner a sizable gain of development. Moreover, as some people use relations to enhance their position, they are able to reproduce the processes that influence governance-outcome. These two contesting forces, bonding and bridging social capital, coexist and help in redistributing the opportunities created by development. Those who are influential in establishing bridging relations could fulfil their aspirations whereas those who are less fortunate remain so despite having strong bonds within.

In the last two decades, development and sustainability have transformed into a new politics of environment whereby development and sustainability means different things to different people. What state and bureaucracy see as development is, in fact, destruction to some. This is being contested at different levels. At one level, it is responsible in politicising the rights and interests of the people. Ethnicity, in this construct, emerges as a political process, within mixed societies, for protecting interests of groups. The bonding social capital in this political process results in forming new identities. The new identity formations help the communities first to organise themselves and then protest against the sort of development that has been forced upon them. Then why a confrontation between the two social capitals is not taking place? We need to answer if there is a sort of modality between bonding and bridging capitals that indicates when one type of trust increases, the other shall reduce. Evidences show that it is not necessary that bond within members of one's own community reduces trust in people from outside. On the contrary, the always non-poor provide clear evidence that it is possible to trust outsiders without losing or reducing trust within the community. Trust within, however, is clearly an important mechanism to cope with the remoteness. But bridging with outsiders provides economic opportunities; those who are well off, derive benefit from governance by dictating development decision-making.

This, however, implies that participation in development decision-making is subordinate to bridging relational outcome. Unless, these social realities are recognised, community participation in development–decision making may remain a distant dream. Moreover, cultural capital need not always bring efficiency in governance; it could work viciously, obstructing options that are virtuous in nature. In economically homogeneous and relatively remote rural areas, the bonding cultural capital is much more vibrant. Transfer of this capital from social sphere to political sphere is possible only if gains of governance are large and equitable. This also indicates that, like in rest of the country, in remote tribal areas community is stratified on economic, social and political lines. The trust and concerns for fellow members is in perpetual conflict with political and economic hierarchy which is self-serving. These stratifications also create variance in the ways people see the world around them. A grand unified policy intervention towards their welfare will, therefore, not work. The ambiguity in use of 'community participation' in development decision-making only reflects naive acceptance of homogeneity in community located in remote rural areas. This perception, in its turn, helps the state to design a blanket intervention for development. The cultural capital and its varied manifestations make policy interventions by-pass a large section of community.

End Notes

1. The importance to agriculture is for the following reasons. First, over half of the rural masses are net purchaser of foodgrains, hence they depend on policies that influence its availability. Consequently, politically it is incorrect to have a open market policy for agriculture. Secondly, there is a misconception in the policy-making circles that Indian agriculture is driven by incentives. As a result trade protection, marketing controls, state investment, price support and input subsidy remains important interventions in regulating the pace and pattern of agricultural growth in the country. Lastly, Bad experiences of late 1960s, when India was dependent on food-aid to survive, are hard to forget. From those haunting years of scarcity, India is self-sufficient in food and the growth of agricultural production has eliminated the threats of famine. This growth has increased the employment opportunities for rural labour and we have seen a rise in real wages.
2. Economic policies are not made in vacuum; serious investigations have guided the policy makers in formulating appropriate interventions. Poverty policies are also influenced by writings of social scientists. In fact, in last forty years, three important conclusions were instrumental in shaping Indian poverty-alleviation policies. It was Ahluwalia (1978) whose seminal work repositioned Indian poverty-debate from estimating poverty to explaining it. Ahluwalia tried to establish that years when growth in agricultural production slows down are also the years when rural poverty worsens. Saith (1981) and Narain (1985), independently, brought another important explanatory aspect in this debate—the agricultural prices. They tried to provide support to the thesis that years when agricultural prices

are high, other things remaining same, are the years when incidence of poverty increases. These researchers argued that as a large section of rural population, including producers, are net purchasers of foodgrains, an increase in prices of agricultural commodities reduces their purchasing power and shrinks their consumption basket, thus, pushing people into poverty. Taking a clue from these findings, the Indian planners developed a two-pronged strategy for poverty alleviation: providing a favourable environment for rapid growth in agricultural production and creating low and stable prices of foodgrains. The strategy, during 1980s and early 1990s, saw no significant departure, till Sen (1996) tried to impel the hypothesis that apart from these two factors, state investment in social sector weakens forces that accentuate poverty. Thus, the three major planks of Indian poverty reducing interventions remained around rapid growth in agricultural sector, stable price environment for rural consumer and social sector investment. The strategy did significantly influence the Indian rural poverty; the poverty ratio reduced from around 57 per cent in 1970-71 to 26 per cent in 1999-2000.

3. The Indian experience with R&R of large project affected PAPs lacks completeness and had been apathetic to local needs and resources. The R&R policy in forced and its implementation creates visible and invisible raptures in the social fabric in the short run and impoverishment in the long run (see Sah, 1999).
4. Revenue official are remembered for their extortion in land sales which cost the seller about Rs. four thousand per acre or for Land Transfer to a son that could be registered only after a bribe of Rs. two thousand per entry. The police have duel images. First as an institution of settling disputes in such a way that each affected party has to bribe in order to resolve the dispute in his favour. Its second image is of a state apparatus that is used in intimidating involuntary relocation of PAPs. The forest officials connote a bureaucratic set-up that has denied *Barelas* access to natural resources. But if one can bribe them, limited access may be granted.
5. The agricultural technology transfer in tribal areas is driven by what migrants learn from irrigated agriculture as migrant farm labour. Use of high yielding seeds with fertilisers under irrigated conditions, marinating plant health during growth stage, use of irrigation and harvesting equipments and post-harvest management *etc.* are introduced to tribals due to migration. As the state machinery has bypassed the tribal area, the process is internalised without any state support.
6. In drought prone areas, migration also works as asset formation device. Successive droughts render agriculture as unsustainable livelihood option

and forces even large farmers join the queue for doles. The marginal farmers and landless labourers accumulate assets due to their access to labouring options owing to migration.

7. This may also break the distrust syndrome with respect to non-tribals as noted above.
8. Nimar tribal belt is an economically divided lot. For example, in Pospur village in Pati taluka of Badwani district a group of young farmers is ready to take risk and associate themselves with schemes like group financing and self help group activities. But the older generation want no outside especially state intervention on schemes like social forestry and soil and water conservation activities on common property land that farther constrains their already constrained access to natural resources (for details see Sah *et al.*, 2003).
9. Social capital comprises of systems of norms, institutions and organisations that promote trust and cooperation in a community. It is considered a form of capital because it helps in accelerating the process of well-being and healthy decision-making in the community. Putnam (1993) is the best-known exponent of the concept, though both neo-institutional economists like North and sociologist like Bourdieu was early proponent of this concept. Durston (1998) argues that five important features of social capital:
   In economic exchange, social capital reduces transaction cost arising when dealing with outsiders in unregulated environment; it helps in honest and efficient governance. Social capital strengthens each time it is activated; social capital, like culture, is perpetuated and it could take a virtuous or a vicious path. Repeated social interaction virtuous or otherwise strengthens civic participation or non-participation; and social capital developed in culture or religious spheres is transferable to political or economic spheres.
10. Agriculture being the main economic activity, division of family due to marriage of a son, leads to weakening of economic hierarchy. The newly formed households are relatively resource deficient and rely on social network for support not only in social interactions but also for economic survival; also see, Sah and Shah (2003), for details.
11. Macro findings have identified Southwestern tribal belt of Madhya Pradesh as one of the economically poorest region in the country. Badwani district in the region has been selected for in-depth study to understand why and how people in Remote Rural Areas are trapped in chronic poverty. Two Janpads, one relatively developed Sendhwa and one resource poor Pati, are selected for the study. One village from each of the selected Janpad, Pospur from Pati, and Kirchali from Sendhwa, were selected based

on the relative remoteness; Kirchali is relatively less remote compared to Pospur. The paper based its evidences from both qualitative and quantitative methods. The qualitative data, using case study method, compare two communities in Kirchali and Pospur. The detailed write-up on the background, demographic, social structure and brief history of communities, see, Sah and Shah (2003). The quantitative data has been generated from 94 randomly selected households from Kirchali village of Sendhwa Janpad and Chilalkuan village of Pati Janpad.

12. As access to quantitative data was denied by villagers in Pospur, for in-depth study this village was replaced by Chilalkuan.

13, The remoteness of Pospur and poor agricultural base has resulted in relatively large population to rely on migration as a coping mechanism compared to less remote Kirchali (Sah and Shah, 2003). In Kirchali, individuals have invested over Rs. 20,000 for digging wells in rocky terrain with high risk of failure and in drawing electricity line from the nearest Distribution Point. There are about thirty individuals who have such connections. This process, though brought economic success to individuals, has stratified the society on economic lines. Remoteness of Pospur — its difficult terrain, high risk and initial failures in such investment — has made the village more homogenous. For details on relative importance of remoteness and investment, see Sah (2005).

14. Of two different approaches of measuring income poverty, either basing on per capita calorie intake or on per capita annual expenditure, the former was not considered an appropriate indicator of poverty. This is so because food consumption does not change significantly under distress situations in comparison to non-food items. In this research, instead of calorie intake, we have tried to estimate incident of poverty based on annual expenditure. The official norm for identification of households that are poor is Rs. 245 per capita per month. This imply that any household that spends less than Rs. 2950 per capita annually can be treated as poor. Among poor households, that have less than Rs. 2000 per capita per annum expenditure have been treated as severely poor. The poverty categories can further be re-categorised by incorporating time dimension of poverty. One way to reach chronic dimension of poverty is comparing the consumption expenditure over time. The major problem in employing this method is non-availability of a panel of data that fixes chronic nature of poverty. Sah and Shah (2003) have used variations in cereal consumption from normal as an indicator of chronic poverty. But identification of chronic poor using fall in cereal consumption from normal may provide underestimation to chronic poverty. This is because

experience shows that cereal consumption is relatively inelastic to shocks. Alternatively, Krishna (2003) has identified that in sequence of changes if there is deterioration in land asset and increase in leasing-in small tract of land, fall in food intake or clothing over time or if debts have remained un-serviced or leaky roof has not been repaired, it is sign of chronic poverty. Since the variations in quality of clothing over time from our sample are not caught properly and the house repair has only labour component using local material, it is not desirable to include these two indicators of identification of chronic poverty. It was also found that short-term land transactions in the form of leasing-in land is more a function of market failure and brings agencies together than a pure indication of sequence of change that points a deterioration in the quality of life of tenant (Sah, 1999). Thus, in this analysis we have proposed that if the household had lost silver in the last 10 years, or could not service its old debts or did not get even the rab (cereals boiled in buttermilk) and hence missed both the meals, the household is a transitory household either chronic poor or transitory non-poor. The two categories of income-poverty — poor and non-poor — thus can further be categorised as poor with chronic tendency, poor without chronic tendency, transitory non-poor and always non-poor.

15. In fact, *caste Panchayat* along with *traditional village Panchayat* are the two tribal institutions that promote community participation in all social decision-making. See, Sah and Shah (2003), chapter 3, for details.
16. Conflicts over natural resources between the state and the community in this tribal belt have a long history. However, the exploitation of natural resources is also from within. But the solidarity created by *outside* (state and *bania*) exploitation did bind the society. Two of the most active NGOs that are mobilising the tribal in the area are Narmada Bachao Andolan and the Adivasi Mukti Sangathan. While the former is mobilising the tribals on failures of development paradigm adopted by the state, the latter is organising them against natural resource depletion, state repression and their rights. See, Sah and Shah (2003), chapter 3, for details.
17. A discussion with the Chief Executive Officer of Pati *taluka*, where the Adivasi Mukti Sangathan is active, brings out the fact that awareness about tribal rights has grown in the area significantly over last 7-8 years. Earlier a tribal would come to the taluka Panchayat always accompanied by the activists of AMS, now they come for any work their own.
18. Even during the fieldwork of the study, because of the nature of the investigation where land, assets, livelihood *etc.* were being discussed, the community was apprehensive of outsiders' presence. There was a

perception, in both Kirchali and Pospur, that such investigation is part of state activities to understand pre-submergence situation so that resettlement package can be identified for individual households. In Kirchali, the community accepted the team after discussions on the nature, scope and implications of the study. But in Pospur, as been mentioned earlier, the situation became ugly and at one stage the social leadership forced the team to abandon its work. In no uncertain terms, it was told to the team that the community is happy in Pospur living as they are, earning their livelihood based on thin agriculture, some on-farm labouring and migration. Fortunately, a group of economic leaders, especially those who have had benefits of *self-help group*, could feel that the study is not for acquisition of land. The social hierarchy in Pospur had strong message: '*Please leave us as we are. We do not need any outside help for our livelihood. We are content with our life and livelihood despite poor agriculture, hard labouring and degrading migration. Do not disturb us.*'

19. This is especially true for forest guards and the police. What is commonly discussed in the village is that traditional local conflict resolution methods are far more just for, the police will settle the dispute by taking money from both the parties and would be biased against the group that has given less bride.
20. Eight committees deal with decisions relating to agriculture; health; infrastructure; education; social justice; defence; development; and assets. The political decentralisation has accepted the role of traditional leaders in both Pospur and Kirchali. Traditional leaders are a crucial part of Village Security Committee that deals all disputes emerging in the village.
21. The individualistic approach towards economic prosperity, which consolidates productivity gains, is regarded more important than social processes. The community initiatives do not pose any challenge to economic leadership. In Kirchali, individuals are investing over Rs. 20,000 for digging wells in rocky terrain with high risk of failure and in drawing electricity line from the nearest Distribution Point. There are over thirty individuals that have such connections. This process, though brought economic success to individuals, has stratified the society on economic lines. Remoteness of Pospur, its difficult terrain, high risk and initial failures in such investment has made the village more homogenous.
22. The remoteness of Pospur and poor agricultural base has resulted in relatively large population to rely on migration as a coping mechanism compared to less remote Kirchali. For details, see Sah and Shah (2005).
23. Tribal economy is based on reciprocity. Apart from performing economic transaction under market failure conditions, the short-term land

transaction, especially share cropping and fixed rent, also create social trust that works as metaphor for social return in exchange of economic gains. This latter (social) function of this exchange is an important as its formal (economic) function of exchange.

24. A sharecropper, Ramesh, said that I will have to look after the aged parents of my close relatives in his absence in any case, but I will have to bring a doctor and spend Rs. 30-50 in an injection or two in case I have leased-in their land.
25. A large number of variations exist when the contracts are agreed upon. With share cropping at one end and mortgage of land at the other, a large number of fixed rent contracts fall in the middle. Depending upon bargaining power of different participants, urgency of the deal to materialise, and perception of cost of enforcing the contract, terms and conditions vary even in a village.
26. Moral hazards are involved in sharecropping: The tribal who is leasing out land would like to ensure that the tenant, as agreed, has applied labour and inputs on the field for he has to share the out-of-pocket cost. Similar is the case when the crop would be harvested and shared for, the landowner has to ensure that he receives the crop output portion as agreed. For enforcing these, the landowner migrant has to either make a number of visits to the village or leave all these monitoring in trust on the other party. In this area the first option is more prevalent, not because of lack of trust but because it re-establishes his ties with the community.
27. In Pospur, seven 'Self-help Groups' comprising around 10 members each are in operation. Member of these groups contribute Rs. 50 to Rs. 100 per month. One of the 'Self-help Group' has provided loan of Rs. 20,000 to a farmer in order to get his mortgaged land back from a trader. Another 'Self-help Group' has over Rs. 20,000 in a nationalised bank and are in process of receiving a loan of Rs 0.3 million for goat rearing.
28. It has been argued that associations that draw on inherited identities and solidarities need to be taken into account as associations that may generate social capital. Rudolph (2000) suggests that only those organisations that are egalitarian, non-interest oriented and voluntary associations would create collaborative and cooperative conventions that can and do mediate between individual and social whole or individuals and the state.
29. Migration keeps a sizeable workforce out of the village for over 6 to 7 months. Moreover, iniquitous distribution of benefits and unfulfilled expectations of the community from the decentralised governance make them empathic towards the institution. See, Sah and Shah (2003), chapters 6 and 7, for details.

30. Widmalam (2004) identifies trust within as bond and trust on outsiders as bridges.
31. In poverty ridden areas, welfare schemes like pension, Indira Awas Yojana, SJGSY, SGRY, irrigation development are meant to transfer public resources to most vulnerable sections. What we find that such redistribution was not done equitably; both poor and non-poor received benefits though the always non-poor received more resources from redistribution than rest (see, for details, Sah and Bhatt, 2004).
32. These differences originate from a strong bonding social capital that de-tastes and vocal against unequal access to developmental gains. We are inclined to use this process in cultural context though Bourdieu (1997) clearly distinguish between the cultural and social capital.

REFERENCES

Ahluwalia M. S., (1978): 'Rural Poverty and Agricultural Performance in India', *Journal of Development Studies*, Vol. 14 (2).

Baviskar, A., (1995): *In the Belly of the River: Tribal Conflicts over Development in the Narmada Valley*, Oxford University Press, Delhi.

Baviskar, A., (2001): 'Written on the Body, Written on the Land: Violence and Environmental Struggles in Central India', Institute of International Studies, University of California, Berkeley.

Breman, J., (1985): *Of Peasant, Migrant and Pauper*, Oxford University Press.

Bowles, S., and Gintis, H., (2000): 'Social Capital and Community Governance', (memio), Department of Economics, University of Massachusetts, Massachusetts.

Bourdieu, Pierre (1997): 'Forms of Capital', in eds., Hasley, A.H., Landere, H., Broen, P. and Wells, A., *Education: Culture, Economy and Society*, Oxford University Press, New York.

Dubey, K.C., (1998), 'Tribal Uprising and Social Movements in Madhya Pradesh', in eds., Singh K. S, *Antiquity to Modernity in Tribal India, Volume 4: Tribal Movements in India*, Inter India Publications, New Delhi.

Durston, J., (1998): 'Building Social Capital in Rural Communities', Social Development Division, UN Economic Commission, Santiago, Chile.

Govinda, R., (2003): 'Dynamics in Decentralised Management in Primary Education,' in eds., Govinda, R. and Diwan, R., *Community Participation and Empowerment in Primary Education*, Sage Publications, New Delhi.

Krishna, Anirudh, (2003): 'Falling into Poverty in High Growth State: Escaping Poverty and Becoming Poor in Gujarat', *Economic and Political Weekly*, Vol. 38 (49).

Narain, Dharm, (1985): reported in Desai Gunvant M., "Trends in Rural Poverty in India: An Interpretation of Dharm Narain", in eds., Mellor, J.W. and Desai, G.M., *Agricultural Changes and Rural Poverty: Variations in Themes* by Dharm Narain, Johns Hopkins University Press, Baltimore.

Pai, S., (2001): 'Social Capital, Panchayats and Grassroots Democracy: Politics of Dalit Assertion in Uttar Pradesh', *Economic and Political Weekly*, Vol. 36, February 24.

Putnam, R. D., Leonardi, R. and Raffaella, Y. N., (1993): *Making Democracy Work : Civic Traditions in Modern Italy*, Princeton University Press, Princeton.

Rudlph, S.H., (2000): 'Civil Society and the Realm of Freedom', *Economic and Political Weekly*, Vol. 35, May 13.

Sah, D.C., (1997): 'Second Generation Problems of Involuntary Migration', *Indian Journal of Agricultural Economics*, 52 (4).

Sah, D.C., (1998): 'Avoiding Impoverishment Risks', *Review of Development and Change*, Vol. 3 (1).

Sah, D.C., (1999): 'Pressure on Land, Employment and Migration', *Review of Development and Change*, Vol. 4 (2).

Sah, D.C., (2002): 'Crop Commercialisation and Migration', in eds., Shah, G. and Sah, D.C., *Land Reforms in India, Volume 8: Performance and Challenges in Gujarat and Maharashtra*, Sage Publications, New Delhi.

Sah, D.C., (2003): 'Social Capital and Governance', *Review of Development and Change*, Vol. 8 (1).

Sah, D.C., (2007): 'Environment, Culture and Development' in eds., Atal, Y. and Sah, D.C., *Exploring Social Frontiers*, Rawat Publications, Jaipur.

Sah, D.C., (2007a): 'Chronic Poverty in Tribal Areas', *Indian Journal of Agricultural Economics*, Vol. 62 (2).

Sah, D.C. and Shah Amita, (2003): 'Chronic Poverty in Remote Rural Areas of Southwestern Madhya Pradesh', (mimeo), MPISSR, Ujjain and GIDR, Ahmedabad.

Sah, D.C., and Shah, Amita., (2005): 'Migration in Remote Tribal Areas', *Indian Journal of Agricultural Economics*, 60 (2).

Sah, D.C., and Bhatt, A., (2004): An In-depth Study of Chronic Poverty: Evidence from Southwestern Madhya Pradesh, (mimeo), MPISSR, Ujjain.

Saith, A., (1981): 'Production Price and Poverty in Rural India', *Journal of Development Studies*, 17 (2).

Sen, Abhijit, (1996): 'Economic Reform, Employment and Poverty', *Economic and Political Weekly*, 31 (35-37).

Sen, Amartya, (1999): *Development as Freedom*, Oxford University Press, Oxford.

Srivastav, P.N., (1970): *West Nimar: Madhya Pradesh District Gazetteers*, District Gazetteers Department, Government of Madhya Pradesh, Bhopal.

Wade, R., (1988): 'Why Some Indian Villages Cooperate', *Economic and Political Weekly*, Vol. 33, April 16.

Widmalam, Sten (2004): 'The Utility of Bonding Social Capital', *mimeo*, Department of Government, Uppsala University.

5 Watershed Approach for Socio-Economic Development of KBK Tribals (Orissa)

S.N. Tripathy

Water, the most important natural resource, is indispensable for the entire living organism as well as vital for the growth of plants, agriculture, fish culture and industrial development. Water shed approach has captured the imagination of conversationalists around the world and as such, watershed development as a strategy for raising agricultural productivity has been indispensable particularly in dry land areas—one that integrates sectors and provides the foundation for subsequent development. National Authority for Sustainable Development of Rain-fed Areas (NASDORA) and other institutional arrangements are indispensable for implementation of programme from national level to local micro watershed level for sustainable development and raising productivity. It is pertinent to mention that the present policy for agriculture growth in the country continues to lay emphasis on conventionally enhancing irrigation potential in different parts of the country. Divergence in normal monsoon causes variations in rainfall intensity and pattern expressed by droughts and floods resulting in serious fluctuations in water availability. The fluctuation in water availability is responsible for variation in agricultural production, which renders rain fed production unstable and inconsistent, exacerbating food security and intercepts the availability of agricultural products. Rain-fed soils is generally infertile and subjected to water and wind erosion, rendering the overall environment endowment rather fragile. Due to erratic rains and infertile nature of soil in uncertain rainfall areas, there are high risk factors associated with agricultural production and the rural poverty in such areas is much higher than in irrigated areas. People in rain-fed areas are resource poor having low-risk taking capacity as these areas extend into remote corners, sometimes almost into inaccessible areas, with poor communication facilities and logistic supports, a cause of demotivation on the part of the service providers and the procurer of output.

Decentralized Governance of Water Resources : A Shifting Paradigm

It has been established that in democratic and developing countries like India, genuinely participatory governance of a common property resource like irrigation at the local level can yield benefits in terms of both efficiency and equity, by giving the water users a sense of ownership, by allocating resources according to people's demand and by utilizing their skills and knowledge. As a result, it is now observed that an increasing number of governments around the world are adopting programme to devolve responsibility for irrigation management to farmers' organizations or to Water Users Associations (WUAs) in their reform process, known as Participatory Irrigation Management (PIM) and is found place in their national policies. Indian irrigation sector in recent years is also in the same PIM trail where attempts are being made to increase farmers' direct participation in decision-making and investment. The level of transfer of management responsibility precisely varies from different types of irrigation system. Thus, in India during 1990s systematic institutional and organizational changes have been undertaken to increase farmers' participation in irrigation management through formation of Water Users' Association. As such, decentralization of governance of Irrigation infrastructure or Participatory Irrigation Management (PIM) through Irrigation Management Transfer (IMT) at various levels is being implemented in different types of irrigation systems in several states like Andhra Pradesh, Orissa, Gujarat, Karnataka, Maharashtra and Madhya Pradesh. The PIM programme in India though implemented initially under externally assisted economic restructuring programmes like Water Resources Consolidation Project (World Bank), system rehabilitation programme (European Commission), irrigation infrastructure development by assistance of Japan Bank for International Cooperation (JBIC) etc. has been spreading to all irrigation commands through Union and State governments' initiative or in some cases spontaneously. Furthermore, steps are being taken continuously for improvement in the strategies to achieve the goals of PIM. It has been observed that the Water Users' Associations have taken up the responsibility of operation and maintenance of tertiary segments of irrigation systems, water distribution among member farmers and collection of water rates from water users.

The Participatory Irrigation Management (PIM) was meant essentially to improve irrigation efficiency and thereby decrease wastage of water by empowering the community through formation of water user associations (WUAs). The main criticism of PIM has been that communities have not provided adequate powers in terms of involvement in the planning process and that the devolution of power to user associations has been primarily a means to an end, namely efficient water use for irrigation purposes (Jai Rath, 1999). The part of governance basically areas of regulatory functions identified to protect the public interest should occur through legislation, regulations and the endorsement of standards of practice, and thorough a dispute settlement mechanism. Financing of research and development, education and partnerships should ideally remain in the domain of the public sector.

For sustainable agriculture, improved irrigation service delivery ensuring equity in water distribution, efficiency in water utilization and sustainability in water use has been indispensable. Water conservation through water harvesting structures for supplementary irrigation for wasteland development, hill terrains, to raise agricultural productivity to meet the growing needs of our teeming millions of population has been considered indispensable. Therefore, WHS have been playing a crucial role in recent years for water harvesting and water recycling should become mandatory for all the states. Rain water harvesting techniques play a vital and indispensable role in the sustainability of ground water resources. The rain water flows from the high areas to downward areas through outlets. The flow takes place from different places to outlet is treated as 'watershed'. Watershed management includes soil and water conservation works such as contour bunds, stone wall pitching, trenches/pits, check dams, spring development etc. The National Water Shed Development Programme for Rain-fed Agriculture in 1990 launched by the ministry of Agriculture was an attempt at restructuring. At the ground level, which is at the cutting edge of the programme and where most of the action will take place, community participation is sought to be achieved by entrusting the responsibility for all aspects of the programme to Panchayati Raj institution.

Watershed management envisages formation of community-based organizations with management of natural resources. But merely devolving responsibility to farmers groups does not necessarily guarantee efficient management. This may be a case especially when farmer groups lack financial resources to effectively participate in irrigation management through payment of irrigation service fees or by way of committing monetary resources towards routine maintenance of irrigation infrastructure.

Watershed management is essentially a resource based approach to livelihood enhancement. It ensures supply of water to every field, remove hunger and poverty from rural areas, restore ecological balance, provide green cover in the denuded areas, bring in more rains and improve environment.

Watershed has been conceived as a catchments area feeding an identifiable drainage system, such as stream or river. Watershed management projects rely on water conservation technology, which is built upon accumulated wisdom of the people. This would not only enhance people's participation but also assist in adopting conservation measures, which are to be adopted on community basis collectively by group action. Community involvement is essential for successful implementation as well as for maintenance of community assets created under the project through which the responsibility of management of land and water resources could be transferred to the people.

The government of India has accorded utmost priority to the holistic and sustainable development of rain-fed areas through integrated watershed development approach. The vital attributes of the watershed approach are conservation of rain water and optimization of soil and water resources in a sustainable and cost effective mode.

Watershed management is a community development program and mass participation is an essential feature of it. Needless to mention that economic development implies creation of employment and generating income of rural people leading to the removal of poverty, ultimately improvement in social, educational, health and cultural aspects of rural life. Development strategy is to ameliorate the socio-economic life of rural poor and to confer benefits of development to the marginalized communities (World Bank, 1975). The mechanism of watershed particularly the soil and moisture conservation techniques have become popular and successful to convert dry land (rain-fed regions) into promising agricultural land.

Watershed development, thus, needs to be integrated into the main stream strategy for agricultural growth, if a large part of it is going to be realized from the hitherto rain-fed areas (Joy *et al.,* 2006). Watershed development as a strategy for poverty eradication, food and livelihood security for millions of marginal, landless labourers and tribals would gain momentum; only if development of rain fed land are assured supply of water (Joshi, 2006).

Mounting pressure on available land other resources, unrestricted exploitation of natural resources, higher demand for food and fodder, impact of increasing consumerism, coupled with rapidly deteriorating socio-economic conditions of larger section of the population of the country have caused severe ecological and environmental problems. The tribal population has suffered a lot due to the geographical location of the area as well as lack of appropriate and integrated programme for their development. The vast natural, human and other resources of the area have not been properly managed. Various land based development programmes have failed to attract the farmers as their production seems to be highly disproportionate to the investment. In order to check further depletion of the existing resources and bring about socio-economic changes keeping a balance between the production and the environment, watershed approach has been taken as comprehensive programme of action with a view to address some of the basic question of survival such as:

(i) Long-term self-reliance and sustainability in the livelihood system,
(ii) Regeneration of bio-mass and the degraded eco-system,
(iii) Entitlement and equitable control over community,

(iv) Economic viability of a self-managed resources system at the micro-level etc.

Watershed programme primarily envisages integration of several development activities such as soil conservation, land and water management, agriculture, reforestation and animal husbandry with special emphasis to relate these actions with human issues and to develop the capability of the target population at the micro level befitting to the local conditions. It also aims at improving and enhancing the purchasing power of the people and facilitating their empowerment for better bargaining power, ensuring food security, through the adoption of an integrated approach of developing the natural and human resources.

A participatory watershed approach as a strategy seems more pragmatic in view of its socio-economic and ecological impacts on the livelihoods of the impoverished tribals and as such, an attempt has been made in this paper to discuss the pro-poor implications of watershed in among the KBK tribals that have occurred as a sequel to the implementation of watershed programme.

Problems of Tribals in Orissa

Orissa is the poorest state in India, with 46 per cent of people living below the poverty line in 1999-2000, as against 26 per cent for the entire country. Tribals constitutes about 23 per cent of total population who are the backward, marginalized and poverty stricken population and KBK districts* account for 19.72 per cent population over 30.59 per cent geographical area

* KBK districts basically refer to the undivided districts such as Kalahandi, Bolangir and Koraput and newly organized eight districts of Orissa namely: (i) Kalahandi. (ii) Nuapara (iii) Bolangir (iv) Sonepur (v) Koraput (vi) Nawarangpur (vii) Malkanagiri and (viii) Rayagada, which are among the most backward districts of India.

of the State and tribals constitutes 38.72 per cent (District Statistical Handbooks, Bureau of Statistics and Economics, Bhubaneswar, Orissa, 2005). Several socio-economic indicators highlight the backwardness of KBK region, which is one of the poorest regions in the country. The low level of income in the region, large scale unemployment, under employment and poverty, ultimately distressed migration of tribals has been due to the lower growth rate in agricultural sector. Such migrant tribals fall prey to exploitative contractors and suffer bondage, social isolation and identity crisis (Tripathy, 1989). There are evidences which enlighten that because of deforestation, restrictions imposed by the Government for the use of forests, pressure on land, recurring drought, unemployment and poverty—the tribals of KBK migrate to outside the state in search of employment and livelihoods in construction projects and brick-kiln and other manual works (Tripathy, 2006, p.17).

The coping strategies of the poverty stricken tribals under stress of water scarcity consist of distress sale of assets, reduced consumption, increased borrowings, migration etc. all tend to add to the human misery. In long run, agriculture suffers in terms of loss of soil moisture, reduced fertility of soil and reduced agricultural productivity and unstable agricultural growth, fluctuating incomes and employment which discourage farmers to invest in agriculture (Rao, Ray and Subba Rao, 1988). Then poverty tends to get concentrated in the water scarcity regions. Water scarcity has bad impact on environment and ecology-depletion and degradation of natural resources, degradation of common property resources and increasing fallow. Social impact of water scarcity affects women the worst and the traditional social security system tends to decline. It results in lesser dependence on kith and kin or lesser sharing risks, family dislocations and decline in social relations (Chen, 1991). Some studies indicate that access to water by marginal groups has not improved (Sainath, 2000).

Table 5.1: Demographic and Literacy Indicators in the KBK Districts, 2001

District	*Population Density*	*Population Indicators*					*Literacy Rate*	
		Total (000)	*Female (%)*	*Rural (%)*	*ST* (%)*	*SC* (%)*	*Total (%)*	*Female (%)*
1	*2*	*3*	*4*	*5*	*6*	*7*	*8*	*9*
1. Koraput	134	1,178	49.96	83.18	50.67	13.41	36.20	24.81
2. Malkangiri	83	480	49.91	92.79	58.36	19.96	31.26	21.28
3. Nawrangpur	192	1,018	49.81	94.18	55.27	15.09	34.26	21.02
4. Rayagada	116	823	50.71	85.98	56.04	14.28	35.61	24.31
5. Bolangir	203	1,336	49.56	88.45	22.06	15.39	54.91	39.27
6. Sonepur	231	541	49.13	92.59	22.11	9.50	64.07	47.28
7. Kalahandi	168	1,334	50.00	92.49	28.88	17.01	46.20	29.56
8. Nuapada	138	531	50.15	94.34	35.59	13.09	42.29	26.01
KBK Districts	*152*	*7,241*	*49.91*	*89.89*	*38.72*	*16.63*	*36.58*	*24.72*
Orissa	*236*	*36,707*	*49.29*	*85.03*	*22.21*	*16.20*	*63.61*	*50.97*

Note: Population density (persons / sq.km).
* As per 1991 Census

Presents a picture about the demographic and literacy position of KBK districts (Orissa).

In the light of the above background, we can examine the ground reality in our study area.

Methodology of Study

Needless to mention that the importance of irrigation in boosting agricultural productivity and farm income by enhancing the crop yield, diversifying the cropping pattern in favour of remunerative cash crops and increasing the cropping intensity has been widely recognized (Bharadwaj, 1974, 1990; Dhawan, 1987, 1988). Also, the experience with watershed development under the new participatory approach in India exhibits that immediate results are positive in terms of the increase in water table, crop yields, employment and income of the participants (Rao, 2000). Moreover, where the use rights on common property resources are well-defined as well as protected, there has been a remarkable decline in the distress migration of labour (Chopra and Gulati, 1997, 2001).

As such, the analysis of watershed-livelihood linkages in KBK districts in our study takes into account various socio-economic indicators like cropping pattern, yield rate of only paddy, cropping intensity, gross revenue, livestock production, fishery, enrollment ratio, drop-out rates, incidence of infant mortality rates, incidence of out-migration and incidence of food insecurity (hunger) etc.

The study was conducted in two sample districts, namely, Navarangpur and Sonepur of KBK region for assessing the performance of watershed programs where watershed strategy has been implemented for increasing the level of ground water and integrated development of both arable and non-arable lands. The various quantitative changes have been analyzed on the basis of sample data obtained by employing quick appraisal techniques like rapid rural appraisals (RRA) and focus group discussions. Different socio-economic and environmental parameters have also been considered to analyze the impact of water shed programme on the development of tribals. The socio-economic impact of watershed has been studied by comparing the present status of different indicators during 2005-06 (Post-project periods) with the corresponding figures in the year 1997-98 (Pre-project period). The marginal changes have been calculated through percentage changes.

Sonepur

The district Sonepur comes under Western Central Table Land Agro-climatic zone of Orissa. The average rainfall of the district stands at 7644mm. Percentage of rural population to total population is as high as 92.5 per cent as per 2001 census.

The EAS watershed in Sonepur has covered 92 villages in 4 blocks, i.e. Sonepur, Tarava, Birmaharajpur and Ulunda with the following objectives:

(i) To mitigate/prevent drought like situation in the drought-prone blocks,
(ii) To halt migration of rural people through provision of employment,
(iii) Integrated use of the existing rural resources.

Because of this convergence program an additional land of 1614 hectors had been treated which is around 10 per cent of the gross treated area. The formation of 876 user groups with 13923 members, promotion of 171 women SHGs with 1992 members, plantation of 383 hectors land could be possible because of EAS watershed Sonepur. Further it has been revealed that 52 per cent of these SHGs were linked with banks and members were engaged in pisiculture, sweep binding, rice processing and grain bank. Watershed wise works included mainly soil and moisture conservation works like contour bunds, water harvesting structures, afforestation, vegetative bounding, farm ponds, percolation tanks and check dams have been undertaken.

Nawarangapur

The district Nawarangapur, located in the southern part of Orissa comes under Eastern part of Orissa, comes under Eastern Ghat high land Agro-climatic Zone of the state. Mean annual rainfall stands at 1329 sq. mm. The national wasteland development board sanctioned the implementation of integrated wasteland development (IWDP) in Jhirigaon and Papadahandi blocks of Nawarangpur district. IWDP, Nawarangpur comprised of 5 micro watersheds in Jhirigaon block and 7 micro watersheds in Papadahandi block. Total treatable area as per project document is 6404 ha. out of geographical area of 6901.57 ha.

In all micro-sheds, 50.10 per cent of private lands followed by community lands (46.98%), forest lands (1.61%), gochar land (1.30%) respectively have been treated. Watershed-wise works included mainly soil and moisture conservation works like contour bunds, water harvesting structures, afforestation, vegetative bounding, farm ponds, percolation tanks and check dams have also been undertaken in the district of Nawarangpur. Out of 12 watersheds in the study area 8 watersheds have reported about nursery. Plantation works in 290.00 hectares of common property resources land have provided livelihood to landless people and marginal farmers.

Impact of Watershed on Tribals

The socio-economic impact of watershed programme has been depicted in Table 5.2. It has been revealed that due to water harvesting structures (WHS), there has been crop shifting from traditional cereals and vegetables to high value of seasonal vegetables.

It was seen that because of crop demonstration programme the farmers have adopted new vegetables. It has been demonstrated that yield rate of paddy has increased by 71.42; cropping intensity has made a record growth of 101.51per cent. Spectacular increase in the gross revenue per hectare has also been manifested. Consequent upon hike in agricultural production and availability of fodder, livestock population has also increased which in turn enhanced the production of milk. It is heartening to mention that fish production also exhibited an increase by 50 per cent in the project area.

The portrait of watershed situation that emerges from the analysis of discourse and ground reality presents a success story with regard to human development. Remarkable changes have been noticed in the sphere of enrolment ratio (50%), drop-out rate has been reduced by 85 per cent, distressed out migration and incidence of hunger has declined by 75 and 72 per cent respectively.

Table 5:2 Socio-Economic impacts of water-shed programme on the tribals

Sl. No.	*Indicators*	*Pre-project*	*Post-project*	*Per cent of deviation*
1.	Cropping pattern (Number of crops)	4(Paddy, brinjal, lady finger, cabbage)	(Paddy, brinjal, lady finger, cabbage, patato, radish, tomato, til, sun-flower, peanut, maize, horse gram, and beans)	120.00
2.	Yield rate of paddy In quintals/acre	7	12	71.42
3.	Gross revenue per acre	Rs. 8,000	Rs.30,000	275
4.	Cropping intensity (Gross cropped area as percentage to land holding)	66.66	134.33	101.51
5.	Livestock population No. in the sample villages,			
	Cows,	140	150	7.14
	buffaloes,	30	40	33.35
	goats	40	60	50.00
	sheep	3	50	66.66
6.	Milk production (liter of milk produced per month)	150	200	33.33
7.	Fish production	100	150	50.00
8.	Enrollment ratio (5-14 years children admitted in the schools)	60	90	50.00
9	Drop-out rate (% of Chil-dren of 5-14 years joined the school but left between the sessions)	20	3	-85
10	Incidence of out-migra-tion(No of persons reporting in a year)	20	5	-75
11	Incidence of hunger (no of households remaining hungry for some days in a year)	25	7	-72

Table 5.3 examines the environmental impacts of watershed programme in the study region which depicts that the number of well and tube wells registered an increase by 50 per cent and 40 per cent respectively with sign of improving water table.

Table 5.3 : Environmental impacts of watershed programme

Sl. No.	*Indicators*	*Pre-project*	*Post-project*	*Per cent of deviation*
1.	No of wells in the two sample villages	20	30	50
2.	No of tube wells	10	14	40
3.	Water table	Below 25 feets	Below 20 feets	-20

Thus, it goes with out saying that watershed programme has enormously impacted the socio-economic lives of tribals and poor people because of availability of farm and non-farm employment and allied benefits.

A perusal of the aforesaid analysis demonstrates that watershed projects are important as they are drought-proofing, increasing crop production, protecting environment and generating employment. In the watershed programme implemented areas, run-off and soil erosion have been reduced, water storage increased the ground water level, increase irrigated area and cropping intensity and finally, increase in the employment of the landless tribals.

Emerging Problems of Water Scarcity

The district Kalahandi, one of the most backward districts of KBK, is widely known for recurring phenomenon of sale of child, starvation deaths, bonded labour and mass migration (Tripathy, 1989, 2006) In recent years due to development projects there has been indiscriminate felling of forests and resulted in acute shortage of water to the tribals thus, necessitating an urgent call for watershed strategy for sustainable supply of water and to tackle the impending danger.

Indigenous people from the Donrgia Kondh, Kutia Kondh and Jharania Kondh groups have inhibited for centuries in the Niyamgiri Mountain near the tribal town in Kalahandi district

(Orissa). They are dependent on farming/agro-forestry and have no others Lanjigarh source of livelihood. The thickly forested and riverine region of Lanjigarh in Kalahandi is under sever pressure from mining development for bauxite deposits and aluminum processing by the London-based Vedanta group, which has initiated its Rs.3500 crore alumina plant in collaboration with Government of Orissa (Press Trust of India, January 16, 2008). The tribes are in apprehension that when the factory will start in its full-spring they will be constrained to leave their place and have to go in search of availability of water as their perennial source of water streams will dry due to deforestation and there will be failure of crops. He devastating effects of bauxite mining on Niyamgiri will have detrimental effect on hydrology and water system, ultimately, the lust vegetation will not only disappear but also the water and irrigation available to the tribal community will not be there. "It is believed that the bauxite layer which is formed through leaching also acts as a layer for imbibing water and releasing it slowly through out the year."* In fact, there has been already shortage of water as the factory requires huge quantities of water. It is a matter of concern that the removal of this layer of bauxite will impact ground water in the region and consequently the quality of forest and also livelihood of the impoverished tribals. Thus, it is apparent that watershed development is the key to tackle such pressing problem.

Policy Paradigms

Deprivation linked to water has been a source of poverty, of

* Quoted in Central Empowered Committee, Report in IA No. 1234n Regarding the alumina Refinery plant being set up by M/S Vedanta Alumina limited at Lanjigarh in Kalahandi district, Orissa, 21 September 2005.

inequality, and social injustice. In terms of poverty, illiteracy and lack of access to social and technical services the tribals have been the most disadvantaged section of our society. Directly or indirectly more than 80 per cent of the tribals dependent on agriculture with primitive agricultural practice for their livelihood, that results in low productivity. Hence, rapid agriculture development through the management of land and water resources has to be adopted as measures to eradicate poverty among the tribals.

Promotion of sustainable livelihoods for tribals through tree based farming approach, plantation of cashew nut trees, adoption of soil and water conservation measures, development of plantation, inter-cropping and introducing new technologies for sustainable productivity in rain-fed areas emphasizing on soil-water-plant conservation seems more urgent as such areas are prone to degradation process in comparison with irrigated areas. Therefore, a developmental strategy based on integrated management of land, water and other production resources coupled with appropriate cropping and other agro-techniques has been justified for sustainable production.

To improve water table we need to build check dams, develop watersheds, clear the inlets and outlets to the ponds and water bodies and recharge the wells. Recently some states have undertaken mini and micro watershed irrigation schemes to improve ground water level in drought prone areas to preserve the local rainwater for irrigation. Collective efforts by government and non-government organizations in collaboration with local communities can help mitigate water stress, paving the way for improvement in the quality of life of the people (Rekha Krishnan *et al.*, 2003).

Deforestation, shifting cultivation, over-grazing and improper cropping of undulating land, plugging of natural drains and other kinds of poor land management have been instrumental for runoff, reduced groundwater recharge and water scarcity. Such activities result in the deterioration of soil, loss of valuable nutrients, lower yield, flooding of lower lands, sedimentation of small tanks and wastages of precious water to the ocean. Changes in land use, in particular degradation of soil, loss of vegetation cover and over extraction of groundwater are likely to affect water availability through their impact on hydrological parameters determining recharge (Tripathy and Panda, 2004, Chopra, 2003). With regard to future requirements of water and possible ways to meet the same has been conceived as crucial as the future water scenario depends on:

The present and future demand for water largely depends on such factors like—the technically feasible and economically viable augmentation of the quantum of surface and groundwater available for use; the quantum of water needed to meet the requirements of consumptive use for crops and for various non-agricultural uses (which is one use of water efficiency), the scope for and prospects of increasing this ratio; and increasing the productivity per unit of consumptive use in agriculture etc. (Vaidyananthan, 2003).

REFERENCES

Bharadwaj, Krishna (1974): *Production Conditions in Indian Agriculture: A Study Based on Farm Management Survey*, London: Cambridge University Press.

Bharadwaj, Krishna (1990): *Irrigation in India: Alternative Perspectives,* ICSSR Research in Economics, Second Survey, Monograph-3.

Chen, M. (1991): *Coping with Seasonality and Drought*, New Delhi: Sage Publications.

Chopra, Kanchan and S.C. Gulati (1997): "Population, poverty and Environmental degradation: The role of property Rights", in Anil Agarwal (Ed.), *The Challenge of the Balance-Environmental Economics in India*, New Delhi: Centre for Science and Environment.

Chopra, Kanchan and S.C. Gulati (2001): *Migration, Common Property Resources and Environmental Degradation-Inter-linkages in India's Arid and Semi-Arid Regions*, New Delhi: Sage Publication.

Chopra, Kanchan, (2003): "Sustainable use of water: The next two decades", *Economic and Political Weekly*, Vol. 32, August 9, p. 3362

Dhawan, B.D. (1987): "Productivity of irrigated Farming: Survey Evidence from Three States", *Journal of Indian Water Resources Society*, 17 (3), pp. 23-37.

Dhawan, B.D. *(1988): Irrigation in India's Agricultural Development: Productivity, Stability and Equity.* New Delhi: Sage.

District Statistical Handbooks (2005): Bureau of Statistics and Economics, Bhubaneswar.

Downloads of RLTAP of KBK districts, *http:www.kbk.nic.in*

Evaluation of Watersheds under EAS Watersheds in Sonepur District (2003): *Watershed Development Mission*, Bhubaneswar, Orissa, prepared by Agricultural Finance Corporation, Bhubaneswar.

Jai Rath, (1999): "Participatory irrigation Management: Experiments in Andhra Pradesh", *Economic and Political Weekly*, 34 (40), October 2.

Joshi, Deep (2006): "Broadening the scope of Water shed development", *Economic and Political Weekly*, Vol No. 27, July.

Joy, K.J., Amita Shah, Suhas Paranjape, Shrinivas Badiger & Sharachandra Lele (2006) : "Issues in Restructuring", *Economic and Political Weekly*, Vol. No. 27, July.

Mid-term Evaluation of Watersheds under Integrated Waste Land Development Programme in Nawarangpur District (2003): Watershed Development Mission, Bhubaneswar, Orissa, prepared by Agricultural Finance Corporation, Bhubaneswar.

Rao, C. H. Hanumantha, S.K. Ray and K. Subbarao, (1988) : *Unstable agriculture and drought*, New Delhi: Vikas Publishing House Pvt. Ltd.

Rao, C.H. Hanumantha (2000): "Watershed Development in India- Recent Experience and Emerging Issues", *Economic and Political Weekly*, Vol. 35, No. 45, November 4.

Rekha Krishnan, Suruchi Bhadwal, Akram Javed, Shaleen Singhal, S. Sreekesh (2003) : "Water stress in Indian villages", *Economic and Political Weekly*, Vol. No. 37, September.

Sainath, P., (1996): *Why Everybody Loves a Good Drought*, Penguin, India.

Tripathy, S.N. (1989) : *Bonded labour in India*, New Delhi: Discovery Publishing House.

Tripathy, S.N. & Panda, Sunakar (2005): *Fundamentals of Environmental Studies*, Delhi: Vrinda Publications.

Tripathy, S.N (2006): *Dynamics of Tribal Migration*, New Delhi: Sonali Publication.

Vaidyananthan, A. (2003): "Interlinking of Peninsular Rivers: A critique", *Economic and Political Weekly*, No. 27, July.

World Bank (1975): *Rural development sector policy paper*, Washington, DC.

6 Livelihood of the People, Companies and the State Administration

An Observation on the Politics of Imbalance

Premananda Panda and *H. Samanataraya*

Introduction

India is known for bundle of contradictions. It has population of increasing ignorance while she has a sharp movement towards revolution in information technology. India is rich in natural resources yet retains chronic poverty in many states. The poverty is manifested in form of farmers suicide, starvation death, growing naxalite infections areas in intensify and extent. It encourages big players to come to her land through market economy yet it promulgates welfare economy as democratic planning. It went for land reformation on equity parameter and goes for acquisition of land for contract farming and development projects like dams, mines and industries and looks for international competitiveness. There has been a qualitative shift in the essence of allocation of funds budget. Thus, politics of imbalance based on equity as well as efficiency parameters reveals a sharp change since the introduction of new economic policies since 1991. Some treat the post globalization era as neocolonial era and for some other it is the governance of imperial power on Indian polity based on Pareto optimum orientation.

It is popularly said that expectations from progress initiatives in India are lofty and our efficiency to deliver the required supports to the industrial giants is grossly unsatisfactory. This has been attributed to the lack of accountability and administrative lapses. The development benefits accrue more in favour of the rich than the poor and as a result new explanations are sprouting for the failure of development initiatives and matches with the salient features of Pareto Chart. As it seems, in a sense, the development is anti-democratic in its orientation as evidenced from the available data and thus calls for reexamination of the system of governance and development administration from holistic perspectives. Most of the failures are attributed to errors in human resources management such as deficient of human skill and knowledge. The development with out hegemony has been an unreasonable explanation. Keeping this in view, the paper attempts to analyze the data and opined that the conventional therapies that implicitly refers to 'wholeness' through the notion of deficiency has appropriately engulfed to Indian society in this ear of globalization. The tall claims of change of Indian society towards betterment has been possible due to the overuse of non-renewal resources and free entry to the global players who control market force. However, these are not free from apprehensions and are likely to have intricate future due to no-accentuate on the existing human resources skills.

Land is most widely acquired for what is described as public purpose. For infrastructure development such as highways, railways, defense industries, public sector undertakings such as industries and mines land acquisition has become essential. Since British colonial period India has been experiencing the land acquisition in which historically the state has acted as an exploitative agency against the people. State repressions are many in India during pre-independence and also during post independent era. There has been no change in the quality of life of displaced and the intensity of state repression in such land acquisition.

Since recently many more projects are being planned in the name of liberalization. These project displaced people who lived in their habitat for centuries. There is hardly any case cited for reference to prove that the displaced have led a better life than what they had in past. Instead of redressing their grievances of the displaced The centre plan to amend the Land Acquisition Act, 1984 and change the fifth schedule to make acquisition easier by removing obstacles in transferring tribal land to private parties, (Fernandes 2002). But the Act does not clearly define what "public purpose" is or what project fall under its purview, says Sanjaya Uppadhyaya (1998). The ground norm for any land acquisition for infrastructure must primarily satisfy some basic question that relates to the livelihood of the people who sacrifice the land for development. Acquisition for whom and at the cost of whom is the big question. Is the quantum of acquisition is necessary for improvement of the quality of life of the people of the area in question?

The implication of Land Acquisition Act, 1984 and its subsequent amendment during post-independence in 1994 can well be analyzed from concrete situation of the people whose land has been acquired and the compensation paid to the *patta* holders (the legal land holders). Although planners, politicians and bureaucrats, pretty well know that compensation is no substitute for the resettlement, and people who sacrifice for the national development loose everything that they had in form of common property resources they argue in favour of the "development".

Mineral Resources of the State and the Nation

Orissa is endowed with varieties of minerals resources and

occupies an important position in India's mineral map. Of the total deposits in India during 2002-03, the reserves of major minerals like chromites, nickel, bauxite, iron-ore, and coal in Orissa were 98.39%, 95.11%, 70.39%, 26.5% and 24.37% respectively.

The total production of minerals and ores in Orissa during 2002-03 was 873.62 lakh tonnes value at Rs. 3694.16 crore compared to the previous year it has an increase of 16.51 per cent in quantity and 26.93 per cent in terms of value.

Several mineral based industries have been set up in Orissa that includes Rourkella Steel plants, Aluminum plant (INDAL) now known as HINDALCO, National Aluminum Company (NALCO), three charge Chromites plants at Bramhanipal, Bhadrak, Chaudwar by Orissa Mining Corporation (OMC) Ferro Alloy Corporation (FACOR) and Indian Charge Chrome Ltd. (ICCL) respectively. At Thiruvally the Indian Metal and Ferro Alloys (IMFA) in Rayagada district has set up a plant for the production of charge chromo/ferro chrome. The other two iron industries established in Keonjhar and a refractory in Dhenkanal . The mineral sand separation and synthetic retile plants of Indian Rare Earth Ltd. at Chhatrapur in Ganjam had raised its head. Several cement industries have along with three coal based Thermal power plants have been set up at Talcher, Kaniha, and Banharpoali. In addition NALCO, RSP, ICCL and Hindalco have set up their own captive power plants. In addition to these there have been many industries and mining legal and illegal have been functional in Orissa. Nuapada district has been identified as the potential diamond mining district in Orissa. In western part of Orissa the gem stone business has been recorded since long. The Gem stone policy of 1998 for the premonition and exploration of precious stones tales measures for illegal trading and theft of gemstones. Of the total 28 identified gem stone localities, 18 have been on mining lease.

However, at the grassroots it has been observed that poor tribal and members of economically marginalized people are being engaged as labor force by the private traders at low wage rate illegally to dig the areas to exploit gem stoners . There are trdaers from Gujarat and Rajstan move into these areas and keep watch eyes so that with least effort there is a great gain . The department of Geology, Government of Orissa, has submitted its report on the prospect and potentiality of mining resources . The area is fast getting spoiled. All these are found in the tribal habitat and the areas exploited for any form of mining are m normally the livelihood resources of the tribal.

The liberalization policy of Government of India in mining sector has opened the doors for foreign investors in Orissa.The multinational firms in mining sector like the giants Rio. Tintu and Empire Gold Mines N.L. of Australia have already entered in to joint venture and made MOUs with Orissa Mining Corporation. The projection is made that with such players coming in will increase the infrastructure development and there by open new vista for the OMC at the global level generating wealth for the government. The balance of power at the grassroots is maintained by the alliance made with the external agencies. The poor remained art the receiving ends. The abettors of gemstone exploitation have connections with the local leaders and with their supports they make good money. There are stories current in the areas that indicate the sources of gemstone. Lucky gemstone pickers from village are duped and forced to sale those at the price not known to them. The tribal and rural people in the gemstone tract retain a sense of fear to the state machinery therefore dare not to raise any voice against the employer of lower wage.

As per the state government's estimate, there were 439 mines functioning in Orissa in 1989, out of which 33 were of manganese, 58 iron ore, 48 chromites, 8 limestone, 22 dolomite,

18 coal, 78 graphite, 28 quartz, three bauxite and 143 of other minerals. All these mines have acquired nearly 1,05,000 hectares of land. Most of the minerals of the state are in the "scheduled areas" inhabited by 62 tribal communities. Tribal people constitute nearly 23 per cent of the state's population. Orissa is termed as the most backward in all indicators of human development. Its child mortality rate of 96 per 1,000 children in 2003 was the highest in Asia. In terms of infrastructure and social sector development, many tribal villages in south Orissa are lowest in Asia. Again, most of the cases of starvation since 1985 have been reported from south-western and south Orissa, predominantly inhabited by tribal lineages. The failure of social policies for tribal empowerment and development, rampant corruption and exploitation of natural resources are the main causes of underdevelopment, deprivation and hunger among the tribes in Orissa.

The underdevelopment of tribal areas started with indirect administration and extraction of excess land revenue by the colonial government. The introduction of formal rules and regulations to control land, forest and mines alienated the tribes from their customary rights over land. In the name of improvement of agriculture, the feudatory chiefs brought peasants from plains who took possession of most of the cultivable land from the tribal families. The tribal rebellions in Keonjhar, Sambalpur, Khurda, Sundargarh, Nayagarh, Ganjam and Kalahandi were mainly in protest against alienation of tribal from the land. Records reveal that they were forced to leave for tea plantations of Assam by the colonial government to weaken tribal rebellions.

The leasing of tribal land to the Asiatic Society of Bengal for mining of coal started in 1884 in Jharsuguda. In 1939, the IB Valley Coal Mines bought 500 acres of tribal land from the village headman in Jharsuguda. The first mining of iron ore started in 1910 in Mayurbhanj and Keonjhar. In all, 62,264 hectares have been acquired for mines, industry and dams displacing 1,442 villages, 81,172 households between 1950 and 1993.

The majority of the people displaced are tribes and primitive tribes. In many cases they have been displaced twice over a period of 50 years of planned development in the process of their empowerment. Between 1947 and 1950, several feudatory states rich in natural resources, such as coal, iron ore, bauxite, etc. were merged with Orissa. The government of Orissa enacted rules for regulating mines, which only maintained the ownership of mines, as during the colonial regime, with private companies. However, the ownership of new coalmines was given to the state government. In 1957 the ownership over iron ores, copper, oil and so on was given to the state government.

In 1973, the coalmines were nationalized. In 1981, the National Aluminum Company in Damanjodi of Koraput displacing 26 tribal villages acquired 1,058 acres. In the "scheduled areas" lands belonging to the tribal communities are given to companies violating the Panchayat Extension of the Scheduled Areas Act, 1996 (PESA) which was passed by the State Government in 1997. There is a provision in the Act, which specifies that no tribal land in "scheduled areas" will be given to companies for mining without prior permission of the Gram Sabhas.

The popular movements of Kashipur in Rayagada district have been against the transfer of tribal land to NALCO. In 2000, nearly 8,000 tribal members in collaboration with social activists and civil society groups, protested against rampant land alienation and pressed their demand for the of the lost lands. In a backward state like Orissa, royalty earnings from mines constitute the main source of revenue for the state. For example, in 2001-02, 53.35 per cent of the state's cash inflow came from the mines. The state government has been leasing out mines to earn more revenue even neglecting the rights of tribes and ignoring the long run affect of the ecological conditions. The government has been giving false hopes of employment to the people in the mines, dams and industries. The number of people engaged in mines was only 59,326, which declined to 45,135 in 2001-02.

The 1991 census indicated that the number of persons engaged in mining and quarrying activities in Orissa in absolute number figured 101247 as against 71842 in 1981 registering a growth of 41 per cent. This includes the direct and indirectly engaged in all types of mining activities. The recent census of 2001 in this connection is yet to come out, however, the number of workers directly engaged in mining activities has declined sharply from 55448 in 1998-99 to 44 416 in 2002-03. The automation in mining operation is likely to reduce the labour requirement severely. With regard to the resources distribution and quality of life of all those engaged in mining operation starting from labourers to the traders the politics of imbalance is observed neatly.

The situation in tribal areas has not changed even 57 years after the implementation of community development projects. The nexus of mining contractors, government officials, middlemen, politicians and even some of the village representatives have siphoned the resources meant for tribal development. The share of the development funds among them is an established phenomenon in each and every programme sanctioned to eradicate poverty and empower the tribal communities in Orissa.

A survey by the New Indian Express in 2000 shows the Panchayati Raj, Revenue and Excise Departments have topped the list of corruption in Orissa. The Public Distribution Systems (PDS) has not benefited tribal households living below the poverty line. The shops do not open in time. In many villages there are no PDS shops. Even if food grains are available, the starving tribal families have no purchasing power.

There are several cases in Kalahandi, Balangir and Koraput districts showing mortgaging of ration cards by BPL households to the rich peasants. This shows the vulnerability of the asset-less tribal people. The politics of unequal development has created more inequality and disparity in tribal areas. Land acquisition for mines has displaced and pauperized the tribes. It is time now to remodel our development strategy, which has a human face.

The State of Orissa occupies an important place in the country having a high concentration of Scheduled Tribe and Scheduled Caste population. In terms of ST population, it is the second biggest in the country. Both Scheduled Tribe and Scheduled Caste constitute nearly 38.66 per cent of the total State Population (S.Ts 22.13% and S.Cs 16.53% as per 2001 Census).There are 13 primitive tribal groups. Of the total 62 Scheduled tribal groups in Orissa 11 groups had revealed negative population growth in 1981 and it has reached to 24 in 2001. The rate of population growth is normally understood as the ratio between gross death rate and gross birth rate + or - out migration. The tribal and rural out migration in Orissa is increasing day-by-day. The food security from land forest and labour is either at threshold or in threat. In search of living people migrate to other part of nation through the labor contractors. The population of the members of the Scheduled Tribes and Scheduled Castes, as per 2001 Census is as follows:

Total population of the state	36804660
Scheduled tribe population	8145081
Scheduled caste population	6082063
Percentage of the Scheduled tribe population to the total population of the state	22.13
Percentage of the Scheduled caste population to the total population of the state	16.53
Total number of Scheduled tribes enlisted	62
Total number of Scheduled castes enlisted	93

Scheduled Areas in Orissa

In exercise of powers conferred by sub-paragraph 6 of the Fifth Schedule to the Constitution of India, the revised Presidential Order titled "The Scheduled Areas (States of Bihar, Gujarat, Madhya Pradesh & Orissa) Order 1977" has declared the full districts, viz. Mayurbhanj, Sundargarh, Koraput (which now includes the districts of Koraput, Malkangiri, Nabarangapur and Rayagada), Kuchinda tehsil of Sambalpur district, Keonjhar, Telkoi, Champua, Barbil tehsils of Keonjhar district, Khondamal, Balliguda and G. Udayagiri tehsil of Khondamal district, R. Udaygiri tehsil, Gumma and Rayagada block of Parlekhemundi tehsil in Parlakhemundi Sub-division and Suruda tehsil (excluding Gazalbadi and Gochha Gram Panchayats), of Ghumsur sub-division in Ganjam district, Thuamul Rampur and Lanjigarh blocks of Kalahandi district and Nilagiri block of Balasore district as Scheduled Areas of the State. After reorganization of districts in the state, 7 districts fully and 6 districts partly are covered under the Scheduled Areas of the State.

Origin of the Department

To look after the welfare of Backward Classes, a small unit named Backward Classes Welfare Section was formed in the erstwhile Planning and Reconstruction Department in the year 1946-47. In order to provide concerted efforts to the problem of Scheduled Tribe, Scheduled Caste and OBC, the Backward Classes Welfare Department was formed in 1948. In the year 1949 the subject 'Village Welfare' was entrusted to the Department and was renamed as "Rural Welfare Department".

Soon after the adoption of the Constitution of India in 1950, the name of the Department was changed and renamed as Tribal and Rural Welfare Department. This name continued for quite a long period after which the Department was renamed as Scheduled Castes & Tribal Welfare Department. Subsequently, the Department was bifurcated into Scheduled Castes Welfare & Tribal Welfare which again was merged to be named as Welfare Department. Welfare Department was rechristened as Scheduled Tribe and Scheduled Caste Development Department since 22nd February 1999 and continues as such.

Mandate of the Department

The Constitution has imposed responsibilities on the Governments for the all-round Development of the Scheduled Tribes and Scheduled Castes. The policies, Programs and schemes of the Department have been designed in consonance with the overall goals and objectives as enshrined in Articles 46 (Part IV), 16, 17, 19, 164, 244, 275, 330, 332, 335, 338, 339, 341, 342 and 366 of the Constitution of India and aim at improving the quality of life of S.T. & S.C. communities.

In exercise of powers conferred by sub-paragraph 6 of the Fifth Schedule to the Constitution of India, the revised Presidential Order titled " The Scheduled Areas (States of Bihar, Gujarat, Madhya Pradesh and Orissa) Order 1977" has declared the full districts viz. Mayurbhanj, Sundargarh, Koraput (which now include the districts of Koraput, Malkangiri, Nabarangapur and Rayagada), Kuchinda tehsil of Sambalpur district, Telkoi, Champua, Barbil tehsils of Keonjhar district, Balliguda and G.Udayagiri tehsil of Khondamal district, R.Udaygiri tehsil, Gumma and Rayagada block of Parlekhemundi tehsil in Parlakhemundi Sub-division and Suruda tehsil (excluding Gazalbadi and Gochha Gram Panchayats) of Ghumsur sub-division in Ganjam district, Thuamul Rampur and Lanjigarh blocks of Kalahandi district and Nilagiri block of Balasore district as Scheduled Areas of the state. After reorganization of districts in the state, 6 districts fully and 7 districts partly are covered under the Scheduled Areas of the state. The details have been tabulated as follows :

Table 6.2 : Distribution of scheduled areas and population of Orissa according to 1991 Census

Sl. No.	*Name of the Districts*	*Detail Tract declared as Scheduled Area*	*Scheduled Area in sq. kms*	*Total Pop. of Tract area*	*ST pop. in Scheduled Area*	*SC Pop. in Scheduled Area*
1.	Mayurbhanj	Whole dist.	10416.60	1884580	1090626	131765
2.	Balasore	Nilgiri Block of Nilgiri Sub. div.	223.60	106468	53080	10780
3.	Keonjhar	1.Keonjhar sub-division a. Kojhar tehsil, b.Telkoi tehsil	5350.20	646857	354605	52498
		2.Champua Sub division a.Champua tehsil b.Badbil Tehsil	1585.40	328437	152986	32487
4.	Sambalpur	Kuchinda Tehsil of Kuchnda Sub-division	2367.30	225.086	125741	27263
5.	Sundargarh	Whole district	9921.40	1573.617	798481	138157
6.	Gajapati	1. R. Udayagiri Tehsil of parlakhee-mondi sub-div. 2. Guma block of Khemondi tehsil of Parlakhe-mondi Sub-div. 3. Rayagada block of Parlakhemondi Sub-div.	2498.80	287799	195497	12525
7.	Ganjam	Suruda tehsil excluding Gazalbadi and Goshha Gram Panchayat in Ghumsur Sub-div. of Bhanjanagar	921.00	142649	12852	29076

(Contd...)

Table 6.2 :*(Contd...)*

8.	Kalahandi	Two Blocks 1.Thu.Rampur of Bhawani-patana Sub-div.	323.80	55777	31042	14170
		2. Langigarh of Bhawani-patana Sub-div.	999.70	60974	29832	14189
9.	Koraput	Whole dist.	8534.00	1029986	521849	138169
10.	Rayagada	Whole dist.	7584.70	713984	400097	101956
11.	Nawaranga-pur	whole dist.	5135.30	846659	467919	127800
12.	Malkangiri	Whole dist.	6115.30	421917	246214	84208
13	Phulbani	Two tehsils Kandhamal tehsil of Kandhamal	2017.60	160205	76587	36180
		Sub-div. Baliguda tehsil and G. Udayagiri tehsil of Baliguda Sub-div.	5628.10	386076	204799	63319
		Total Area	69613.80	8871071	4762207	1014542
		State total	155707.00	31659736	7032214	5129314
		Scheduled area as a share of the State	44.7%	28.2%	67.72%	19.78%

The problem of land alienation in scheduled areas in India is not merely a 'structuralist–legalist' one, it is rather deeply connected phenomena with lot of contradictions within the framework of the existing socio economic order (Rao, 1987). Available documentary evidences revealed that ed the Scheduled Tribes in India in general and Orissa in particular have been subject to exploitation and had to relinquish their livelihood resources to the state power and other non-tribal agencies for various purposes. Of many purposes one of the major processes of land alienation in scheduled areas is due to the fact that state promotes development projects like Hydro-electricity power stations, mining and industries. The National Commission of Backward Areas Development (1980) says that : "In a number of areas new industrial and mining complexes established ...... the reservoirs of many major irrigation projects were located in the areas resulting in the submergence of extensive lands belonging to the tribals". Apart from traditional way of getting land alienated, the process of victimization of the tribal communities starts since the date of notification of acquisition. Land everywhere has been a major factor in conditioning political and socio-cultural order of the society. The economy that is dominated by the private property relations encourages concentration of land in the hand of a few. Rao writes when land assumes the status of a commodity it becomes the source of exploitation (1987).

These development activities do not confer any benefit on the tribal people directly even if the state administration have been trying to safe guard the interest of the tribal communities by power of implementation of the protective laws. National policy for the development of tribal communities seeks to tackle the tribal land alienation by stipulating that :

- Tribal communities have accesses to village land records
- Land records be displayed at the local political forum like Panchayat
- Oral evidence be considered in the absence of records in the disposal of tribal land disputes
- State prohibits transfer of land from tribal to non-tribal
- Tribal and their representatives be associated with land survey
- Forest tribal villagers be assigned *pattas* for the land under their village since ages
- Sate launching development projects take adequate care to keep tribal land intact and when not possible, allot land even before a project takes off

Brief Note on Land Alienated Tribal families in Orissa

The tribal communities are in subsistence economy based on collection, hunting, fishing as in case of Birhor, Hill Kharias. The tribes like Juang, hill Bhunya, Langia Soara Kondha have mixed subsistence from collection, hunting, fishing and shifting cultivation. The settled plough cultivating tribal peasants often supplement their economy with hunting and collecting and woodcutting for market consumption. They have simple technology, simple division of labour small-scale unit of production and no investment of capital. Social unit of production, distribution and consumption is limited to family and lineage. The ecological and historical conditions are beyond their control. No knowledge of efficient exploitation of natural resources lack of capital harsh physical environment, chronic poverty often responsible to push them to utter poverty. Often the contingencies made the tribal families to sale their land, the raised produce and other valuable articles.

The animistic life style of each tribe is distinct and can be best internalized in the paradigm of nature, man spirit complex. The Kondhs of Kondhmal as per their tradition believe that their ancestors are the owners of the land they cultivate and the members of present generation are merely the custodians to protect their ancestral property so that whatever they left for them must be ensured for their next generation. The communal property concept was very much there with them since centuries. The deities own the forest and water. They abode in forest and dwell into the village to take stock of the resources that includes bovine and kin.

The types of land the Bhunyas own are the *Biringa* used for *podu* cultivation during first year, Kaman used for *podu* cultivation in second year, *Guda* used for the third year *podu* cultivation, the Nala is an open patch of fallow land taken up for cultivation, Bila is a permanent paddy plot made by individual families and *Bakadi* is the kitchen garden of the Bhunyas. For them the *Jhad* is the forest nearer to the village, which is targeted for future use of cultivation. The owner ship of the *podu* cultivable patches are individually owned by family and as and when the family stops any more use and abandon it goes to the village ownership. In Sambalpur the land types are *Bahal, Berna, Mal* and *Atta.* The hill areas have either mal or atta type land with the owners hip of the tribes like Kssans, Gonds, Binjhals, and Oraons. These are less productive dry land susceptible to drought.

In the history of tribal villages the communally own land and clan-based settlements are distinct socio-cultural features. In due course of time the internal arrahement of sheltering the kin members had made the uni-clan settlement a multi-clan one and later the intruders and other ethnic 'brothers' who initially took shelter with the due mercy of the tribal; leaders and later became an exploitation made the community contribute some land for newly entered non kin families' sustenance and gradually through various tactics the outsiders grabbed land. On genealogical analysis it is evident that across four generations the tribal who once were the landowners and now work and wage earners on those land now owned by outsiders. In fact the movement of land from tribal to non-tribal can be traced to numerous reasons however the easy way was the ritual friendship to risky friendship top evil necessity. The money lending mechanism of the usurers made the tribal to go for distress sale of their land and other vital resources. In most cases the contingent expenditure in tribal family has brought land to market. Some where the rich non-tribal for their socio-economic position were closer to the state power and got supported by bureaucratic machineries including the revenue department. Thus the tribal families were alienated from their all forms of resources and turned to paupers.

In Rayagada district of South Orissa during the fieldwork among the Kondh in Mukundpur *panchayt* area it was found that some landless tribal families who recently got alienated from land were given *patta* against the two areas of cultivable land and 20 decimal of house sites in 1976 during Nandini Satpathy as the Chief Minister. They have been paying the revenue against the land but to our surprise the *patta* holder have never seen the land against which the *patta* were allotted. When it was brought to the notice of the administration the isolated reported case was only handled and no action was initiated to find out how many such cases exist. In another case the land that was under the physical possession of the tribal of Kondh shifted its physical ownership to a non-tribal Kumuti. Neither the tribal family had the desire to get back the land not the Kumuti was willing to leave it from its occupancy and the owner is now a worker in the same land. The land in this case was alienated due to non-payment of loan for food. The distress sale has been a practice in many places. In another case in Kalahandi scheduled areas the land contour of land and the flow of water to the filed was manipulated by the non-tribal to grab the tribal land and successfully forced the tribal to leave the use right of the land at his disposal. This implies that any form of development that does not contribute to the change in the quality of life of the people concerned and majority of the people who scarified for the national growth and development is antidemocratic.

PESA in Orissa is expected to function as a part of Constitution without diluting any portion of the PESA Act. But the *Pali Sabha* is yet to function in real terms. The decisions are taken at the district level. Since PESA Act has a content indicating that the community/private land in scheduled areas (tribal area) can be taken by government if it is for public purposes provided only when the *Pali Sabha* gives consent or with the consultation of *Pali Sabha* it can be acquired by government. The government till date bothers to consult and ignores the consent of the *Pali Sabha*. The term consultation means that it needs no approval or consent. Although the Andhra High Court in recent years gave a judgement in favour of the Samata—an NGO that fought for the tribal in which the consent term is upheld and not the consultation (the judgement is available in web site of http// www. Samata.org). Keeping this in view the State need to amend the Act so that the people will be protected for their livelihood. As one examines the PESA Act one is sure to react and will be tempted to recommend as follows:

That the natural resources extend to all cultivable wasteland, all types of water bodies; forest land which is traditionally accessed by the community, burial grounds, sacred grove, cemeteries, grazing grounds, mines and minerals, bio-diversity (NTFP) within the jurisdiction of the *Pali Sabha*; PESA also protects traditional way of life including the traditional rights. All laws that come in conflict with provisions of PESA are not sustainable. These rights are also subject to compensation and should be considered in the process of resettlement. Traditional cultural right should be included within the rehabilitation plan. Non-farm employment is one of the factors of poverty alleviation. This implies industrial and activities other agriculture. It is suggested that the *Pali Sabha*, as certified by Collector for promoting industrial activities, should use the instrumentality of lease. The *Pali Sabha* may also use the Public Private Panchayat Partnership mode for promotion of industries with the Panchayats providing the adjudication process. The Sub-Group notes with distress that none of the nine States where PESA is applicable have even begun to implement the provisions of the Act. They should immediately draw up an time bound Action Plan for the implementation of PESA. All laws inconsistent to or not in conformity with PESA should be brought in alignment to the same expressly giving effect to their provisions within a definite time frame. The State should set up a strong administrative support system for the Panchayats. This should include putting in place a responsible officer as the Secretary of the *Pali Sabha* under the full administrative control of the Panchayat. All officers working at the Panchayat level should be placed under the control of the *Pali Sabha*. The State should undertake an Activity map for every district for devolution of functions, functionaries and finances to the Panchayats. The State Government should devolve a part of its budget as untied funds to the *Pali Sabha* as a policy decision. The State should put in place a system of electronic transfer of funds to the *Pali Sabha* with monitoring system. A strong system of social audit should be evolved and put in place internalized within the Panchayat system. A formal system of audit with the local fund auditor should be put in place for the Panchayats. The ownership of the MFP should vest with the GS. A superstructure should be put up based upon the Panchayats. Bamboo and cane should be included in the MFP Act/Forest Act amongst the MFP. The right to grant the lease for the minor minerals should vest into the *Pali Sabha* along with a supporting mechanism for working this provision and providing administrative support. The Biological Diversity Act, 2002 already vests the command over the total range of bio-diversity and Intellectual Property Rights vested in the Panchayat. A separate system for providing capacity building for the *Pali Sabha* in the Scheduled Areas should be put in place. This should permit local variations. It shall be the responsibility of the technical officers to ensure that the members of the GS are fully trained. The successful *Pali Sabha* should be used as training models.

The concealed forms of land alienation are more intense than the exposed ones. The processes of land alienation are observed due to the debt trapping, encroachment, and manipulation of land developments and the like. The phenomena has further aggravated with the emergence of new forces of production such as mining, industries, irrigation projects. The right of a common man who sacrificed for the development has a right to life like any other citizen. The development agencies like MCL could not generate better quality of life of the displaced who have been alienated from their livelihood resources. This seems the government have not able to take necessary steps for discharging the constitutional responsibility.

Initially right over land was limited to use of land. The personal right over land initiated when survey started and entitlement was given in form of *patta*. The Bhunyas struggled in their own way to have a secured life. Instead the vested interest got the support through the use of Acts and policies. The attitude of the NGO, Government and the Coal authorities do not differ much in dealing with the cause of the poor as evidenced from of coal mining.

The Balco experience of Gandhamardan hills in Bargarh district of Koraput Nalco one realizes that at the process of development and MCL in all these developmental projects the government takes away the land under the colonial land acquisition Act of 1894 in the name of "public purpose" and gives the land to the concerned industries or projects. The rehabilitation is left at the level of promises, largely unfulfilled, except when the affected people agitate and convert the promises into some form of social contract. Symbolically it is these unfulfilled promises possibly that made the architect of modern temple in India to remember in his last days other poems of Robert Froast. For people, however, it is the different poem the promise have to be converted into accountable social contract. The displaced people whether due to mining, industry or Dam are asked to sacrifice for the welfare of the nation. Naturally the academic is saturated with then discussion on how to make the gainers compensate the losers and how best to see that the welfare is at the optimum/maximum. In reality the case is contrary, where the losers are asked to sacrifice (a holistic notion) for the benefit of the society. Taking as an example of MIP on Dungiuri Jahran, the estimated cost about 65 lakhs to irrigate about 100 acres, the project ignores the alternative indigenous technological use of water of the Jharan along the length of the stream.

In a country where the legal contracts do not represent the social contract fully, the officials and the government get away by giving promises which are part of the local contract and which the people believe as contract and break them at will of the personnel for implementation. Thus for affected there are no legal contract to implement the social contract. Victims of development had the notion that promises are mirages. Mirages like false consciences are subjectively and to an extent objectively real phenomenon. To overcome the collective social experience will help through effective negotiations based on industries—community interfacing else at the level of individual it will result in a suicide.

Although proclaimed by the state and the companies to serve the common interest of the people character of welfare economy failed to manifest its essence in presence of the market economy. In the process not only many tribal families are sacrificed but the general environment I also got severely affected. Despite the crucial differences the tribal people across the districts face more or less similar problems like a form of re-colonization of their territories, general economic subjugation, socio-economic stigmatization in which the tribal families are leading towards different degree of ethnocide due to fundamental asymmetry in decision making capacity. The Orissa experiences would be similar to other empiric situation in other parts of the nation.

The tribal are bound to live under the cultural hegemony of dominant economy. The aggressive articulation of the company personnel and their allies made the tribal suffer. The ideology of individualism advocating modernization and nation building could not properly realized the essence of customary holistic concept of nature, cognitive heritage and consensus decision making process generic and corporate character of land, community oriented values, collective identities, self-management systems rater these are being derecognized and castigated resulting creation of voiceless mass in presence of economically powerful global organizations.

Examining the PESA Acts and the rapid denigration of natural resources, the present scenario of mining operation and the role of the state, it is felt that since anthropology as a profession is committed to the promotion and protection of the right of people and peoples everywhere to the full realization of their humanity, which is to say their capacity for culture. When any culture or society denies or permits the denial of such opportunity to any of its own members or others, the American Anthropological Association has an ethical responsibility to protest and oppose such deprivation. This implies starting from the base line of the Universal Declaration of Human Rights and associated implementing international legislation, but also expanding the definition of human rights to include areas not necessarily addressed by international law. These areas include collective as well as individual rights, cultural, social, and economic development, and a clean and safe environment. The politics of imbalance in the context of Development is an inbuilt mechanism in Indian polity.

7 Paradox of Development in an Era of Globalization

The Case of Santhals in Jharkhand

Jitender Prasad

The governance of post-colonial states have exhibited several contradictory features negating the positive elements of its democratic socialist content. The institutional framework of democracy evolved during the freedom struggle movement revealed several paradoxical features finding its expression in communal, linguistic, regional and ethnic conflicts in post independent India. Considering the paradoxical character of state quite a few social scientists have highlighted the positive features of civil society which is, "commonly identified with a non-statist, somewhat romanticized, set of institutions that stand for liberalism in the form of free market in economic sphere and democracy in political sphere"(Dhanagare, 2001:171). While Gramsci (1976), Shils (1991), Gellner (1994) and Hall (1998) have all pointed out its origin in European society, the Indian democracy after the withdrawal of colonial regime has witnessed challenges that emanated from political rumblings, insurgencies and secessionist and separatist movements. One of the major challenges that Indian democracy has faced pertains to its failure in not promoting and protecting rights in a socio-culturally plural society of different conflicting interests of different caste, communal and ethnic groups.

The Santhals of newly formed Jharkhand state are one some

such major tribal group which faced the tyranny of both the colonial and post colonial state. And in response to the oppressive nature of state functioning, the Santhals protest found its militant assertion in the form of Santhal Insurrection of 1855 and the Kherwar Movement of 1872 and subsequently in the first quarter of 20th century when (the horizontal consolidation of the various tribal groups led to the formation of a major tribal political front in the form of Jharkhand party) the Jharkhand Movement started.

T.K. Oommen has recommended a cultural pluralist view, wherein, "peoples of diverse racial, cultural, linguistic and religious background have a right of claim common nationality an equal citizenship rights if they share territory, communicate with each other and affirm a sense of belonging expressed through duties no less than rights and through symbols and sentiments" (1997:5). In the present paper an attempt has been made to discuss the case of Santhals a major tribal group in Jharkhand state and analyse the government's scheme of development to alleviate their sufferings. The idea is to examine the role of tribal leaders in preserving their ethnic identity of the tribal communities.

The Santhals are considered to be one of the largest homogenous tribes of Jharkhand State bifurcated from Bihar constituting about 8 per cent of India's total tribal population. They constitute about 90 per cent of the total population of the erstwhile Santhal Pargana district of Bihar. Barring two districts of newly formed Jharkhand State, i.e. Palamau and Ranchi, the numerical preponderance of Santhal population is consipicuous in the districts of Hazaribagh, Singbhum, Giridih, Dhanbad, Dumka, Sahibganj, Pakaur and Godda. Besides Jharkhand they also constitue a significant number in other states of West Bengal, Orssa, Bihar and Madhya Pradesh. When Jharkhand was part of Bihar, the percentage of the Santhal population in the state was reported to be 36.23 per cent. If we keep the districts in mind we find that in all the districts of

West Bengal and Bihar, the Santhals are not represented in a significant number. In certain districts their concentration is more than half of the total population. Thus, in Bihar, Santhal concentration was quite pronounced in the districts of Santhal Pargana. There are some other districts of Chotanagpur division where the Santhal's population is quite significant but it is not as dominant as it is in Santhal Pargana. In West Bengal it was 51.24, in Orissa it was 8.87 and in Madhya Pradesh it was lowest with .005.

Paradox of Government's Schemes of Development

In order to examine the development measures and their impact on social, economic and political spheres in the state, it would be useful to examine the process of development under various schemes introduced in diverse settings. Since we have chosen the Santhals of Santhal Pargana specifically for discussion we propose to examine the developmental schemes carried, out by the government at the village level.

In the present study four villages of two different blocks of Santhal Pargana district, i.e., Jama and Shikaripara were selected for field research. The main criteria behind choosing the villages were the homogenous (the village of Santhals inhabitation only) and heterogeneous character (the village where Santhal and non-tribal Hindus both lived together) of the village. But even while using purposive sampling methods to choose villages which met the criteria mentioned above, sufficient care was taken to select those villages where the conflict between the Santhals and non-Santhals over the question of encroaching tribal land was pronounced. Keeping this in mind, *Jama* back from where Shibu Soren, the revolutionary leader of Jharkand Mukti Morcha contested election was selected and the two villages were Thandar Dumaria and Madhuban. Thandar Dumaria is a mixed village having heterogenous character whereas Madhuban is a homogenous village dominated by the Santhal population only.

Similarly Shikaripara block was chosen because it was found that in the block conflict between the Santhal and non-Santhal population was pronounced resulting in an incident of firing in 1980. It also experienced tense situations during 1984-85 parliamentary and assembly elections. From Shikaripara block the two villages chosen were Partappur and Jamuguria. Partappur was a homogenous village exclusively populated by Santhals whereas Jamuguria is a mixed village where both Santhal and non-tribal population live together.

There could be two ways of judging the positive and negative impact of the government measures. The first is by looking at it from the planner's point of view who have an instrumental role to play in providing the infrastructural facilities to the tribals. Another is by looking at these schemes from the tribal's point of view. In this light we will examine the government's schemes of development.

A number of developmental schemes were undertaken in the Santhal Pargana district. For example, over a period of five years starting from 1980-85, it was only in the year 1983-84 when the target set up under IRDP schemes was achieved both at the district and at the block level. In the surveyed blocks of Jama and Shikaripara the target fixed (i.e. the number of beneficiaries) was 783 and 861 and the achievement shown was 885 and 954 respectively. This scheme's progress in 1984-85 in various sectors, i.e. primary, secondary and tertiary, was directed to extend irrigational facilities to boost productivity in agricultural field. Also by distributing milky animals and goats it was meant to provide means of subsidiary occupations. In the secondary sector it was directed towards encouraging the tribals to go in for sericulture and in the tertiary sector it extended the facilities to encourage them to have bullock carts, craftsmanship and the small business, etc. Two years' figures for the district make it evident that the benefits of IRDP scheme are more confined to primary and secondary sectors only.

Under the IRDP schemes of the government, the progress

made in case of Jama block was quite impressive. Since 1980-81, out of a total of 315 villages in the Jama block, 220 villages had been covered by the scheme till 1985 for extending the benefits of the scheme. The details about the number of Scheduled Tribes who benefited from the scheme are contained in Table 7.1.

Table 7.1 : Beneficiaries under IRDP for JAMA between 1981-82 to 1984-85

Year	*Number of beneficiaries*			
1981-82	374	18	48	440
1982-83	254	22	28	304
1983-84	511	76	258	845
1984-85	516	56	279	851

Note: Number of total village = 315, Number of total covered villages = 229
Source: B.D.O. office, Jama.

The progress report of NREP in the district (See Table 7.1) for the year 1984-85 also reveals that the target was not achieved. The allotment made for the year 1984-85 under NREP scheme was Rs. 1,49,71,347 out of which the total expenditure incurred was Rs. 1,30,42,121. Similarly the total schemes taken up during the same period were 691 but only 497 schemes had been completed in the financial year 1985-86. The progress made under RLEGP during the year 1984-85 in social forestry, social conservation, road works, school building etc., also reflected a similar pattern (see Table 7.2).

Table 7.2 : Progress report of NREP and RLPGP for 1984-85, Dumka

Sl. No.	*Name of the scheme*	*Total schemes taken up*	*Total schemes completed*
1.	Social Forestry	52	40
2.	Social Conservation	63	43
3.	Minor Irrigation work	54	–
4.	Road Works	19	–
5.	School Building	63	–

Source: B.D.O. Office, Shikaripara.

Apart from the development activities being carried out at the district level, the possible impact could be examined at block level by going through the official statistics under various schemes. In Shikaripara block the members having landholding of large size and those having of medium or small size both received money through cooperatives, Gramin Banks and LAMPS (see Table 7.3).

Table 7.3 : Loans distributed through cooperatives: 1981-82 to 1984-85

Year	*Kharif Seasons*			*Rabi Seasons*		
	Cash	*Kind*	*Total*	*Cash*	*Kind*	*Total*
1981-82	5.20	1.86	7.06	0.46	0.54	1.00
1982-83	0.62	0.24	0.86	–	–	–
1983-84	0.63	0.41	1.04	–	–	–
1984-85	2.66	1.77	4-43	–	–	–

Source : B.D.O. Office, Shikaripara.

Apart from the development activities being carried out at the district level, the possible impact could be examined at block level by going through the official statistics under various schemes. In Shikaripara block the members having landholding of large size and those having of medium of small size both received money through cooperative, Gramin Banks and LAMPS (Table 7.3).

In the Shikaripara block in various years the LAMP organized its camp for the distribution of the amount both in cash and kind. Similarly the figures given for the Jama block show the loans given through cooperatives in cash and kind. The Social Welfare Department also extended loan facilities to the tribals for various purposes. The prominent feature of the loan extended to them was that the loans were given to the tribals for medical and academic welfare (Table 7.4).

Table 7.4 : No. of the beneficiaries in Jama block for 1980-81 to 1984-85

Year	*No. of beneficiaries*	*Medical loan*	*Agriculture loan*	*Students stipend*
1980-81	1089	31	1	1781
1981-82	1033	41	10	1800
1982-83	1093	31	7	2011
1983-84	967	27	11	1987
1984-85	–	65	–	2499

Source : Social welfare Department, Jama

The figures of the beneficiaries of the scheme included both the stronger and the weaker sections. The weaker section included the members of the Scheduled Caste as well. In the sample villages of Shikaripara and Jama block it was noticed that the weaker sections especially the Santhals who received money either in cash or kind were not in a position to utilise the benefit in a productive manner because of their poor economic condition. In the surveyed villages the respondent's economic condition was so bad that the quality of seed given for sowing was used for meeting their consumption needs. Needless to say that the money received in cash was frittered away in consuming liquor.

The Santhal subsist on loan and therefore, agricultural loans given to them are likely to be utilized for meeting their consumption requirements only. In order to utilise money for productive purposes they need to be given consumption loans first. Majority of the tribals were found to be defaulters, simply because they did not have any means to pay back the loans received from the government's agencies. The collection of short term loans advanced to the tribal was extremely poor. In 1980-81, only 21.65 per cent of the loans could be recovered and subsequent years, i.e. the years 1981-82 and 1982-83 were perhaps the worst years as the recovery of loans was 7.53 per cent and 2.46 per cent respectively. The situation improved in

1983-84 when the recovery of loan rose to 21.06 per cent but in the following year, i.e. in 1984-85, recovery of loan fell down to 7.29 per cent.

There is a considerable degree of difference between the formal and non-formal sources of credit. While the non-formal sources of credit involve the obvious hazards for the tribals (i.e. moneylenders charging compound interest and later forcing the Santhals to mortgage their land) even the formal sources of credit have latent structures of exploitation (i.e. the corrupt officials in the office). The formal sources of credit consist of cooperatives, commercial banks, regional rural banks, land mortgage banks and societies such as LAMPS etc. The lending policies of various formal institutions regarding size of loan, subsidies granted to the tribals, the schedule for its payment etc., are closely regulated by the government still it has not succeeded in freeing the tribals from the clutches of the moneylenders. Whatever success the Santhals could achieve in freeing themselves from the moneylenders in Shikaripara and Jama block has a long history of tribals persistent and organized struggles directed against the exploitation of moneylenders.

The following factors acted as deterrents to the various operation of the non-formal network of credit systems in the tribal region: (a) Since 1970 the militant posture adopted by the santhals of Hul Jharkhand and Jharkhand Mukti Morcha dissuaded the moneylenders of non-tribal origin from continuing with their earlier operation, (b) Various legislations against moneylending partly prohibited the moneylenders of tribal as well as non-tribal origin to be as ruthless as they used to be earlier, and (c) Long term and short term loan facilities to the tribal communities under various schemes of the government have noticed the large scale practice of moneylending through non-formal agencies.

The administrative machinery has also developed vested interests in the schemes launched by the government for the development purpose. The Gramin banks which extend loan facilities to the Santhals to purchase bullocks hardly prove beneficial to them. The Santhals, even if they want to buy good bullocks with the loan money, are not permitted to do so. They are required to purchase only those bullocks which are certified by a veterinary doctor. The Santhals purchase of such bullocks sometimes turned out to be a liability. For example, we found that in Thandar Dumaria in 1985 about a dozen bullocks had died within a span of six months from the date of their purchase. The inferior quality bullocks purchased by the Santhals were sick and diseased and for those sick cattle they had paid Rs. 1800 each.

The loan giving agencies such as cooperative and banks operating in tribal areas have also got infected with the spoil system flourishing in the district. In Pratappur village, for example, Vikram Murmu, the big cultivator of the village, narrated his plight by recollecting his experience. He was approached by an agent named, Sidu Marandi who informed his that he could get a pumping set without investing a heavy sum because the government was giving heavy subsidy to the tribals for buying pumping sets. Similarly another Santhals, named Kisto Soren in Pratappur village was approached by one official named R.C. Mandal who informed him by saying that if he wanted a pump set he could get it by paying Rs. 250 only for seven years. He paid Rs. 100 only and after about three months he got the pump set which he utilized for irrigation purposes.

In Pratappur village due to the nonavailability of water the Santhals could not think of cultivating the rabi crop and, therefore, after having got the pump set, he could harvest the rabi crop as well. He could get about 5 maunds of wheat, the year he cultivated rabi. Next year he was served as notice from the bank for clearing the loan. He went to the head office of the land Mortgage Bank located in Raneshwar block where he was asked to pay the amount Rs. 700 only but he could pay only Rs. 400. Again in 1985 he received a notice asking him to pay Rs. 1000 which he could not deposit.

Some of the Santhals who took loan to buy pump sets had to sell their bullocks to clear the loan. Similarly the land mortgage bank and its functioning had caused serious problems for the Santhals. In Jamuguria and Pratappur there were quite a few Santhals who had bought pumpsets by securing loan from the land mortgage banks. After having bought the pump sets all of them felt cheated. First of all the pump sets that they bought were not of good quality. It required frequent repairs for which they neither had money nor did they known where to get it repaired. Secondly, the Santhals who bought pump sets were also cheated by the touts of the land mortgage banks, who wrongly informed them that the bank was giving them more than 50 per cent subsidies to buy pump sets. Thirdly, those Santhals who were asked to buy pump sets did not have enough land and without taking note of this aspect they were persuaded to buy pump sets by the touts. Fourthly, in order to use the pump sets, it was essential for them to have well or pounds, etc. where water was available to them in abundance. Most of the Santhals who were forced to buy pump sets through the bank had neither the ponds nor any other source of water which could be exploited for agricultural purposes.

The bureaucrats instead of being oriented towards the people, simply stuck to the letter of the rules and procedures to accomplish their target. Such an inflexible attitude of the bureaucrats alienated the tribals from the developmental schemes. Their callous attitude was also noticed in pursuing the family planning schemes in tribal areas. For example, in one of the family planning camps organized at Shikaripara, sterilisation of 400 cases through laparoscopic method was recorded. The laparoscopic method of sterilization is a blinding method of family planning (it is performed without surgery) and if it is performed hurriedly keeping in mind only the target the risk multiplies. Apart from multiplying the risk before sterilisation of a person, if his/her case history is not studied, there is likely to be duplication of operation being performed which may negate the very purpose of operation. It was noticed that in some of the single unit families, both wife and husband were operated. The general impoverished condition of the tribals made them vulnerable to double sterlisation. Since the officials were seized with the idea of achieving their target, both husband and wife were sterilized.

In Madhuban village of Jama block, Lukku Hembram an illiterate Santhal went to one of the family planning centres for Hernia operation. Without paying adequate attention to his problem, the medical experts vasectomised him. When he discovered that he had been operated for something else he informed the officials about his problem. He was told that if he wanted operation for Hernia he will have to forgo the amount of Rs. 60 (Paid as an incentive to one who volunteers for this operation). He consented to be operated for hernia only to invite future problem for himself. After having been operated in the family planning camp, he developed some complications and his condition became critical. He was later advised to go to Mohlpahari (a village where the Mission hospital is located) for his treatment. He had to sell his bullocks to arrange for the money.

The bureaucracy is supposed to be an important agency of development. The sub-plan scheme introduced for tribal welfare and the eradication of poverty etc., can help the tribals only when it is committed to the cause of tribal welfare. The officials and bureaucrats have developed vested interests in various development schemes meant for the tribals. Thus the bureaucracy has developed into a spoil system having its own design of exploiting the tribals. In a situation like this the government's planned strategy of development from below will remain a utopia so long as the vicious network and the vested interests of the contractors, merchants, moneylenders, zamindars, bureaucrats and administrators are not broken.

Role of State and Question of Ethnic Identity

When we examine the state policy in providing tribal community the opportunity to develop their own culture and ethnic identity, we find certain paradoxes. The issue that immediately comes up for the discussion is the role of state and its management. The management of state is linked with those who hold power and authority. When T.K. Oomnen pointed our attention to this element, he dropped a line of caution by suggesting that "the statists tend to hijack the nation in the interests of a section of the people and the nationalists tend to demonise both the state and the cultural mainstream". He writes.... "the state nation coterminality is not an empirical fact but a distorted vision or an ideological preference. To view everything from a Nationalists perspective is to produce hegemony and chauvinism" (1995 : 233).

The Santhals leaders who were fighting for the formation of a separate state called Jharkhand tried to forge an ethnic identity by seeking horizontal consolidation of different tribal groups. Thus they could easily be termed in T.K. Oommen's Parlance as 'ethnicist' who, "invariable forgets that all cultures have both assets and liabilities and hence it is not desirable to preserve all aspects of cultures. At any rate, the nation of cultural purity is a myth and even if it were a fact. Cultures cannot be preserved in their pristine purity in a fast changing world" (1995 : 233).

Considering the paradoxical governance of state the question that becomes pertinent to raise here is whether the paradoxical elements in governance of state would disappear under the leadership of tribals holding state power? Will the tribal leaders work towards minimizing the tyrannical nature of state governance when the Jharkhand state was bifurcated from the erstwhile Bihar state? Yet another concept of 'civil society' which has not become part of popular sociological discourse would crystallize under the tribal leadership who until recently remained marginalized, oppressed, discriminated and exploited? Neera Chandok (1995,28) thinks that 'civil society' in India has "a fluid association of social groupings which are based on caste and kinship linkages or on religious mobilization". Consequently "in India meaning if not the terminology of civil society has been widely used to delineate the upsurge of popular movements against the state".

When we consider the possibility of evolving civil society with the appointment of State Reorganization Commission (1954) in recommending the formation of state on linguistic basis by first forging the unity of India by recognizing the social pluralities and cultural diversity and second, the unity of India should transcend community and language and recognize the nation as one integrated unit—we find state lacking in its intent to pursue any consistent policy. It would be worthwhile to consider recognising the Santhali, Bhils, Gonds and Kurux so that formation of Jharkhand as a separate state becomes meaningful.

The colonial rules denied tribals their home land by vivisecting the Chotanagpur and the Santhal Paragana regions in four states, i.e. Bihar, Orissa, Bengal and M.P., Bihar bifurcated from Bengal in 1911 and Orissa in 1936. The divisions meant dilution of ethnification which enabled the colonial ruler to keep the rebellious tribals separated from each other. And it also made all the four states share the rich mineral resources of the Chotanagpur and Santhal Pargana regions. It is somewhat intriguing to note that even the national state pursued a pragmatic policy towards the tribals by co-opting the leaders into the Indian National Congress, engineering factions within the Jharkhand Party, plundering the tribal economy by creating enclave economy and when the decision to concede the formation of a Jharkhand state was taken it was also guided by consideration of parochial political gains and that was to destabilise the RJD government which was hostile to the NDA led Central Government.

After the formation of Jharkhand state on November 15, 2000, quite a few seemingly contradictory features that have emerged in the newly created state and they are first, the political aspirations of the tribals belonging to different tribal groups have risen significantly. Their political aspirations have given way to the brokerage politics due to which the so called 'dikus'(i.e. non-tribal migrants in tribal lands) have become their potential allies. Second, the political parties which were hostile to the tribal demands for the formation of a separate state may now become the coalition partner. Thirdly, the rhetoric of ethnic politics have to be sustained in order to consolidate the support base among the tribal groups. And now the question of granting domicile status only to the original inhabitants of the population living in the tribal land is the pragmatic approach pursued by the state leaders to woo the tribals and win the sympathy of people. Fourthly, the pragmatic consideration of reviewing the state policy in its planned strategy of development may not see any consistency in pursuing policies which were close to their heart before the state was formed.

The process of industrial development in and around the Jharkhand regions saw a major shift of population from the North Bihar and adjoining regions (i.e. U.P. and West Bengal) from ABC group called Arrah, Balia and Chapra. They are all Bhojpuri speaking people who are perceived by the tribals as their exploiters. The migration of the so called non tribals into the tribal regions is not new as even during the colonial regions the non-tribals belonging to the landowing caste groups, i.e. Rajputs, Bhumihars and Bania had maintained their hold over the tribal land by alienating the tribals of their land. The fire and fury with which the Santhals targeted the 'dikus' during the Santhal Hul is the reminder of the outside exploiters consisting of zamindars, merchants and moneylenders who plundered the tribal by exploiting them and their resources in league with the bureaucracy and the corrupt police force. Thus the goals of economic development even during the governance of tribal leaders may not provide succour to the subalterns from within the tribal groups. The economy and politics of the Jharkhand region is likely to be dominated by the non Jharkhand who constitute about 70 per cent of the Jharkhand population and in the economic field as well they might just find the Jharkhand as their internal colony. That is why T.K. Oommen in his perceptive observation has noticed several conflicting trends. The paradoxical features have aptly been summed up by him when he laments. "..... mobilisations by the underprivileged social categories are geared to bring about dignity also for them, the thrust being emancipatory identity. In contrast, mobilizations by the dominant categories are efforts to reinforce and perpetuate their hegemony" (Oommen; 2001, 234)

The formation of Jharkhand State might still witness the paradoxical features of state governance even under new leadership because of both the elite formation within the tribal groups and the migrant non-tribals on the one hand and the under privileged belonging to the tribal groups and the migrants form within the non-tribals on the other. The former might try to maintain its supremacy whereas the latter would always work towards greater mobilization of subaltern groups by exploiting ethnicity as the basis of forging greater solidarity. Rightly observed Piven (1995,166) when he wrote, "for the subordinate groups, identity politics was a vehicle of psychycic emancipation as well as 'political empowerment'. And that may set the tone for the future course of political ferment in the newly created Jharkhand state.

REFERENCES

Chandok, Neera (1996): *State and Civil Society: explorations in political theory* New Delhi: Sage Publications.

Dhanagare D.N. (2001): "Civil Society, state and democracy: contextualizing a discourse", *Sociological Bulletin*, Vol. 50, No. 2 Sept. pp. 167-191.

Gellner, E. (1994): *Conditions of Liberty: Civil Society and its rivals*, London: Hanish & Hamilton.

Gramsci, A. (1976): Selection from the Prison Notebooks of Antonio Gramsci (edited and translated by Q. Hoare & G-Normell Smith) London: Lawrence & Wishart.

Hall, J.A. (1998): "The nature of civil society", *Society*, May-june pp. 32-41.

Oommen, T.K. (1995): *Alien concepts and south Asian Reality: Responses and Reformulation*, New Delhi: Sage Publication.

Oommen, T.K. (1997): *Citizen, Nationality and Ethnicity: Reconciling competing identities*, Cambridge: Polity Press.

Oommen, T.K. (2001): "Civil Society: Religion, Caste and Language in India", *Sociological Bulletin*, Vol. 50 No.2, September pp. 217-235.

Piven, Francis Fox. (1995): "Globalising capitalism and the rise of identity politics" in Leo Panitch (ed) *Socialist Register*. London: Merlin Press.

Prasad, Jitendra. (1991): *Structure of exploitation and styles of protest: the case of Santhals, 1855 to 1985* (Unpublished Ph.D. thesis) CSSS/SSS, New Delhi: Jawaharlal Nehru University.

Shils, E. (1998): "The virtue of civil society", *Government and Opposition* 26 (1), pp. 11-23.

8 Plight of the Autonomous District Councils in Sixth Schedule Areas

J.J. Roy Burman

Most parts of North-East India by and large do not share a common history with rest of the country. Though the indigenous peoples are not very poor in the region and incidence of beggary among the autochthones of the area is almost absent, there is a deep sense of alienation among them from the rest of 'mainstream' India. In order to assuage their feelings and undo the trajectory of colonial history, the government of India on the recommendations of Gopinath Bordoloi (Ex-Chief Minister of Assam) brought about the erstwhile 'Excluded Areas' in certain areas of tribal concentration in Assam, and Tripura within the ambit of Sixth Schedule as a measure of positive discrimination. Later with the separation of Meghalaya from Assam, all the three Scheduled Areas were retained intact. For administering the Scheduled Areas Autonomous District Councils (ADC) were created. In Scheduled Areas where there are too many different tribal communities, by the notification of governor autonomous regions with separate Regional Councils have been set up. The ADCs became functional from 1952.

According to Gassah (1998) the ADCs were created in response to the demands of the tribal people for autonomy out of their apprehensions about the preservation of their ethnic identity and their rights over the lands, natural resources, customary laws, traditions, etc. They were conceived to ensure the right of self-rule of the tribal people to manage their affairs according to their own genius, to enable them to preserve their ethnic identity and to face the forces of assimilation squarely from their more advanced neighbours in the plains.

There are two ADCs in Assam – North Cachar Hills District and Karbi Anglong District; three in Meghalaya – Khasi Hills District, Jaintia Hills District and Garo Hills District; One in Tripura – Tripura Hills District and three in Mizoram – the Chakma District, Mara District and the Lai District. There are six ADCs in Manipur but they are not within the ambit of Sixth Schedule.

The District Councils and the Regional Councils have the power within their jurisdiction to make laws regulating (a) the allotment, occupation or use, or the setting apart, of land, other than any land, which is a reserved forest for the purpose of agriculture or grazing or residential or other non-agricultural purposes or for any purpose likely to promote the interests of the inhabitants of any village or town. Provided that nothing in such laws shall prevent the compulsory acquisition of any land, whether occupied or unoccupied, for public purposes by the government of the state concerned in accordance with the law of the time being in force authorizing such acquisition; (b) the management of a forest not being a reserved forest; (c) the use of any canal or water course for the purpose of agriculture; (d) the regulation of the practice of *jhum* or other forms of shifting cultivation; (e) the establishment of village or town committees of the councils and their powers; (f) any other matter relating to town or village administration, including village or town police and public health and sanitation; (g) the appointment or succession of chiefs or headmen; (h) the inheritance of property; (i) marriage and divorce; (j) social customs. All these laws need the assent of the Governor.

There is a provision for the Regional Councils and the District Councils to form Village Councils or courts within their respective jurisdictions for the trial of suits and cases (Except certain categories of cases mentioned in the Schedule) between the parties all of whom belong to the Scheduled Tribes.

The District Councils may establish, construct or manage primary schools, dispensaries, markets, cattle ponds, ferries, fisheries, roads, road transport and waterways in the district and may, with the previous approval of Governor, make for the regulation and control thereof and, in particular, may prescribe the language and manner in which primary education shall be imparted in the primary schools in the districts. Besides, the Governor may, with the consent with any District Council, either conditionally or unconditionally to that council or to its officers functions in relation to agriculture, animal husbandry, community projects, cooperative societies, social welfare, village planning or any other matter to which the executive power of the District Council extends.

The District Councils and regional Councils may receive funds for which the Governor sets up rules and regulations. The Councils can also generate their own revenues from the lands as per the rules of the respective States. Revenue can also be generated by levying various kinds of taxes like professional tax, taxes on animals, vehicles, ferries etc. But the regulations for all these require the requisite assent of the Governor. The District Councils may as well receive royalties for the extraction of coal, minerals as agreed upon with the State Government. Any dispute in these matters is referred to the Governor and amount payable is settled as per his discretion.

Though the Sixth Schedule has provided some sense of autonomy and administration through customary laws, at the empirical level the actual provisions of the statute seems to have maintained the form but not the spirit of the approach.

Community process was just accommodated but the institutions created under provisions of the Sixth Schedule were subordinated to state control. In due course they tended to draw their legitimacy mainly from the state process rather than the community process. The position of the Governor with regard to the District Councils is too contentious. While Justice Hidaytullah viewed that the Governor is not bound by the advise of the State Government, Justice Hansariya viewed it the other way round.

B.K. Roy Burman (1998) points out that with the promulgation of the 73rd Amendment the position of the ADCs have become considerably diluted, "When all the provisions of the 73rd Amendment about the powers, scope of function and financial support for the exercise of the powers and discharge of the responsibilities by the Panchayati bodies are compared with those attached to the Autonomous Councils under the Sixth Schedule, it is found that while the ADCs have several regulatory powers subject to state control the Panchayati bodies are in a more advantageous position in respect of developmental functions. In fact in the matter of exercise of developmental function the ADCs are at the mercy of the State Governments. Eleventh Schedule of the Constitution on the other hand, ensures that a large number of developmental functions come within the operational jurisdiction of the Panchayati bodies. For instance, whereas the ADCs may establish, construct or manage primary schools, the functional jurisdiction of Panchayati bodies cover even secondary schools. Similarly whereas the ADCs may have dispensaries established by them, hospitals and primary health centres come within the purview of the Panchayati bodies. The ADCs witness further hindrances as they are often starved of the legitimate finances by the State Governments".

Roy Burman further states as compared to the provisions of

the 73rd Amendment which ensures election for the Panchayats within six month of the date of their dissolution, the ADCs have to depend on the discretions of the Governor.

Roy Burman also indicates how the States create barriers to the ADCs in financial matters through an illustration. "One of the sources of finance of the ADC is the share of royalty accruing each year from the licences and leases for the purpose prospecting for extraction of minerals granted by the state government in respect of any area within an autonomous district. In 1989, the Khasi Hills District Council alleged that they were not paid their share of royalty since 1972-73. Further the same District Council alleged that though for convenience of operation vehicle tax is collected by the state on terms of equal sharing, the state government takes over the 50 per cent share; out of the remaining 50 deducts 40 per cent as collecting charge and gives only 10 per cent to the District Council". Due to such constraints the ADCs become compelled to sell off the timber from forests within their jurisdiction and meet the expenses for fulfilling their administrative obligations.

Dutta (2005) points out the fallacy of extraordinary powers delegated to the Governor with regard to the ADCs in Meghalaya. The share of royalty in respect of any area between the ADC and the State Government as agreed upon was 60:40 ratio (e.g., share of royalty on coal). A dispute rose later on and the case was referred to the Governor who determined the share as 25:75 between the ADC and the State respectively.

Assent or approval of the Governor to the Bills passed by the ADC is often accorded after a considerable period of time. This defeats the very purpose of the Bills and the Council is not in a position to implement its developmental programmes properly.

In certain cases, like in Mizoram the State have bulldozed their way through and directly taken over the community lands.

In 1954 when the Chiefship was abolished, the lands under their disposal were handed over to the newly formed ADCs. But after Mizoram attained statehood, the Lushai Autonomous District Council was abolished and all the community land was taken over by the government. In Mizoram it has been seen that the domination of the Mizos have curtailed the freedom of the indigenous Lakher and Pawi communities from using their own language as medium of instruction in the schools even within their respective Autonomous Regional Councils (Prasad: 2004).

The other anomaly commonly witnessed in the ADCs is that they are often manned by the personnel deputed by the state government and they are not controlled by the local bodies. Their primary allegiance is therefore to the State and not to the ADCs. Besides, the District Commissioners wield considerable power as the law and order responsibilities are conferred upon him along with several developmental responsibilities. Thus in the dual authority structure, at the district level, they wield considerable leverage of power in spite of the rhetoric of autonomy.

Rajesh Dev (2007) writes that in Meghalaya the existence of ADCs have resulted in inter-institutional power struggle. The institutions of the state, the institutions of the ADCs, municipalities and the traditional Syiemships (Chiefship) in Khasi Hills, Nokmas in Garo Hills and the lower local level institutions are locked in endemic conflicts. Besides, the Acts of these Councils which permit them to appoint chiefs from any clan or suspend them violate the traditional customary law. The conflicts often emerge on the matter of sharing the financial resources.

Gassah (op. cit.) writes that due to lack of statutory support and financial dependence on the State Government the ADCs become compelled to rely upon the political parties in power,

"If the same political party is in power both at the State and the District Council levels, the latter may have a smooth sailing in programme of development activities. If it is otherwise, a number of obstacles and hurdles may be created by the party in power at the State level to jeopardize the plan of action that might be framed by the District Council."

While there are many limitations of the Sixth Schedule in the devolution of power and autonomy to the tribal peoples of North East, it definitely has conveyed some positive message and many of the tribes in the region where Sixth Schedule is not in vogue are demanding the same to be included within its ambit as well. The Bodos in Lower Assam have succeeded an institution of its kind. In Manipur too several tribal groups are fighting to attain Sixth Schedule in their areas. In fact, the states like Mizoram and Meghalaya gained statehood due to community mobilizations based on the political boundaries conforming to those of the Scheduled Areas. The Karbi Anglong ADC and North Cachar Hills ADC are too demanding formation of separate states.

The limitations of the ADCs are now coming handy to the State bureaucracy and ignorant academics from 'mainland' India who are recommending replacement of the Sixth Schedule Areas by the Fifth Schedule and Panchayati Raj Institutions. An expert Committee formed by the Ministry of Panchayat Raj in 2006 makes this absolutely clear. The Committee fails to register that the most poverty stricken areas of the country are the tribal predominant areas falling within the jurisdiction of the Fifth Schedule Areas. The Committee recommends that the institutions like Village Development Boards (VDB) in Nagaland may also replace the Village Councils. They may disburse the State Government and Central assistance funds. The Committee also recommends otherwise that even the ADCs may receive the Central funds directly by passing the State. These may become part of decentralized planning and development. Unfortunately the Committee ignores the fact that decentralized planning cannot omit the local revenue generation component. Otherwise the Central and State funds can lead only to a parasitic existence. In fact, the VDBs in Nagaland have failed to generate any local revenue and do away with insurgency and secessionism. The Committee also fails to note the existence of an underground government in Nagaland and the adjoining Naga predominant areas of Assam, Arunachal Pradesh and Manipur. The Committee has recorded the displeasure vented by the members of the Karbi Anglong ADC against any imposition of Panchayati Raj system as it would dilute the traditional system of chieftainship. The Committee failed to realize that chieftainship in most parts of the tribal areas of North East means stewardship and custodial role over land and natural resources. In the given situation chiefship has to reorient itself to the democratic principles of ADC and not the other way round. The ulterior motives of State hegemony underlying formation of such Committees should be nipped at the bud before any serious damage is done.

To conclude with, it must be realized that the ills of tribal administration and participatory planning and development is not rooted to the malfunctioning of the ADCs. Rather the tribals in states like Manipur are demanding the extension of the Sixth Schedule in their areas as well. More than that, the region itself finds virtually no place in the political process of the country. In a house of 544 members in the Lok Sabha while U.P. also has 80 seats, the eight North East states have only 25 members. The colonial legacy of population logic for formation of constituencies is at the root of such anomaly. In a just confederation of states all should be represented by equal members. It is a pity that at the grassroots level, the merits of the ADCs functioning within the Sixth Schedule Areas are not properly highlighted and macro dimensions linking to the nation-state formation are totally ignored.

REFERENCES

Dev, R. (2007): "Negotiating Diversities through Institutional Strategies" in *Eastern Quarterly,* April-June, Vol. 4 Issue No. 1.

Dutta, S.K. (2005): "Basic Functions of the KHADC" in S. Kothari *et al.* (eds.) *Indigenous Perspectives,* New Delhi: Intercultural Resources.

Gassah, L.S. (1998): "The Sixth Schedule and the 73rd Amendment: An Analysis" in M.N. Karna *et al.* (eds.) *Power to People in Meghalaya,* New Delhi: Regency Publications.

Ministry of Panchayati Raj (2007): "Report of the Expert Committee on Planning for the Sixth Schedule Areas", New Delhi: Government of India.

Prasad, R.N. (2004): "Sixth Schedule and Working of the District Councils in North State" in *Dialogue,* December 2004, Vol. 6 No. 2.

Roy Burman, B.K. (1998): "Constitutional Framework for Tribal Autonomy with Special Reference to North-East India" in M.K. Raha (ed.) *North-East India: The Human Interface,* New Delhi: Gyan Publishing House.

9 Socio-Economic Transformation in Tribal Areas

A Telescopic Study in Western Tribal Belt of Madhya Pradesh

Y.G. Joshi

Introduction

The present paper is based on a research project undertaken by the author in collaboration with Dr. Sandeep Joshi at Madhya Pradesh Institute of Social Sciences, Ujjain, sponsored by the Ministry of Tribal Development, Government of India in the year 2003. The study pertains to the tribal dominated Jhabua district of western Madhya Pradesh and is a telescopic study, that is, it is based on the comparison of the base line data collected during a project in the same area during the year 1984 with the data collected for the same villages in the year 2003.

Social change and development are complex phenomena, involving a much wider range of physical, locational, economic, socio-political, technological and behavioral variables. The outstanding feature of Indian economic scene today is that we have all the different stages of economic development coexisting, i.e. folk or preliterate society, pre-industrial peasant, urban, industrial urban and corporate system. As such, in spite of a number of existing development models conceived by sociologists, economists and geographers, the process cannot be viewed, as stressed by Prof. Yogendra Singh, under a structural mode of thinking (Singh, Yogendra, 1993). This is all the more true of backward tribal areas, such as Jhabua, where the totality of situation has to be analyzed in its particular context, and not with reference to overall considerations (Sundaram, 1982). A temporal evaluation of development process, based on some authentic base line data, will not only be valuable to analyze the trend and overall process at work, but this grassroots level information will not only be helpful in theory building, but in the prediction of trends as well.

Typical Characteristics of the Study Area

The tribal areas of India are generally associated with inaccessibility, under exploited forests and other natural resources, and relatively sparse population. The Jhabua district of western Madhya Pradesh with a tribal ratio of 86 per cent, however, presents quite a different scene. Some of the typical characteristics of this tribal area may be summarized as follows:

1. Jhabua is not an inaccessible area, as is generally perceived about a tribal region. This *Bhil* region had been in turmoil for centuries but the tribal community of the area had opportunities of interaction with advanced communities continuously and much more intimately than other tribal communities had. In fact, the dividing line between the Rajputs and Bhils in this region has been very thin (Sharma, 1997, p.33). Seasonal migration in search of employment is quite common in this district and lakhs of tribals migrate as unskilled workers to big cities like Ahmedabad, Surat, Vadodara, Kota, Bhopal and Indore, for periods ranging from 6 to 8 months, and are thus not cut off from the modern world.

The physical accessibility in the area is also good; the district has one of the highest road densities in the Province.

2. Even with good accessibility, the degree of in-migration in the area had been relatively much less and in spite of the fact that the traders and other immigrants occupied better class of land and held high social position, there had not been any noticeable sectional tendencies. The community, by and large remained an "assimilationist society" (Joshi, 1997, p.59), a characteristic feature, resulting in an easier economic and social integration.
3. The area is basically of scanty resources but these are over-exploited. The one time friendly equation of forests and tribals has completely broken down in the last few decades. The stocked forests are reduced to 5 per cent and the contribution of forests to household income is negligible. The resource base of agriculture, which is the main source of livelihood of the tribal people, is also fragile. The rainfall is scanty and highly variable, making the entire district a drought-prone area. The rate of erosion had also been very high so much so that 36 per cent of the so called agricultural land has virtually no top soil. There are also no mineral resources worth mentioning. The rate of urbanization and industrialization has also been quite low.
4. Compared to scanty resource base, the population density, as per 2001 census, was 206 persons per sq. km, as compared to 195 for the province. Since 1961 the district recorded a growth rate of 171 per cent. In between1981-91 the growth rate was 42 per cent, against provincial average of 26.8 per cent. The area thus presents essentially disequilibrium between the available man power and resources.

5. The district ranks quite low with respect to technological and human resource development. In spite of rapid improvement in literacy level in the last 15 years, female literacy is half as compared to provincial average. With a high work participation rate (both for male and female), a majority of them are unskilled workers and marginal workers. The marginal workers in the district are nearly three times higher than the Provincial average.

Background of the Study

Looking to the typical characteristics of the area of study, as stated above, the area has attracted attention not only of academicians but also of governmental agencies.

Because of such socio-economic peculiarities Jhabua is one of the tribal districts of Madhya Pradesh where a number of programmes of the State and Central Governments have been launched on a very large scale, both for the improvement of the socio-economic conditions of the tribals as well as for the restoration of Natural Capital Stock (NCS) of this drought-prone and over-exploited area. Lately it has been claimed that the minor irrigation projects, Rajiv Gandhi Literacy and Watershed Development Missions, and the intensive efforts made by Forest Department have changed the face of the district. With a perceptible rise in the water-level and rabi crop area, there have been significant improvements on socio-economic, technological and ecological fronts of the region.

In last ten years there is a perceptible rise in the political consciousness of the people because of the emergence of panchayati raj institutions and the enhanced contacts of younger population with urban people. In this period Hindu organizations have also made deeper penetration, bringing about a change in the original tribal value system.

However, the success stories about the people and the region as a whole appearing in the press are not based on scientific evaluation done on the basis of any measurement of actual change with reference to some primary baseline information. A base-line data on a number of socio-economic indicators was scientifically documented for 20 sample villages during 1984. This was a research project sponsored by Madhya Pradesh Council of Science and Technology, Bhopal. The report was later published in book form in 1995 (Joshi, 1995). A study conducted on migration in the same area during 1995 showed an increasing trend of migration from the area, despite government claims of improvement in the carrying capacity of the area (Joshi, 1997).

With the availability of authentic base line survey information, it was thought proper to re-survey the same villages during 2003. It was thought that a precise measurement of change recorded for a period of around 20 years will be very useful for measuring the quantum and character of change and for analyzing the contributing factors to these processes. This comparison is claimed to be scientific on the following two grounds :

(a) The initial selection of sample villages was made from all the micro-level agro-economic regions and;
(b) Statistically the villages were found to represent the over all condition of the district.

Objectives of the Study

The objective of the present paper is :

- To measure the quantum of change in the socio-economic and techno-ecological parameters of Jhabua both with reference to secondary block-wise data and primary information collected for 1984 and 2003,

- To analyze this change with reference to various factors involved in this change process,
- To analyze the process and trend of this transformation taking place in the area, and
- To outline strategy on the basis of collected data and work out a model of social change for the region under study.

Methodology

The basic aim of the research project was to assess the quantum of change that had occurred in the drought-prone and over-exploited tribal district of Jhabua during the last twenty years or so, with the objective of analyzing both the direction and the process of change initiated under the intensive development efforts made by the State. To have a scientific evaluation based on some authentic base line data, the initial survey of 20 villages conducted during 1983-84. The survey design was, therefore, kept the same as it was adopted in the earlier survey conducted during 1984. Details of the same are described as follows:

Sampling Frame

Basically the area sampling framework, involving selection of villages representing different agro-ecological conditions, was adopted. This was done in view of a wide micro-level differentiation existing in the district. The steps involved in the selection of villages may be described as follows:

(i) Based on the 1:50,000 topographical sheets, numbering 20, a large-sized transparent base-map was prepared.

(ii) On this map forest land, cultivated land and barren land was marked, using different colours.

(iii) With the help of 'majumili maps' the boundaries of 242 patwari 'halkas' was drawn over the base map.

(iv) The patwari halka-wise calculated data pertaining to population density, land-use, irrigation, double-cropped area, and crops grown was transferred over the base map.

(v) On the basis of the pattern of distribution of agricultural land, crop and land-use statistics, together with the personal experience of the area, the district was divided into the following agro-ecological regions:

I. Negative area, forested or barren with patchy agricultural land, low double cropping, smaller villages, scattered settlements, millets being predominant :
   (a) Predominantly forested,
   (b) Predominantly barren land with intermediate patches of cultivated land.

II. Agricultural land with intermediate patchy barren land
   (a) Low irrigation, low double cropping,
   (b) Higher double cropping with irrigation.

III. Comparatively continuous tract of agricultural land with smaller patches of barren land. Higher irrigation :
   (a) Double cropping not high, maize and cotton with irrigation,
   (b) Higher irrigation with higher double cropping.

Selection of Sample Villages

At the time of initial survey in 1984 there were 1313 inhabited villages in the district, as per the census of 1981. Out of these 279 were very small having a population of below 200, and therefore, were not considered to be viable units for sample survey. Looking to the intensity of fieldwork required in each village and the cost constraint, it was decided to cover nearly 3 per cent of the villages whose population was above 200. Thus, a total of 20 villages were included for intensive study. However, to have a proportionate representation of all the agro-ecological regions and the population size class, the villages were selected from each agro-ecological region in proportion to its areal coverage and also proportionately from each size class.

Selection of Respondents

From each sample village approximately 10 per cent of the families were interviewed. During the random selection of the respondents it was ensured that the respondent was from cultivators only and there was a fair representation of the beneficiaries of different schemes.

Looking to the growth of population from 1981 to 2001 the number of sample households during the survey in 2003 was enhanced by 76 per cent.

The list of the sample villages and the number of respondents in each village during the survey in 1984 and 2003 are as follows:

Source of Data and Tools

Data was collected both from the secondary and primary sources. Besides the utilization of 1:50,000 topographical sheets of the Survey of India for the demarcation of agro-ecological regions, patwari-halkawise and block-wise data was compiled from the District Census Hand book, records of the Land Records Office, Department of Agriculture and the Office of the District Statistical Officer, Jhabua. The tabulation of village information was made with the help of the Village Information Schedule. The basic information regarding the village and the individual respondent was collected by the interviewer, respectively by the use of group discussion and household schedules.

Table 9.1 : Sample villages and surveyed household during the survey in 1984 and 2003

Sl. No.	Village	Block	Agro-ecological region	No. of surveyed households	
				1984	2003
1.	Amagragh	Petlawad	IIC	14	25
2.	Sarangi	Petlawad	IB	27	48
3.	Charanpura	Petlawad	IA	08	14
4.	Bavdi	Meghnagar	IA	06	11
5.	Patdi	Meghnagar	IA	08	14
6.	Pawagoi Choti	Meghnagar	IIIA	08	14
7.	Talai	Meghnagar	IIB	13	23
8.	Aamli	Thandla	IIIB	08	14
9.	Amba	Rama	IIC	26	46
10.	Mokampura	Rama	IIIA	08	14
11.	Amlipada	Rama	IA	10	18
12.	Kheda Andharbad	Ranapura	IIA	10	18
13.	Masuria	Jhabua	IIB	11	19
14.	Barkheda	Jobat	IA	09	16
15.	Amankuwa	Bhabra	IIA	31	54
16.	Mendhar	Kathiwada	IA	08	14
17.	Kiti	Sondwa	IA	06	11
18.	Silota	Sondwa	IIA	11	19
19.	Kund	Alirajpur	IIA	10	18
20.	Machalia	Alirajpur	IIA	15	26
Total				*247*	*436*

Profile of Jhabua District

Jhabua district is located on the south-western border of Madhya Pradesh and forms the core of the western tribal belt of India. The district is constituted of 2 tribal sub-plan areas, 8 tehsils, 12 tribal development blocks, 612 village panchayats, 1313 inhabited villages and 8 towns.

Jhabua lies on the western margin of Malwa Plateau with an average elevation of 450 metres. The general physical appearance of the area is of an undulating plateau with steep hilly terrain, heavily eroded slopes, and degraded forests. The remnants of Vindhya and Satpura ranges extend from east to west in the district.

The climate of Jhabua is subject to greater extremes than the open lands of Malwa. The mean monthly maximum and minimum temperatures are 32°C and 18°C respectively. The summers are hot and the temperatures many rise even up to 48°C. The winters are mild.

The average rainfall of Jhabua is 845 mm. It is not evenly distributed. Petlawad tehsil and the Katthiwada forest area of Alirajpur tehsil receive higher amount of rainfall, as compared to other regions.

The rainfall suffers from high variability, ranging from 29 to 37 per cent. Low rainfall, high annual fluctuation, loss of original forest cover, and lack of proper water management result in frequent droughts. Due to the abnormal behaviour of climatic conditions there is hardly any village in the district which can be considered consistently free from drought condition, and therefore, the whole of the district has been included in the drought-prone areas programme. In the recent past 1966-67, 1968-69, 1972-73, 1985-86 and 1987-88 were severe drought years. Years 2001 and 2002 were also water scarcity years. The year 2003 has been a year of abundant rainfall.

The tribal areas are generally associated with sparse population, inaccessibility and unexploited forest and other natural resources. The tribal scene of Jhabua, however, presents quite a different picture. Here the resources have been overexploited and the one time forested area has now turned into barren land, devoid of any tree vegetation. With the increasing pressure of population the available resources have further shrunk, and at present, Jhabua is a region of scare and depleted resources where there exists a large disequilibrium between the available manpower and resources.

The physical appearance of the district is that of waves of

bare hillocks, strewn with loose pebbles of different sizes. As per the land classification of the Land Records Office, the net sown area is 60 per cent, forest area is 12.2 per cent, while the rest is either barren or is uncultivable.

It is evident from the land-use data and land set imageries that a sizeable portion of the district is converted to barren land where bare rocks have been exposed. The condition of the cultivated land in the area is also quite different from the general perception about a cultivated area. The quality of land is very poor. The soils have abundant stones and pebbles, and due to low retention capacity, these dry up quickly, and even with small deficiency of rainfall, the crop failure is total.

Within a short span of 60 to 70 years the large-scale devastation of forest-cover has resulted in a virtual total loss of soil layer, leading to desert like situation. The problem of soil erosion is severe throughout the district. However, during past 20 years significant efforts have been made to check soil erosion, conserve moisture, and restore vegetation cover.

Jhabua is a poor district as far as minerals are concerned. The only mineral worth mention is rock phosphate which is mined by the Mining Corporation in Thandla an Meghnagar tehsils. Some limestone is mined around Alirajpur. The contribution of mineral resources in the total income and employment of Jhabua district is however, negligible.

Water is a scarce resource in Jhabua. The average rainfall of the area is 845mm. The rainfall is erratic and is not evenly spread; the average variability is as high as 29 to 37 per cent in different parts. Large-scale deforestation in past 80 years has reduced the infiltration capacity of soils. The soils are mostly gravelly with abundant stones and have low water retention capacity. Frequent rain failure, coupled with bare treeless surface and low retention capacity of soils, has made this area an area of chronic deficiency.

The drainage of the area may be divided into two systems,

the Narmada and the Mahi. The Narmada flows on the extreme southern boundary of the district in a gorge, while the Mahi makes the northern boundary of Petlawad tehsil. None of the rivers flowing through the area are perennial, excepting the Narmada which has no practical significance for the area. All the rivers convert into dry beds during summer with some ponds.

The status of ground water resource in the district is not good. Merely 1.4 per cent of the area has very good groundwater potential. The area having good, moderate, and poor potential is respectively 2.9, 32.0 and 63.7 per cent (Joshi, 1997, 42-43).

Under the drought relief programme nearly all the villages have now been provided with hand pumps for the supply of drinking water.

The gross irrigated area in between 1987-88 to 1991-92 was only 7.0 per cent of the gross cropped area, which increased to more than 23 per cent in recent years. Out of this total irrigated area, 31 per cent is by wells or tube wells, while the canals, minor irrigation tanks and rivers or nalas contribute a share of 16, 9 and 44 per cent respectively. The percentage of area irrigated varies considerably in different parts of the district, ranging form 8 per cent in Sondwa to 34 per cent in the Petlawad block.

Forests are the integral part of the tribal ecosystem. However, excepting few tracts of Mathwar range and Katthiwada, this association has become the story of the past in Jhabua. Due to increasing population pressure, lack of alternative resources, and increasing demand of wood for fuel and timber in industrial areas, Jhabua which was covered with thick forests just a few decades ago, has now been converted into bald naked hillocks, devoid of tree vegetation. The destruction of forests in the area was completed within comparatively short time. The forests now exist almost in the ruined state. Now only few pockets around Katthiwada, Bhabra, and Mathwar region in the southern parts of the district can be seen as reminiscence of those old forests. Less than 5 per cent of the total forest area of the district is now having stocked forests.

Nearly 97 per cent of the tribal population depends on agriculture. However, due to low productivity, agriculture alone is not able to provide bare sustenance to 55 per cent of the population. The salient characteristics may be summarized as follows:

(i) The average size of land-holding in 2000 in the district was 2.2 hectares, which was higher, as compared to the Province as a whole.

(ii) Due to the poor quality of soil, lack of irrigation facilities and the low investment capacity of the farmers, the agricultural productivity of the district is one of the lowest in the Province.

(iii) Kharif is the main cropping season of the Jhabua and these crops together occupy nearly 88 per cent of the gross cropped area. Food crops dominate the scene, commanding a share of 83 per cent.

(iv) Maize and black gram, are the two main crops of the district, covering nearly 41 per cent of the gross cropped area. Gram, wheat and soybean have now figured as important crops. Kulthi (horse gram), cotton and groundnut are other important crops.

(v) High crop diversification and large-scale variation within the district are two important characteristics of the cropping pattern of Jhabua.

(vi) The general cropping pattern of the area represents poor quality of soil. Crops like black gram, horse gram, minor millets and fodder grass are restricted to areas from where top soil has largely been washed away. As large as 36.7 per cent of the gross cropped area is under these crops.

The best class of land is devoted to wheat and cotton whose share is only 13 per cent.

(vii) As far as the recent changes in the crop pattern are concerned, there has been increase in the area under soybean, wheat and gram, while the area under jowar, groundnut, cotton and minor millets has declined.

As compared to the provincial average of 38.7 per cent of irrigated area and 33 per cent of double cropped area, these figures are now respectively 23 per cent and 31 per cent for Jhabua, showing thereby a significant improvement during last 20 years. During 1980-85 the corresponding figures were comparatively less than half the provincial average.

Milk production as an economic activity is pursued by few farmers only and all of these are non-tribals. Due to shortage of fodder in dry years and due to extreme poverty, cows and buffaloes are not properly fed, resulting in low milk yield.

In spite of the fact that the availability of fodder in the normal years is sufficient, in drought years there occurs an acute scarcity of fodder, resulting in large-scale distress sale of cattle by the tribals, and therefore, in last 20 years there has been a reduction of animal resources.

Jhabua is the district of highest tribal concentration in Madhya Pradesh. The tribal ratio in the district is 83.5 per cent, as compared to the National and Provincial averages of 8.1 and 19.9 per cent respectively.

The area is dominated by 'bhils' who trace their origin to Rajput tribes. The earliest mention of this culture is found in the epic literature which refers to the bhils as forest people of lower status and famous archers. In Jhabua there are three sub-groups of bhils, namely, 'bhils', 'bhilalas', and 'patlyas'. Bhilalas are considered as offsprings of the ruling chiefs and their bhil wives, while the patlyas are considered to be offsprings of bhil men and Rajput women. Patlyas trace their origin from Gujarat and are comparatively progressive farmers. Surprisingly, bhils are themselves regarded as the lowest in the hierarchy.

From the point of view of human resource, Jhabua district is an area of surplus man-power, as compared to the resources. From 1911 to 1991 the district has recorded a growth of 630.9 per cent, being more than twice the provincial average. The total population of Jhabua in 2001 was 13.94 lakh. The growth rate of 42.1 per cent during 1981-91 surprisingly shows a sharp decline to 25.5 per cent in between 1991-2001. This drop may possibly be ascribed to large-scale migration.

Widespread illiteracy is an important aspect of the human resource in Jhabua. As per 2001 census, total and female literacy in the district was respectively 27 per cent less and one-half of the Provincial average.

As regards workforce structure, the participation of female in the workforce is higher and the percentage of marginal workers is significantly higher than the Provincial average. The dependence on agriculture is very high. Cultivators and agricultural labourers together constitute 94.8 per cent of the main workers. The level of urbanization is very low. More than 50 per cent of the workforce seasonally migrates out of Jhabua for work.

Quantum of Changes Recorded based on Secondary Data

Jhabua is one of the districts in India where intensive efforts have been made by the Government, especially during last 20 years, both to check further eco-degradation and to improve the agricultural production by providing irrigation facilities. Besides, larger investments have been made to improve transport and communication and to provide basic amenities like basic education, drinking water and health facilities.

Based on the available secondary block-wise information

for the 5-year average period of 1980-85 and 1995-2000 and on secondary data collected from the surveyed villages for the base year of 1983-84 and for 2001-02, the salient changes which were noted may be summarized as follows:

1. In spite of the fact that a large portion of the cultivated land in Jhabua is of poor quality and is devoid of top soil, a further increase of nearly 38 thousand hectares had been recorded during the last 15 year period.
2. The additional cultivated land had been diverted from either village forest area or from grazing land. However, this change was notional because most of the so called diverted land was already under encroachment and was later on regularized. Except Sondwa, the increase in the cultivated area was recorded throughout the district.
3. In between 1980-85 to 1995-2000 there had been a phenomenal average increase of 13.6 per cent in the irrigated area of the district. The increase had been more marked in the northern and north-eastern part, comprising Rama, Thandla and Petlawad blocks.
4. The irrigation is solely linked with groundwater recharge, and therefore, a very high degree of variation in irrigated area occurs on year to year basis, depending of course on rainfall. For example, during 2000-01 the sample villages did not show any significant rise of irrigated area in spite of the fact that there had been 193 per cent increase in the irrigation pumps. However, during 2003-04 a drastic change, both in the irrigated area, and rabi crop area has been observed during the field visit.
5. Comparing the data of investment made for irrigation with irrigated area, it emerges that there had been a sharp increase in the cost of irrigation because infrastructure remained unutilized in years of low rainfall.
6. Together with the irrigated area, the double cropped

area had also recorded a significant increase, especially in the central part.

7. From the point of view of agricultural development, the gap within the district between the northern and southern portion had widened. The southern portion, especially Sondwa block, had largely been stagnant as far as agricultural development was concerned.
8. The change in the very base of agriculture from subsistence to commercial is clearly apparent. Most of the low remunerative crops, like minor kharif millets, horse gram and jowar and those which were having lower productivity, viz., groundnut, have been replaced by crops like black gram and soybean.
9. Due to increase in irrigated area, the area under wheat and gram has considerably increased.
10. Along the railway track in Thandla, Meghnagar and Petlawad blocks vegetable growing is developing as a new economic activity.
11. Maize still remains the main staple food and its importance has further increased.

Quantum of Changes Recorded based on Primary Data

Last two decades have witnessed a rapid change in this tribal area. The area has become relatively more prosperous in spite of the fact that labour migration from the area has simultaneously increased, a fact which is astonishing in the tradition way of thinking. The changes with respect to a number of socio-economic indicators, computed from the villagewise survey data, have been set out in Table 9.2. A mere glance at the table brings out the fact that there has been a statistically significant and positive improvement in the economy of this tribal area on all fronts during the period under review.

Table 9.2 : Summary of socio-economic indicators of surveyed household and surveyed population in the years 1984 and 2003

Sl. No.	*Variable*	*1984*	*2003*	*Level of significance*
1.	Total household surveyed	247	436	–
2.	Total family members	2540	3481	–
3.	Average size of family	10	7.98	**
4.	Per cent literate	16.1	27.9	**
5.	School-going children (% of children below 15)	12.6	62.5	**
6.	Percentage of family members who cannot be supported by agriculture with their minimum standard	53.0	62.5	**
7.	Persons engaged as labourers within the village above (% of persons above 15)	20.5	15.1	**
8.	Persons going out as labourer (% of persons above 15)	45.3	62.4	**
9.	Persons desirous to go out for work (% of persons above 15)	55.3	59.7	NS
10.	Persons who want to settle permanently out of Jhabua for work (% of persons above 15)	12.2	44.6	**
11.	Average size of land holding (hectare)	3.8	2.3	**
12.	Holding per individual (hectare)	0.4	0.3	**
13.	Fragmentation index (No. of fragments/ total holding × 100)	98	249	**
14.	Area irrigated (% of NSA)	14.7	20.9	**
15.	Double cropped area (% of N.S.A.)	7.3	17.7	**
16.	Area under improved varieties (% of gross cropped area)	10.8	29.6	**
17.	Score for the use of improved techniques	6.6	3.0	**
18.	Organic manure used (Rs. per hectare) @	122	222	**
19.	Chemical fertilizers used (Rs. per hectare) @	97	692	**
20.	Insecticides and pesticides used (Rs. per hectare) @	61	282	**
21.	Capital formation score	32.5	38.1	NS
22.	Paid up cost per hectare per year @	375	850	**
23.	Percentage of commercial crop production	34.6	43.8	**
24.	Annual agricultural production (in Rs./ hectare) @	3568	6999	**
25.	Gain in Rs. per hectare per year @	3198	4745	**
26.	Outstanding loan per hectare (Rs.)@	1927	217	**
27.	Outstanding loan per individual (Rs.) @	701	484	**

@ Prices of 1984 stepped to 2003 level, using consumer price index base 1981 (1984 = 125, 2003 = 447)

** Difference significant at 0.01 level

N.S. Difference not significant at 0.05 level

The result of this analysis is summarized in the following two sections, namely, the pattern of change and the process and trend of change.

The Pattern of Change

The economy of this tribal area was based basically on agriculture and earning from unskilled labour. Forests, minerals, industry and dairying played an extremely limited role in the household economy of an average tribal. Last two decades witnessed a rapid improvement in the agricultural base, bringing about increase in agricultural income to a level of more than 50 per cent, at constant price level. To those farmers whose agricultural resources were limited, relatively higher wage paid employment in towns of Gujarat, Rajasthan and Madhya Pradesh provided them cash saving, decreasing their dependence on money-lenders. The increase of household income, together with a large population of those youths who remained constantly in contact with urban area, initiated a process of social change that has paved way for rapid transformation of the socio-economic scenario of the area. The large-scale public investment under sub-plan strategy, in spite of large leakages, helped to build an infrastructural base of the area, thus, providing strong ground for this transformation. For convenience, the pattern of change recorded during the investigation, may be summarized under the following sub-headings:

Resource Front

(i) Due to consistent effort made under water, soil, and forest conservation programmes, there had been a check on the rate of resource depletion.

(ii) Due to construction of a number of stop dams and ponds the groundwater availability has improved. In years of normal rainfall the water storage capacity is much higher than it was in the past.

(iii) Nearly 38 thousand hectares of additional land has been put to cultivation in the last 15 years, as per land records. This is, however, largely notional because most of the so called diverted land was already under encroachment.

(iv) As per land records data there has been a decrease in village forest area, especially in the northern blocks.

(v) Though the availability of fodder from forests is still scanty, its availability from agricultural sector has improved.

(vi) Due to mechanization and increasing trend of migration, there has been a reduction of cattle population.

(vii) Due to undulating terrain, soil erosion and scarcity of water, the supporting capacity of land resource in the area is generally lower. With rapidly increasing population and division of land holding, the availability of even this poor quality land at household level, is fast declining. In the surveyed households, between 1984 and 2003, the land holding per household declined from 3.8 hectares to 2.3 hectare, a decline of 39.5 per cent. With a decline of available land resource at household level, its fragmentation has also drastically increased. The disparity of land asset ownership is also high and is increasing. The variability of land asset ownership in the period under review among the surveyed households increased from 79 to 121 per cent.

Infrastructure Front

(i) The overall accessibility to villages has significantly improved, though the quality of roads in many parts in still poor.

(ii) There has been a manifold increase in the access to information through Public Call Centres, mass media and Gyandoot scheme.

(iii) Despite a general complaint of non-availability of power for long hours, the access to power upto village level has significantly improved in last two decades.

(iv) In spite of the fact that many hand pumps and bore wells dry up in years of scanty rainfall, the availability of drinking water has been much better than it was in the past.

(v) The teacher guarantee scheme and *'anganwadies'* have now reached even upto *'phalia'* level. The quality of education is, however, poor.

(vi) There has been manifold increase in the infrastructure for irrigation, both at individual and community level. Banks have also significantly contributed towards group irrigation schemes. In spite of the fact that a large percentage of this infrastructure remains unutilized during years of scanty rainfall, during years of normal and above normal rain this enhanced potential pays rich dividend.

(vii) The effectiveness of infrastructure created for providing medical facility and public distribution system is, on an average, poor.

(viii) The effort made in developing industrial centres in Meghnager-Bamania belt during 1980s had not been successful. Many of the industries have closed down.

Human Resource and Seasonal Migration

(i) Jhabua is a district of highest tribal concentration of 83.5 per cent, more than 10 times the national average. There has also not been any significant in-migration of non-tribals in the area during last two decades.

(ii) The growth of population has been twice than the Provincial average in between 1911 to 1991. This has significantly slowed down in between 1991 to 2001, as per Census figures.

(iii) Due to high population growth rate and scanty resources, the district may be classed as an area of surplus man power. The density of population of the district, as per the census of 2001, stands higher than Provincial average, in spite of the fact that from resource point of view, the district ranks as one of the lowest. Therefore, in the surveyed population, in spite of 50 per cent growth of net agricultural production in last two decades, the percentage of family members, who could not be supported from agriculture alone, increased from 53.0 per cent in 1983 to 62.5 per cent in 2003.

(iv) With a high percentage of young population, the work participation, especially of female, is much higher than the Provincial average. Though in the Census of 2001, 88.6 per cent of workforce is shown as cultivators, a majority of them are part-time cultivators. During village survey it was revealed that 77.5 per cent of the persons, above the age of 15, were working as labourers, apart from working as cultivators. This percentage was 65.8 in 1984, showing thereby, that in spite of increase in agricultural production, the ratio of off-farm workers increased by 11.7 per cent in a period of two decades. Added to the fact that there has been a very high increase in young population, the actual number of off farm work seekers has drastically increased during last two decades. A new feature of seasonal labour migration in the area had been that previously non-tribals did not migrate at all, however, now the non-tribals have also joined the stream of migrants.

(v) Generally it is perceived that when the agricultural production increases, the seasonal migration should reduce. However, in Jhabua the scenario that has emerged is, that in spite of a perceptible increase in agricultural production, the survey shows that the percentage of family members, above 15, migrating out for work increased from 53.0 in 1984 to 62.5 in 2003. Besides the fact of a rapid increase of off-farm work seekers, as discussed in para (iv), the other factors contributing to the increase of migrant workers have no significant increase in local labour market potential, a high wage differential, and a possibility of cash saving. The attraction of permanently settling out of Jhabua has also increased. The percentage of family members who were desirous to settle out of Jhabua increased from 12.2 per cent in 1984 to 44.6 per cent in 2003.

(vi) In spite of the fact that the male and female literacy is respectively 27 per cent and 50 per cent lower than the Provincial average, during the period under review the literacy level of the surveyed population showed an increase from 16.1 to 27.6 per cent. There has also been a significant change in the attitude of the tribals towards sending their children to schools. Tribals at the time of out migration are now increasingly leaving their school-going children at home. This has resulted in a remarkable increase in the percentage of children (between 6 to 15 years) going to school, in the surveyed population, from 12.6 in 1984 to 62.5 in 2003. However, despite rise in general literacy level, the level of technical or professional achievement is very low.

(vii) The workforce can largely be classified as unskilled workers. However, the enquiry has revealed that due to urban contact many youths have gained skill in scientific farming, construction work and a number of urban jobs. Especially they have become more skilful in bargaining and getting more wages by getting contractual type of work, in stead of daily wages. That is why now migrating out is not just a mere compulsion, but is also a gainful attraction.

Economy

1. The economy of earlier Jhabua was based on two components, i.e., agriculture and wages earned from labour. The same pattern still continues.
2. In spite of the fact that the survey recorded an increase of more than 50 per cent in the net agricultural income, this is restricted to only those who have irrigation facility. For nearly 68 per cent of the farmers who do not have any irrigation facility, there has not been any significant increase in agricultural income. Added to this fact, the decrease of landholding and increasing fragmentation has further reduced the dependence on agriculture, and therefore, a majority of so called cultivators so categorized in Census records, are actually off-time farmers and their major component of the household income is acquired from wages. This trend is steadily increasing.
3. An interesting feature which emerges from the survey is that, in spite of rise of agricultural income, the percentage of family members who could not be supported by agricultural alone have also gone up in last two decades.
4. The economy of the district itself could not provide significant job opportunities during past two decades. The percentage of surveyed population who could

acquire work locally, reduced from 20.5 to 15.1 per cent from 1984 to 2003. Within 78.7 per cent of the surveyed households not even a single labourer was working locally.

5. Non-availability of work locally, a seven to eight month of off-farm period in the single cropped area, demand of wage paid employment in towns of Gujarat, Rajasthan and Madhya Pradesh, a large wage differential, the ease of getting work due to now established relations, and an attraction of the younger group to go to cities have acted together for increased interest in seasonal migration. This has recorded an increase from 45.3 per cent to 62.4 per cent from 1984 to 2003 in the surveyed population. The earning from migration now is the main source of income to above 60 per cent of the tribal households.
6. Leaving aside some forest villages of southern Jhabua, income from forests in negligible. Dairying as an economic activity could not find any place and the income earned in towns in tertiary activities is also restricted to non-tribals. There has not been any improvement in the industrial and mining sector in last two decades which may have any significant contribution to tribal economy at the household level.
7. During last two decades the effort made in water conservation, groundwater recharge, and investment in irrigation has paid rich dividend. The flow of information, especially due to contact with farmers of Gujarat, Malwa and Nimar, has also contributed towards changing the face of agriculture in the area. This change is more apparent in the northern and central Jhabua. Sondwa block has remained more or less least affected by this change. The noticeable change in the agricultural sector based on the survey may be enumerated as follows:

(a) Due to the use of PVC pipes, connected to pumps, it has been possible to irrigate uneven fields, resulting in an appreciable increase in irrigated area, especially in years of normal rainfall. However, more than 68 per cent of tribal farmers still depend upon rain-fed farming.

(b) Due to irrigation, double-cropped area has appreciably increased. Wheat and gram are now important crops of the area.

(c) During the period under review the change in the very base of agriculture from subsistence to commercial is apparent. Most of the low remunerative crops, like minor Kharif millets, horse gram, jowar and those which were having low productivity, viz., groundnut have declined and have been replaced by commercial crops, like black gram and soybean. Along the railway track in Thandla, Meghnagar and Petlawad blocks, vegetable growing for metropolitan markets is fast developing as a new economic activity. Being a staple food crop, maize still remains the main crop of the area.

(d) There has been a remarkable development in the use of modern farming technology, especially the use of high yielding varieties, chemical fertilizers, insecticides/pesticides, recommended techniques, and modern agricultural implements. Wherever irrigation is available; the gap between tribal and non-tribal cultivators with respect to the use of modern technology has also appreciably reduced.

(e) The survey shows a drastic increase in the cost of farming in last two decades amounting to an increase of 2.8 times at constant price-level. The main increase had been in labour cost and the cost of chemical fertilizers and pesticides.

(f) With increase in input, the output and profitability has also increased. However, as compared to a rise of input cost of nearly 3 times, the profitability has increased by 1.5 times, meaning thereby that the cultivation is becoming costlier and more risky, especially for small and marginal farmers, day by day.

(g) Together with enhanced production, the disparity level, both intra-regional and intra-community has significantly increased. The tribal farmers having larger farm size and irrigation facility have become quite prosperous in the last two decades.

8. Earning from wages, mainly earned from outside of Jhabua, is a main source of household income to nearly 62 per cent of the surveyed tribal households. Workers now prefer contractual type of work in which a worker is able to earn more, based on the work completed. Wages earned during migration is a main source of cash saving for a majority of small and marginal farmers and has reduced their dependence on money-lenders.
9. The increase in agricultural production and inflow of money from wage paid employment is clearly reflected in the economy, purchasing power, and the general standard of living. The most noticeable change is in the houses. In the past most of the houses of the tribals were made of bamboo and grass: now a large number of these are made of bricks and titled roofs. A number of tribal households now own items like tractors, threshers, and motor cycles which were rare at the time of previous survey. The investment in irrigation equipment has also drastically increased. The contribution of government programmes and banks in the acquisition of fixed assets has been quite significant.

10. The general dependency on loan amongst tribal has shown a declining trend, mainly due to the saving made during migration. The per hectare loan liability from institutional sources amongst the surveyed tribal household has also increased only marginally in two decades, in spite of manifold increase in the investment in agriculture.
11. The micro credit concept has become popular in last ten years and a number of self-help groups are now functioning effectively. These groups have also helped the tribals to reduce their dependence on moneylenders for day-to-day requirement.
12. Excepting large and medium farmers whose agricultural production is significantly large, a majority of small farmers generally sell their produce to local traders and migrate out as early as possible.

Socio-cultural

1. Due to urban contacts, increased exposer to media and the political process of Panchayat Raj which reached up to village level, process of assimilation of the tribals has been quite fast. This is clearly reflected in the economy, life style, dress, eating habits, and in attitudes. Adoption of modern dress by young generation, wearingof under garments by ladies, increasing popularity of bear in place of 'toddy' may be quoted as some examples. Difference between tribal and non-tribal farmers with respect to the use of modern technology and commercialization has also narrowed down.
2. There has been a change in the attitude towards education. Now more tribals are sending their children to school. Many migrating families now leave behind their school-going children.

3. People are now opting for modern medicine in place of 'badwa'. Due to lack of facilities in government dispensaries, private doctors are making good business in the area.
4. Political awareness has improved in a big way. The one time one party scenario has totally changed. The grassroots organizations like RSS, VHP and Sewabharti have made deep inroads in this tribal area.
5. The process of Hinduization is clearly seen. The traditional tribal gods are being replaced by 'Hanuman' and other Hindu gods. Many Hindu organizations run by VHP, Asharamji, Khoobsingji, Ramsharanam, Kamalkishore Nagarji are very active and many tribals have adopted vegetarianism and left drinking. Such bhils are called as 'Bhagat bhils'.
6. Unfortunately fundamentalism has increased both in the Christian and Bhagat bhils, resulting in clashes.
7. Crimes have significantly reduced. Especially in Alirajpur area where in 1984 it was not safe to go even in day time, crimes are now rare. This has been possible due to education and increased income from agriculture and migration.

The Process of Change

Social change is a complex process which has been analyzed by hundreds of authors with anthropological, sociological, economic, political, geographical, historical and behavioural perspectives. A number of models of social change have also been put forward. However, none of these can be termed as universal that may be applicable to all societies in all time frames. In a fast transforming primitive society, such as the tribals of western India, situational analysis with an emphasis on process, will lead to better results.

When viewed in a broader perspective, the tribals of Jhabua are an assimilationist society, and therefore, the process of transformation should be analysed within the framework of social and cultural integration, rather than in the conflict framework. The present study also indicates how certain processes, such as seasonal labour migration, which emerged out of survival compulsion, later on helped the society to increase their productivity and pave a way for faster transformation. Marx has also asserted that the character of society depends on the way in which economic problems are solved by that society. In the case of Jhabua, besides this in-built mechanism, the intervention of the State in terms of planned inputs has also significantly contributed towards providing a strong infrastructural and capital base for bringing about this transformation.

The rapid change witnessed during last two decades, as is evident from the study, should be viewed in a frame of multi-causality with chain reactions. The basis of this change had been those processes which helped to increase household income at the grassroots level, i.e., both to those who were cultivators and those who were wage earners, as depicted in part A of the diagram. The enhancement of income, coupled with the awareness generated due to urban contact, mass media, increased accessibility, political process, and education started a social process (part B), resulting in decreased crimes, accelerated process of assimilation, and creation of separate identities among bhils themselves.

The Strategy

1. The basic planning philosophy of Jhabua must be governed by two priorities, i.e., rebuilding of natural resource base through water, soil and forest conservation

programmes and providing options to the people which strengthen the survival base.

2. The study clearly shows that the key to the prosperity seen in the area during last two decades is the rise of income in the farm sector due to irrigation and use of new technology and increased income earned by labourers from outside Jhabua. Therefore, these basic sources must be strengthened. There is much scope to further increase the irrigation potential by water harvesting and group irrigation schemes, especially in the southern Jhabua.

   It is not practically possible to check migration; therefore, the role of the government should be to act as facilitator. Information network upto block level should be developed to provide information about the availability of work outside Jhabua, SMART cards be provided through self help groups to migrating workers which could be used for providing food grain at subsidized rates at the work sites. Provision of education to children at work sites should also be made.

3. Micro finance concept has helped a lot in bringing the tribals out of the clutches of money lenders. Government should come forward in a big way to strengthen the self help group network in the area.

4. Village markets or '*hats*' are not only the centres of economic exchange but also act as focus of cultural activity and centers of diffusion of knowledge. In Jhabua 38 such centres have been identified, along with their tributary area (Joshi, 1997, 27-29). Looking to the fact that disequilibrium between available resource and man-power is the basic problem of the area, this cluster planning framework should be adopted for man-power planning in the region, as a long-term measure.

5. Drought is still a serious chronic problem of the area and therefore, instead of *ad-hoc* measures it should be managed on a permanent basis. In all panchayats a separate 'corpus' for short-term drought relief measure may be created on a permanent basis. The funds for these may be generated by putting levy in *hat* bazars, on labour contractors, DPAP and other sources, to be decided by the State Government. The minimum fund to be generated for individual panchayat should be worked out on scientific basis. A detailed guideline, giving a variety of options suited to local conditions, should be prepared for the utilization of this fund in local *bhili* language. The total decision of when to declare a drought and how to manage the relief activities, in tune with the requirements of people, should be vested with the '*gram sabha*'. The panchayat be linked to fodder banks located at cluster points for their requirement of fodder and for establishing cattle sub-centres at panchayat level at the time of drought.
6. From the point of view of social fabric this tribal dominated district is on an advantageous position, in that, there is neither any separatist movement, nor there exists any tension between tribal and non-tribal population. The crime graph of the district has also significantly come down in last two decades. However, in recent years new cleavages are appearing between tribals on religion and political lines. There is a need to check these disrupting tendencies in the beginning itself, to prevent the vested interests to create tension for their own benefit.

REFERENCES

Doshi, S.L. (1997) : *Emerging Tribal Image,* Delhi: Rawat Publications.

Dube, S.C. (1992): *Understanding Change : Anthropological & Sociological Perspective,* New Delhi: Vikas Publishing House Pvt. Ltd.

Joshi, Y.G. (1983): *"Impact of Urbanisation on the Typological Characteristics of Agriculture: A Study Around Indore City,"* published by University of Indore under the scheme of population of learned research work by U.G.C.

Joshi, Y.G. (1990): *Process of Tribal Development in Over-exploited Tribal Region,* New Delhi: Inter India Publishers.

Joshi, Y.G. (1997) : *Tribal Migration,* Jaipur: Rawat Publications.

Joshi, Y.G. (1999) : *"Perception of Drought and Reaction Towards Strategy in Jhabua,"* Monograph M.P. Institute of Social Science Research, Ujjain.

Mandal Dabarata (1998): "Life and Culture of the Bhils of Malwa" in Mehta, P.C. *Changing Face of Bhils,* Udaipur: Shiv Publishers & Distributors.

Pattnaik, Renuka (2000) : *Tribe : Ecology and Development,* New Delhi: Rajat Publications.

Raina, G. (2001): *Politics, Development & Modernization in Tribal India,* Delhi: Rawat Publications.

Sachchidananda (1979) : *The Changing Munda,* New Delhi: Concept Publishing Co.

Sharma, B.D. (1997) : "Tribal Development in Scarce Resource Regions" in Gupta Ranjeet (ed.) *Planning for Tribal Development,* New Delhi: Ankur Publication House.

Singh, R.S. (1986) : *Changing Occupational Structure of Scheduled Tribes,* New Delhi: Inter India Publishers.

Singh, Yogendra (1993) : *Social Change in India : Crisis and Resilience,* New Delhi: Har-Anand Publications.

Sundaram, K. (1982) : *"Rural Urban Migration : An Economic Model and the Indian Experience"* in Rao M. S. A. (ed.) *Studies in Migration,* New Delhi: Manohar Publications.

10 Tribal Livelihood Options : Socio-Ecological Changes, State Intervention and Sustainable Development

D.K. Verma and *A. Sohrot*

During last five decades the socio-ecology of tribal people has changed substantially. Traditionally, tribals had not only been the part and parcel of forest ecosystem, but forests also significantly contributed towards their livelihood. The relationship of tribals with forests for centuries had been mutual, integrated, supportive but based on sustainable subsistence rather than exploitation. Socio-ecology of tribals started changing since the exploitation of forest resources started in 1864 with the constitution of forest department and gradually transferring the ownership of forest to the State by enacting forest law in 1865. Abruptly the tribals, who could freely utilize the forest for their livelihood, were left without substantial alternatives and were even looked down as intruders and thieves. Albeit in the name of forest conservation, tribals were denied their traditional rights, yet there is no denying the fact that during British era forests were exploited for railway sleepers, shipbuilding, construction activity and a variety of uses meant for the non-tribal section of the society.

After independence also the forests were largely considered as a source of revenue for the state and there was no element of partnership with the tribals. With increasing cost of timber and other forest produce the unabated commercial exploitation of forest continued. Besides, a large portion of forest cover was lost due to large-scale irrigation, mining and industrial activities in the tribal dominated areas of the country. In the early years when the population pressure was not high and the level of awareness among the tribals was low, the conflicts were not to the extent, which could have forced the States to re-look at their policy and make conceptual shifts to ensure food security and livelihood options for tribal people.

The present paper discusses the empirical studies concerning livelihood options for scheduled tribes of Madhya Pradesh under changed socio-ecological conditions. The linkage of food security with tribal livelihood has two conceptual dimensions. Firstly, the tribal economies in our country still largely operate under the mechanism of survival compulsion with a bare minimum livelihood base and that too being traditionally dependent upon natural largely forest based resources. Secondly, food security essentially includes three dimensions, namely, food availability, food access and food absorption. While food availability is a function of production and food absorption is a function of physical health and hygiene of an individual, food access is essentially linked to livelihood access, *i.e.* the capacity of an individual to procure food when it is readily available in the market. The paper recommends that livelihood options for tribal people could be made sustainable if tribal development policy is reoriented ensuring expanded livelihood resources base for alternative options of food availability, multiple access to food and enhanced capability of food absorption.

Forest and Tribal Issues in Five Year Plans

The Constitution of India incorporates several special provisions for the promotion of educational and economic interests of Scheduled Tribes and their protection from social injustice and all forms of exploitation. In the very first five year plan of Independent India, it was emphasized that the welfare programmes for tribal people need to be based on respect and understanding of their culture and traditions and an appreciation of the social, psychological and economic problems with which they had been facing. The welfare and development programmes in tribal areas inevitably involved a measure of disturbance in relation to traditional beliefs and practices. In their implementation, therefore, the confidence of the people and, in particular, the understanding and goodwill of the elders of tribal communities, was considered of the highest importance. It was, therefore, considered necessary that welfare extension workers of all kinds should be found as far as possible from amongst the educated youth in tribal communities. In commending the adoption of new techniques tribal leadership should have a major role and any suggestion of imposition should be avoided, and for each step the ground should be carefully prepared in advance. It was also felt that the anthropologists, the administrators, the specialists and the social workers had to work together as a team, approaching the problems of tribal people with sympathy, understanding and knowledge of social psychology and needs of tribal communities.

However, in the document of the First Five Year Plan vital role of forests in India's economy was also emphasized. Forests were seen as an important source of fuel and also of raw materials, such as timber, bamboos, lac, gum, katha, etc. useful for domestic, industrial and agricultural purposes, and also as source to provide materials for defence and communications as well as grazing for cattle. Accurate statistics regarding the area under forests were not available at that time. "Indian Forest Statistics" placed the area under forests in 1949-50 at 147.7 million acres

(230,789 sq. miles) *i.e.* 18 per cent of the total land area. That figure included a considerable area of unwooded waste land too. The Forest Policy Resolution of May 12, 1952, suggested that India as a whole should aim at maintaining one-third of its total land area under forests. Considerable improvement was planned by renovating large areas which, even though classified as forests, had been deforested or had not been properly managed, such as, about 40 million acres of *Zamindari* forests that had became vested in State Governments on the abolition of *Zamindari* and *Jagirdari*. Further, over felling of trees occurred during the war, as in 1945-46, where production of timber and fuel wood had increased by about 62 per cent. In the First Five Year Plan, consumption of timber (total 2110 thousand tons of round logs) was classified as follows :

		(In thousand tons of round logs)
(a)	Government consumption—	
	Railway sleepers	340
	Other railway demands	80
	Defence and other Civil Departments	160
(b)	Manufacturing industries—	
	Match industry	120
	Packing case industry, Tea Chests	115
	Plywood industry and others	100
(c)	Balance available for other Industries	
	Domestic and building purposes	1195

About 73 per cent of the total timber was thus being utilised in the private sector and the off-take by the Government was about 27 per cent. During that period, demand for timber for defence, as well as for domestic and building purposes had increased considerably as a result of increasing urbanisation and the rehabilitation programme. Further, as the availability of steel was far short of total requirements, a policy of conserving steel and replacing that by timber had become imperative and was adopted in the following cases :

- Treated timber was used for telephone, telegraph and

electric power lines as were done in most countries of Europe. The annual demand for poles and the means of meeting demand that in various parts of the country was worked out in consultation with the State Forest Departments. About 50 thousand poles were obtained annually from the Andamans and 30 thousand poles from the Sunderbans and Mahanadi areas. The Communications Ministry took steps to utilize those poles and the States were made responsible to see that the poles were supplied according to specifications.

- The Central and State Public Works Departments were asked to explore the possibilities of greater use of treated timber in building construction and major and minor engineering structures.

Although forests fell within the State Governments' sphere, in view of the important place of forest products in the national economy and for national defence, it was considered necessary that the forest policies of State Governments in respect of development and conservation should be coordinated with Centre. The plan also considered various tribes inhabiting forest areas. However, the bulk of the forest produce was collected through contractors who exploited the tribesmen. Useful work was noted in Bombay in organising co-operatives of forest tribes to replace contractors. It was seen as the object of State policy throughout India to organise the tribes into co-operatives for the collection of forest produce, and for that a phase-wise programme was drawn up. Responsibility for organising co-operatives was laid on the forest departments.

Second Five Year Plan and successive plans considered forests along with soil conservation and environment. The forests of India were seen as the source of many kinds of timber with varied technical properties, which subserved the requirements of the building industry, of defence and communications, for expanding range of industries in which wood forms the principal raw material, and as the major source of urban firewood and of small timber required by rural communities. Apart from those direct benefits, plans considered that forests perform a vital function in protecting the soil on sloping lands from accelerated erosion by water and on flat lands from wind erosion. Plans appreciated that every advance in industrialization was reflected in an increased demand on the produce of the forest. Thus forests were considered of having more close links with the industrialization than the livelihood of tribals.

During the early period of the Fourth Five Year Plan, it was understood that problems of development of members of the Scheduled Tribes varied in different regions. The Fourth Five Year Plan observed that the development of forest resources was an integral part of the programme for optimum land utilisation, but close interlinks between tribals and forests were not given much priority.

In the Fifth Plan for the first time a strategy of earmarking funds for the development of scheduled tribes was evolved. For the scheduled tribes, because of their population concentration in specific areas, the instrument of Tribal Sub-Plans was developed to ensure flow of benefits from all sectoral programmes and to provide integrated delivery of services in the tribal areas. High priority was accorded to protective measures and elimination of exploitation.

The main thrust of the policy thus, for development of the scheduled tribes during the Sixth Plan, was fourfold:

(a) integration of services at the delivery point to the beneficiary with a view to develop self-reliance,
(b) development of services from the bottom-upwards instead of top-downwards,
(c) development of skills to diversify the occupations, and

(d) introduction of latest technology based on local materials and local skills to reduce drudgery of workers.

Sixth Five Year Plan, 1978-1983 was called as the "Janta Government Plan" which rejected the "Nehruvian Model" of economy and stressed on village and cottage industries, natural mobilization of resources, and increase in employment. During the Sixth Five Year Plan, physically and socially integrated environment became the major concern in conservation and management of natural resource including forests. Environmental problems in India were classified into two broad categories :

(a) Those arising out of poverty and under-development.
(b) Those arising as negative effects of the very process of development.

The first category concerned with the impact on the health and integrity of natural resources (land, soil, water, forests, wildlife, *etc.*) as a result of poverty and the inadequate availability, for a large section of population, of the means to fulfil basic human needs (food, fuel, shelter, employment, etc.). The second category dealt with the unintended side effects of efforts to achieve rapid economic growth and development. The concern for environment was essentially a desire to see that national development proceeded along rational sustainable lines. Environmental conservation was considered, in fact, the very basis of all development albeit traditional rights of tribals over forest resources were largely ignored. State continued to protect and conserve forests without inviting participation of tribals for the purpose.

In spite of that, the forest area continued to decline. The paucity of India's forest cover was realized and the fact was accepted that of the 75 million hectares classified as forest lands, less than half was actually under adequate tree cover and as much as about 20 million hectares of forest land was affected by erosion. No more than about 12 per cent of the country's land surface was actually under adequate tree cover as against the target of 33 per cent prescribed by the National Forest Policy of 1952. Further, although 13 million hectares were classed as "permanent pastures", those areas were in fact, without any vegetation on account of either overgrazing or encroachments.

During the Seventh Plan, there was substantial increase in the flow of funds for the development of Scheduled Tribes, resulting in expansion of infrastructural facilities and enlargement of coverage. However, it was noted that there was limited involvement of Scheduled Tribes in the formulations and execution of programmes resulting in non-adaptability of schemes/policies to cater to their specific needs. For the economic development of Scheduled Tribes, two national level institutions were set up: (i) Tribal Cooperative Marketing Development Federation in 1987 as an apex body for State Tribal Development Cooperative Corporations; and (ii) National Scheduled Castes and Scheduled Tribes Finance and Develop-ment Corporation, primarily to act as a catalytic agent in developing schemes for employment generation and financing pilot projects. But no importance was given to search for forest based livelihood options for tribal people.

The Seventh Plan recognised that environmental factors and ecological imperatives must be built into the total planning process, if the long-term goal of sustainable development was to be achieved. To provide greater systematic impetus and focus to environmental issues at the Central and State levels, new organisational structures were created. The developmental programmes were gradually diverted towards the basic goal of achieving a rapid increase in the standard of living of tribal people through measures, which promoted equality and social justice.

In the nineties, there was an intensification of efforts to

bridge the gap in the levels of development of Scheduled Tribes and other sections of the population so that by the turn of the century, those disadvantaged sections of the population were brought *at par* with the rest of the society in all spheres of national endeavour. Effective steps were taken to prevent the serious problem of displacement of tribals and ensuring their effective rehabilitation; to prevent the growing incidence of tribal land alienation and restoration of alienated land to the tribals in accordance with the provisions of the Fifth Schedule; effective enforcement of existing legal/protective measures along with the provisions made under the Fifth Schedule to prevent tribal indebtedness, bonded labour and other exploitation; involving tribals, especially those engaged in shifting cultivation, closely and gainfully in joint forest management, social forestry, agro-forestry etc. and facilitate rightful collection and gainful disposal of minor forest produce (MFP); and strengthening the grass root democratic institutions viz., Panchayat Raj Institutions and *Gram Sabhas* as per the provisions of 73rd and 74th Amendments and PESA Act, 1996. Thus, a shift could be noticed in the tribal and forests inter-linkages.

The Ninth Plan, besides population control, considered protection of the environment and preservation of the natural resource base of the nation as the second important element of sustainability. Rapidly growing population, urbanisation, changing agricultural, industrial and water resource management, increasing use of pesticides and fossil fuels were seen resulting in perceptible deterioration in the quality and sustainability of the environment. It was realised that environment protection did not only involve a prevention of pollution and of natural resource degradation, but had to be integrated with the over-all development process and the well-being of people. That approach was based on and as articulated in the Agenda 21 of United Nations Conference on Environment and

Development. A synergy between people's well-being, environment and development was recognised.

The Tenth Five Year Plan approached to solve the persisting tribal problems through providing basic minimum services, viz. food, nutrition, safe drinking water, primary health care, education, safe environment, productive assets at least at the level of survival and sustenance with a special focus on women, children and Primitive Tribal Groups; promoting educational development among the tribals especially through reducing drop-out rates and encouraging enrolment/retention with a special focus on women and the girl children; making education relevant and suitable to their *milieu*, local situations and functional needs besides vocationalisation of education to equip the tribal youth with the most wanted technical knowledge and upgradation of skills; developing Forest Villages, on priority basis, by ensuring basic infrastructure and with basic minimum services for those tribals living therein; ensuring food and nutrition security so as to prevent deficiency diseases due to hunger, under-nutrition, starvation and malnutrition.

The above review of the five-year plans with respect to forests and tribal issues reflect that initially, whether the planners being from non-tribal communities and/or their non-tribal perspective, could not appreciate the mutual and close links of tribal communities with forests. During later five year plans' period forest based livelihood options were given due consideration. But, in many parts of the country the non-tribals continued an intensive and yet unsystematic exploitation of forests, with very little consideration to economic welfare of local tribal people.

Madhya Pradesh : Development and Political Concerns

The First Human Development Report of Madhya Pradesh

came in 1995, which benchmarked the status on human development indicators in the state. The first Report led to UNDP organising a national seminar at Bhopal coordinated by Richard Jolly and persuaded other state governments to prepare similar reports. Several state governments have since produced their respective state-level Human Development Reports. The Second Report in 1998 highlighted changes in the human development situation. The Nobel laureate and the eminent economist Prof. Amartya Sen released the Second Human Development Report of Madhya Pradesh.

The Third Human Development Report of Madhya Pradesh was released in 2002. In the report, livelihood security was considered the utmost important challenge in the State. The agenda for the socio-economic development of Dalits (SCs & STs) was seen as a means using the power of democracy for development. The greater importance of the Human Development Report lies in the recognition that disparities in Madhya Pradesh and in that sense in India too were not merely a class or gender dimension but also a caste and tribe dimension.

Hence, the report suggested developing in India, like the UNDP did the Gender Development Index in 1995, a Scheduled Tribe-Scheduled Caste Development Index to capture the inequality in opportunities to human development faced by the Scheduled Castes and Scheduled Tribes. Besides, there were two important political events that reflect upon the concerns for tribal livelihood options in the changed socio-ecological conditions in Madhya Pradesh.

The Bhopal Document: Charting a New Course for Adivasies for 21st Century

The opening sentence of the Bhopal Document (Bhopal Conference, January 12-13, 2002) stated, that it was an attempt by the then ruling political party, to put forward an unexpurgated agenda and invite a free and frank debate on the future of 250 million *Adivasis* and untouchables of the country. It was reported that 64.8 per cent of the landholdings among Scheduled Tribes were small and marginal with poor irrigation facilities.

The document emphasized the prioritized Land Reforms and restoration of tribal land besides Food Security, Grain Bank and empowering cultivators. On March 4, 1998, the state government issued order to all District Collectors to reduce the *Charnoi* (grazing) Land area from 7.5 per cent to 5 per cent. 2.5 per cent of the *Charnoi* land so spared was distributed among SCs & STs. The *Charnoi* land of 5 per cent was further reduced to 2 per cent in September 2001 and the 3 per cent land so recovered was redistributed among them.

Thus, in the phase I, 1.54 lac acres of land and in phase II, 6 lac acres of land, a total of 7.54 lacs acres of land (market value Rs. 3750 crores) was redistributed to about 4 lacs of SC & ST families (more than 15 % of the total) landless agricultural labourers (26.06 lacs including 11.42 lacs SCs and 14.64 lacs STs) in Madhya Pradesh. The Bhopal Document and the Bhopal conference tried to consolidate Scheduled Castes and Scheduled Tribes under one umbrella, *dalits*. The *MP Model of Economic Development* considered the indicator, the rate workers' shift way from the primary to two other sectors, a very crucial one.

Mhow Sankalp Patra

The then political party in opposition in Madhya Pradesh organized a two days Dalit Sammelan on April 25-26, 2003 at Mhow. The land redistribution was seen as a statistical play and was infusing class struggle, as a larger position of the distributed land was either encroached or was already in possession of *Dalits* or other weaker sections of the society. The direction set in the *Sankalp Paper* was towards social harmony, empowerment and all-round development of scheduled classes.

The *Sankalp* was dedicated to scheduled castes. Ideals of inspirers like Mahatma Gandhi, Dr. Bhim Rao Ambedkar, Sant Ravidas, Mahatma Jyotiba Phule and Pt. Deen Dayal Upadhyaya were said to be incorporated in schemes to be formulated for the upliftment of Scheduled Castes. The aim declared was to ensure social dignity to Scheduled Castes, their economic upliftment and participation in power.

The *Sankalp Patra* recommended to distribute 5 acres of land to all landless labourers and Rs. 1000 per acre as grant, to link education and employment to increase opportunities for self-employment and to encourage entrepreneurship. The party made a declaration that Madhya Pradesh would be developed as a "*Model State*" for *dalits*. The *Mhow Sankalp Patra* discussed mainly the problems of Scheduled Castes and considered problems of Scheduled Tribes distinct from them.

Forest based Livelihood Programmes in Madhya Pradesh

The Government of Madhya Pradesh has launched several important programmes to link forests and tribal livelihood. A brief review of some of them is being discussed.

World Food Programme (WFP)

The primary goal of WFP is to play a catalytic role in the state's efforts to eliminate hunger and food insecurity. The WFP has both the long term and immediate objectives. Long term objectives of the programme mainly emphasize to improve the long-term household food security of the most disadvantaged people through preservation and creation of assets like forest, while the immediate objectives focus on enhanced livelihood base through forest regeneration and forest access to the targeted population.

A total of four projects have been implemented in the state

so far. The first project of World Food Programme was implemented during January 1986. The second Project was started in all 45 districts for a period from July 1990 to June 1996. The third Project began in 11 districts of erstwhile Madhya Pradesh in October 1997 and from April 1998 in Seoni district. These 12 districts were split into 21 districts under district reorganization. Subsequent to the reorganization of the State in November 2000, 10 out of 21 districts had gone to Chhattisgarh State.

The programme was implemented in 11 districts in Madhya Pradesh including Balaghat, Chhindwara, Dindori, Harda, Hoshangabad, Jhabua, Mandla, Shahdol, Seoni, Sidhi and Umaria. The fourth and present Project was commenced from April 2003 and would continue for five years in 7 districts of western Madhya Pradesh, viz. Betul, Khandwa, Burhanpur, Khargone, Barwani, Dhar and Jhabua. The direct beneficiaries of the WFP are households from the Scheduled Tribes, Scheduled Castes and other backward castes. The income transfer value of the food ration provides a significant additional support to households. Women comprise at least 50 per cent of the direct beneficiaries in the Food for Work activities and comprise at least 30 per cent (50 per cent in the long run) of the members in the village development committees/user groups created.

In 1987, WFP started using funds generated under the food-for-work programme for development of projects in tribal areas. Since then, funds have been utilised for forestry, agriculture, community infrastructure and income generating activities that help forest dependent families shift their livelihoods to other vocations. A Pilot Project, "Food for Human Development" is being undertaken in a cluster of about 50 villages in four districts, namely, Balaghat, Mandla, Seoni and Chhindwara of Madhya Pradesh. The duration of project would be 12 months and the targeted beneficiaries would be 100 per cent women of SC/ST category, below poverty line and preferably 48-50 years of age.

Joint Forest Management (JFM): The programme, emerged from the policy of involving rural communities living close to forests in protection and management of forest resources as enshrined in the National Forest Policy 1988. Madhya Pradesh pioneered in implementing JFM programme, when it issued the first resolution in that regard in 1991. Learning from experiences, the State Government revised JFM programme to integrate the local institutions by involving the Gram Sabha in the formation and functioning of JFM Committees. The Government Resolution makes provision for three kinds of committees:

(i) Forest Protection Committees (FPC) for protection of well-stocked forests,
(ii) Village Forest Committees (VFC) for rehabilitating the degraded forest areas,
(iii) Eco-development Committees (EDC) in and around Protected Areas (PAs) with a view to ensure biodiversity conservation in National Parks and Sanctuaries.

As per assessments undertaken by Forest Survey of India and published as State of Forest Reports (SFR 1999 and SFR 2001), there has been betterment in socio-economic status of the rural poor. Mutually cordial and sustainable relationship between the local committees and the forest department is developing.

Lok Vaniki

In order to achieve the overall goal of conservation and sustainable development, the Government of Madhya Pradesh launched a scheme based on private forestry, called *Lok Vaniki* in April 1999. The Madhya Pradesh *Lok Vaniki* Act 2001 and the Madhya Pradesh *Lok Vaniki Niyam* 2002 have been enacted. *Lok Vaniki* aims at arresting degradation in private forests and improving their productivity by linking scientific management of these areas with the livelihood system and economic returns. *Lok Vaniki* aspires to bridge the increasing gap between the demand and the supply of forest produce by improving the productivity of private forests, tree clad areas and wastelands. The major thrust of the scheme is on 'handing back' to the people, the management of their own forests for economic and environmental benefits by "unlocking" the neglected and degraded forests on private holdings. The scheme is being implemented in all districts of the state.

Empirical Studies: Livelihood Options for Scheduled Tribes of Madhya Pradesh

Several empirical studies conducted in the form of various projects focused on Scheduled Tribes at Dr. Babasaheb Ambedkar National Institute of Social Sciences (BANISS), Mhow, reflect upon the socio-ecological changes and search for livelihood options for Scheduled Tribes of Madhya Pradesh. The salient findings of such studies (Verma and Sohrot, 2002) could be summarized as under:

> Among tribal migrants from Jhabua district of the western part of Madhya Pradesh, nearly 97 per cent of them were cultivators but the contribution of agriculture produce to the total family income was 32.6 per cent only. The livestock contributed 7.9 per cent while the income from forest produce was as low as 1.1 per cent. Nearly 53 per cent of the family workers, besides cultivating their own fields, also worked as labourers. The wages earned as labourers were the main source (54.7 %) of family income.

The quantum of the seasonal migration was very large and on an average 46.3 per cent of the tribal population migrated out and that went as high as 70 per cent in some parts of Jhabua. Although in the drought years the migration was on a larger scale; in the normal years too, the migration was not less than 43 per cent. The season of migration was from October to June. The tribals migrated in all directions, especially to the urban centres of Kota (Rajasthan); Surat, Vadodara, Ahmedabad, and Dahod (Gujarat); and Indore, Bhopal (Madhya Pradesh).

The migration from Jhabua was a part of the strategy for survival and therefore was not selective with reference to age, sex and marital status. Barring very old people, all the family members migrated out. Small children also accompanied their mothers. The level of skill in the workforce was extremely low. The percentage of skilled workers was merely 1 per cent. Nearly all the migrants were unskilled workers and 80 per cent of them were engaged in construction activities followed by agricultural operations and working in brick kilns or quarries rank.

In the eastern part of the then Madhya Pradesh, among tribal migrants from 100 villages of 90 development blocks in 5 districts, viz. Rajnandgaon, Durg, Raipur, Bilaspur and Raigarh (Chhattisgarh region of undivided Madhya Pradesh), a special nature of the economy in the region was noticed where to migrate in off-season had not only became a compulsion but also an important economic asset for the Scheduled Tribes. In spite of the agriculture being the main economic activity of 69 per cent of the households, to migrate out in search of livelihood options became necessary as the income from agriculture was very low due to very small land holdings, and a vast majority of them were landless labourers besides, innovations in their traditional agricultural practices were almost nil.

Among the Baiga Primitive Tribe Group of 40 villages in Shahdol, Sidhi, Mandla, Balaghat, Surguja, Bilaspur and

Rajnandgaon districts of undivided Madhya Pradesh, it was noticed that the inter-generational occupational mobility depict a negative trend in which more and more farmers were compelled to leave farming and join the workforce as unskilled labourers. The skill element in the Baiga workers was more or less missing even in the existing generation while comparatively in other communities the skill component had increased perceptibly. A sizeable share of agricultural land cultivated by the Baigas was acquired through encroachment of forest land. Nearly 90 per cent of the Baiga farmers did not have any source of irrigation. Further, innovations did not take place in the traditional techniques among Scheduled Tribes.

An analysis of Tendu Patta Policy in 15 villages of Indore, Dewas, Raisen, Sagar, Mandla and Bilaspur districts showed that functionally the policy had resulted into the bureaucratization of the trade. The cooperative societies, though involved the target groups mainly the tribals, could not handle the trade independently due to lack of training. The increase in wages had been ineffective due to decreased plucking days and the increased cost of living.

Another analysis of Social Forestry programme in the Indore Social Forestry Range revealed that availability and accessibility to resources, particularly the forest-based resources were the crucial factors disturbing the expenditure pattern of the weaker sections, as they used to get such needs fulfilled without any cost from the nearby forest areas. The study showed that 84 per cent of the beneficiaries belonged to SCs and STs and 78 per cent among them were landless. However, the low survival rate of the plantation and the improper selection of the species planted, (Eucalyptus, 75%), compounded by lack of training and guidance, insecurity of plantation and water scarcity, defeated the purpose and adversely affected expected benefits intended from the scheme. Besides, no participation of women in such programmes affected them adversely. The economic status of women particularly those of belonging to Scheduled Tribes in Madhya Pradesh was also found very low and little change had occurred in their economic options and development since Independence.

The above review of empirical studies reflect upon the trend and scenario with regard to the socio-ecological changes that have taken place among scheduled tribes of Madhya Pradesh. Traditionally dependent upon the forests, tribals were given option for agriculture but lack of proper infrastructure and training compelled them to migrate from their areas and work as labourers. Though the scheduled tribes have become politically aware of their status and privileges but the social and ecological system under the control of non-tribals is not providing them a proper platform to reap the benefits.

Land Distribution to Scheduled Tribes in Madhya Pradesh

In the Bhopal Document, released in January 2002, the government of Madhya Pradesh reiterated its commitment to make available agricultural land to all landless agricultural labourers of SC/ST category, either by allotment of surplus land or by purchasing agricultural land for such allotment. To solve the problem of local resistance and other bottlenecks coming in the way of the execution of the programme, a detailed guideline was also issued by the Revenue Department on 2nd March 2002. The definition of landless persons was elaborated and two categories of landless persons were formed. Category 1 included such actual cultivators and agricultural labourers who were residing in M.P. for the last 12 years and did not own any land singly or jointly with their family members and category 2 included such actual cultivators or agricultural labourers who were resident of the State for 12 years and who were landless, or owned one hectare or less of hilly or stony unirrigated land, or less than ½ hectare of other class of agricultural land. For all calculations 1 hectare of irrigated land was considered equal to 2 hectares of unirrigated land.

The allotment procedure of the surplus land due to reduction of grazing land from 5 per cent to 2 per cent was decided giving first preference to the persons of SC and ST communities who belonged to category 1. After completing allotment to category 1, allotment was made to category 2. Only cultivable land was to be distributed. Table 10.1 shows the distribution of surplus land to SC/STs in Madhya Pradesh.

Table 10.1: Distribution of surplus land to SC/STs in Madhya Pradesh

Sl. No.	*Item*	*Number*
1.	Total villages	54,496
2.	Total available land for distribution (Hec.)	3,47,933
3.	Beneficiaries upto 28 February 2002	
	(a) SC beneficiaries (number)	98,348
	(b) Land allotted to SC beneficiaries (Hec.)	85,036
	(c) ST beneficiaries (number)	56,273
	(d) Land allotted to ST beneficiaries (Hec.)	48,196
4.	Beneficiaries from March 2002 to September 2002	
	(a) SC beneficiaries (number)	1,04,165
	(b) Land allotted to SC beneficiaries (Hec.)	79,425
	(c) ST beneficiaries (number)	52,172
	(d) Land allotted to ST beneficiaries (Hec.)	42,943

Source : Office of Land Records and Settlement, Government of Madhya Pradesh, 2002.

A survey of 16 sample villages including 8 tribal villages in Madhya Pradesh by BANISS, 2004 revealed that, in most of the cases either the same encroacher was given the legal entitlement, or if the size of land encroached was more than 2 hectares, the surplus was allotted to some other tribal, preferably to his near relative. However, most of the conflicts were reported where the encroachers were from non-SC & ST category. During group discussion, it was reported that some influential persons from other communities were still holding the government land and their encroachment was either not reported by *patwari*, or due to their political alignment, no serious attempt was made to free that land for distribution. Instead poor quality piece of government land was allotted to them.

Table 10.2 shows that in a majority of cases the allottees were actually holding the land. The position was most significant with respect to ST households where 96.1 per cent of the allottees were found to actually holding the land. On an average nearly 55 per cent of the allotted *pattas* were on levelled land. However, a marked difference was noted between the surveyed SC and ST households. In the case of tribal allottees 64.3 per cent *pattas* were on slopping land, while for SCs 72.3 per cent were levelled fields. Due to hilly location of tribal villages 27.1 per cent of the allotted land was stony in nature while that percentage was only 6.0 in the case of SC households.

The average size of *patta* worked out was 0.97 hectare, however, there was a marked difference between the SC and ST allottees. The average size was 1.25 hectare for the SC sample, as compared to 0.65 hectare for the tribal allottees. As per the guideline, no one was to be allotted land below 0.5 hectare, albeit 27.1 per cent of the *pattas* distributed were below 0.5 hectare in size.

The overall annual net financial gain worked out was Rs. 4131.00 per household, without taking into account their own labour cost. The gain was significantly higher for SC respondents at Rs. 5287.00, against Rs. 3591.00 for ST counterpart. That difference might basically be ascribed to the quality of allotted land, which was generally relatively poor in tribal areas. The average amount was, however, not that meaningful because the net gain varied considerably from farmer to farmer depending on the quality of land, availability of irrigation, types of input and the type of crop grown. The net gain was also not

Table 7.2 : Information about the allotment of *patta* to the surveyed households

Sl. No.	District	Block	Sample Village	Whether actually holding land (% of household)	Status of cultivation (% of actual holding)			Ownership category (% of allottees)		
					Self	Given or sold to other	Not cultivating	To male member	To female member	Joint ownership
1.	Dhar	Nalcha	Golarzhiri	100	100	–	–	80	20	–
2.	Dhar	Nalcha	Nai Baroda	84	100	–	–	56	44	–
3.	Hoshangabad	Bawai	Ganera	93	71	–	29	–	–	100
4.	Hoshangabad	Bawai	Nangwada	67	100	–	–	67	–	33
5.	Sehore	Sehore	Satpiplya	100	80	–	20	–	20	80
6.	Sehore	Sehore	Jattakhedi	20	100	–	–	–	–	100
7.	Ujjain	Ujjain	Karohan	100	100	–	–	87	13	–
8.	Ujjain	Ujjain	Panthpipliya	100	100	–	–	29	50	214
9.	Sagar	Sagar	Sanodha	100	100	–	–	13	13	73
10.	Sagar	Sagar	Gidwani	100	100	–	–	27	7	67
11.	Mandla	Mandla	Ghughra	100	53	47	–	53	27	20
12.	Mandla	Mandla	Hardaynagar	87	77	–	23	87	7	7
13.	Shehdol	Suhagpur	Lalpur	100	100	–	–	93	7	–
14.	Shehdol	Suhagpur	Kotma	100	100	–	–	100	–	–
15.	Chhindwada	Chhindwada	Khunarzhiri	100	100	–	–	73	27	–
16.	Chhindwada	Chhindwada	Mujawarmal	100	100	–	–	100	–	–
17.	Morena	Ambah	Bilpur	93	100	–	–	13	20	67
18.	Morena	Ambah	Joha	33	100	–	–	–	–	100
	Total SC			*81*	*94*	–	*6*	*24*	*12*	*64*
	Total ST			96	92	6	3	81	16	3

meaningful to a majority of ST farmers (77.5%) who themselves occupied the same land, prior to the allotment. On the contrary, nearly half of them had to part away with some of their initial encroachment, and thus, lost that income.

Nevertheless, a sense of security developed in them due to legal entitlement of the land. They could now get loan on that piece of land. They could also make capital investment on that land without a fear that the land might be taken back by the government. Becoming landowner from landless increased their social prestige. They could bargain better spouse for their children and also higher bridal price.

Nearly 50 per cent of those tribals who had to part away with some of their land, the feeling was different. Even though no serious clashes developed since in most cases land was transferred from ST to ST and also from SC to SC or to their near relatives, but a sense of bitterness developed and the relations became strained. The general feeling among such cases was that the step had created bitterness and strained family and social relations between the people of their own castes or tribe. However, those who were land less and received legal entitlement, the step anyhow helped them to build self-esteem and enhance their prestige in the society.

Land distribution programme under the Dalit Agenda is an example of a programme which in spite of good intention of the government and a bold step towards providing social justice to the weaker sections, could neither fulfil the desired expectations of the *dalits*, nor yield fruitful political gain for the then ruling party. Land distribution programme was a widely publicized programme applauded as a leap forward towards its commitment to empower the weaker sections. The programme, therefore, generated high aspirations among *dalits*, which turned into discontentment when it was realized that at ground level they had to face many barriers. On the other hand, a feeling was developed among non-SC/ST counterpart that government was snatching their land and distributing it to dalits, just for political gain. In operationalization of the programme the ground reality was not given proper weightage and the so called surplus *Charnoi* land which was, in fact, mostly under encroachment and was not freely available to the administration for distribution.

Food Security Measures for Tribals in Forest Areas of Madhya Pradesh

A study concerning checking felling of trees and food security measures for tribal families (Joshi and Verma, 2003) was conducted in 4 eastern districts of moist deciduous forest belt, i.e., Mandla, Shahdol, Dindori and Sidhi and 5 districts of the western dry-deciduous forest belt comprising Jhabua, Khargone, Dhar, Badwani and Khandwa districts of Madhya Pradesh. The problem of the felling of trees and the related deforestation continued to be a complicated issue in Madhya Pradesh. Besides the large-scale illegal felling by mafia groups and individuals in connivance with the personnel of forest department, a conflicting situation involving a larger section of population, especially the tribals often arose due to the failure of the system to provide the basic requirement of fuel, building material, and fodder to the increasing population adjoining forest areas, on the one hand, and the absence of year the round employment resulting in increased dependence of the tribals on forest wood for their sustenance, on the other.

Quite a large section of tribal population carried head loads of fuel wood to sell to the nearby urban areas, an economic activity which kept them busy from 4.00 a.m. to 3.00 p.m. but hardly provided them Rs. 30 to 35 per day, i.e., much less than the specified minimum wages. An average tribal family of 6 to 8 required on an average 10 to 12 kg of wood for fuel per day.

For brewing liquor the requirement was around 75 kg per litre and for cremation it was 300 kg. For cremation, generally all the relatives and friends of grieved tribal family carry with them some wood, and therefore, no separate arrangement was required to be made.

In the western tract of Khandwa, Jhabua, Khargone and Dhar where the forests were scanty and were located at longer distances, the requirement of fuel was largely met from left over of agricultural produce. In the eastern sector of Mandla, Dindori and Sidhi where rice was the main crop and the forests were easily approachable and their dependence for fuel was mainly on forests, dead wood and bushes were enough to meet the daily requirement of tribals and no felling of trees was reported for meeting their genuine needs. Construction of residential houses was the second essential need for which wood was required. For construction of 2 unit house, known as *'Chasma'*, 200 to 300 small and big logs were required. The requirement of the main frame could not be made from dead wood, which was permitted to be collected, and therefore, it was either to be purchased from the government depot or cut illegally from the forest. It was reported during survey that, albeit the government had subsidized rate of wood for such needs, but that was still beyond the capacity of an average tribal family.

Further, the depot supply for such purposes was less in number of logs (*ballies*), and secondly, there was no scope to select the logs as per the requirement. Therefore, the tribals preferred to cut trees from the forest. It was reported that no problem arose, if bribe was given to the forest guard. However, whenever the forest people were not given their due share, cases of illegal felling of trees were recorded and the woods cut for construction of huts were ceased. A number of such conflicts took a serious turn, as was the case in Mehendikheda episode of Dewas district, where four tribals were killed in police firing.

Due to large scale unemployment, even those tribals who were not engaged in wood cutting, resort to that work in absence of any other alternative. As per the information, in 662 villages of Madhya Pradesh, (Table 10.3) the illegal felling for subsistence was reported to be a more serious problem.

Table 10.3: Number of villages where high incidence of illegal felling of trees for subsistence is reported

Sl.No.	*Forest circle*	*Number of Villages*
1.	South Shahdol	44
2.	North Shahdol	40
3.	East Sidhi	57
4.	West Sidhi	61
5.	West Mandla	79
6.	East Mandla	47
7.	Dindori	66
8.	East Nimar	60
9.	Burhanpur	151
10.	Dhar	32
11.	Katthiwada (Jhabua)	20
12.	Bhabhara (Jhabua)	05
	Total	662

Source : Forest Department, Government of M.P.

Though, the subsistence cutting of wood was a common feature throughout the State, regional differences were noted both in the seriousness of the problem and the mechanism.

The eastern belt (Mandla, Dindori and Sidhi) there is a wet deciduous belt of relatively dense mixed forest with *sal* as the dominant species. The belt is largely inhabited by Gonds and Baiga tribes. It was found that there were some tribal households whose only subsistence was based on selling of wood. Especially Baigas who did not migrate to other places, were engaged in wood collecting and cutting for livelihood during lean periods.

Tribals who generally preferred to work as labourers also cut wood during scarcity periods. A more serious concern was the growing nexus of tribals with local merchants, saw mills, furniture traders, and local mafia which had prompted the tribals to earn easy money by cutting timber wood. Some tribals cut timber wood overnight and the traders in Rs. 200-300 purchased a log costing Rs. 2000.00. That was either transported out or was converted into furniture wood.

The western belt comprised Jhabua, Khargone, Dhar, Barwani and Khandwa districts and was a dry deciduous forest belt where the forests were largely in the degraded state and there were only limited tracts where dense forest still existed. As compared to eastern belt the dimension of damage to forest due to subsistence cutting, especially along railway lines, had been considerably high. During survey of Khandwa tract, it was observed that quite a large number of people depend on forests for livelihood. All the trains in the area were loaded with fuel wood brought by the people for selling it in towns. It was reported by the forest department personnel that besides collecting dead wood and broken twigs, the people used to cut branches and even newly planted trees. Besides fire wood, teak and Anjan wood was also cut and the logs were sold to traders at much cheaper rates.

In the western belt a system prevalent among tribals, called as *'Newad'*, was also found to damage the forest on a large scale. It was also found to be the cause of a number of conflicts. In the system of *'nevad'* a forest patch was illegally cleared and was encroached upon for cultivation. It was largely reported that the illegal system of *newad* was also due to non-availability of alternative source of livelihood and could be checked if employment was provided.

After analyzing the problem and related aspects of the illegal felling of trees in tribal areas, the food insecurity position, needs of the people, and the condition of livelihood options, the policy formulation in the light of the social obligation of the State, could be understood in the following terms:

(i) The problem of felling of trees in tribal areas was a serious problem and was becoming more serious in every coming year.

(ii) The problem was more pronounced in the western belt where the forests were scanty and the pace of regeneration was relatively slow.

(iii) The problem acquired appalling dimension during drought years.

(iv) Besides ecological degeneration, that problem became a source of a large number of conflicts arising between the tribals and the administration and resulted in human rights violations, law and order problem and related socio-cultural fall outs.

(v) The economy of tribal areas of Madhya Pradesh still largely operated under the condition of survival compulsion with limited livelihood options, and therefore, there was a direct linkage between subsistence woodcutting and the availability of livelihood alternatives.

(vi) Within the existing condition of overflowing food reserves in the country, that was also a reality that at least for 3 to 4 months the access to food in the tribal areas of Madhya Pradesh became extremely limited and food insecurity was a serious problem, especially for a large section of small and marginal farmers and landless labourers belonging to Scheduled Tribe communities.

(vii) During the survey of the eastern and western forest belts, it was stressed by the tribals that the programme would be widely welcomed by them, if that was run on a sustainable basis, with a fixed and regular time schedule.

Scheduled Tribes: Search for Sustainable Livelihood Options

The empirical analysis of livelihood options to scheduled tribes of Madhya Pradesh reveal the basic fact that for sustainable development, which basically means meeting the needs of the present generation without compromising the ability of the future generations to meet their own need (World Conservation Strategy, 1987), strategies and approaches need to be reoriented. The current policy and planning towards Scheduled Tribes concern physical target achievement only, but do not ensure their livelihood in qualitative terms and their ability to meet the same in future, which is the most crucial dimension and prerequisite of sustainable development (Verma, 1994, 1995, 1997, 1998, 2002; Verma and Sohrot, 2003).

It is not the question of environment or people, environment or development, or forest or tribal communities. It is a matter to integrate both in a harmonious way. A basic understanding is needed that the problems of inequality and injustice are the major obstacles on the path of sustainable development. In socio-ecological perspective, particularly of Scheduled Tribes, sustainable development needs to be conceptualized as a progressive diminution in discrimination (asymmetry of socio-ecological relations in intergenerational terms); exploitation (asymmetry of ecological-economic relations), deprivation (asymmetry of distribution, consumption of resources and capability explained by Sen, 1992; 1999) and oppression (asymmetry of rights to livelihood).

More importantly than the mere allotment of a physical piece of land to Scheduled Tribes, qualitative support to sustain livelihood is essential. The land distribution programme in Madhya Pradesh could have yielded much better results if qualitative dimensions of the productive assets were also given due consideration besides ensuring physical possession of the land. Forest Land would be such an important asset with the Scheduled Tribes that for their coming generations quality and productivity base of livelihood could be ensured leading to their sustainable development. However, the present policies are not only erroneous but also unsustainable for STs. It should also be therefore, a necessary and prerequisite condition with the proposed bill of Scheduled Tribes (recognition of Forest Rights), 2005, that the state and its machinery should ensure sustainable livelihood from the redistribution of forest land.

On the other hand, Scheduled Tribes also need to be reoriented towards conservation. As seen in the study on felling of trees and food security measures (Joshi and Verma, 2003), Scheduled Tribes indulge in unsustainable means to degrade forest areas mainly due to their survival compulsions. Therefore, checks and balances are also necessary to ensure that the provisions for distribution of forestland and exercising recognition of forest rights result in sustainable development of Scheduled Tribes. The National Forest Policy, 1988, had a separate section on 'Tribal people and forests' which stated that: "having regard to the *symbiotic* relationship between the tribal people and forests, a primary task of all agencies responsible for forest management, including the forest development corporations should be to associate the tribal people closely in the protection, regeneration and development of forests as well as to provide gainful employment to people living in and around the forest."

The symbiotic interrelation between forests and tribal communities need to be understood in current socio-ecological conetxt. Tribals who are compelled to play in the hand of non-tribals particularly land and forest mafias, would never respect that symbiotic relationship. The empirical studies and observation made in this paper clearly reflect that tribals under a socio-ecology of sustenance compulsion behave differently than their traditional culture and they start behaving as non-tribals do or in that case any human group would behave. In other words, for sustainable development, qualitative options for livelihood to tribal people should be the prime concern. Socio-ecology of tribal communities can only work for their sustainable development and for conservation of forests, provided they are not compelled to adopt unsustainable and illegal means for their sustenance.

Therefore, redistribution of forest land should not be a continued part of traditional land reforms in the country. Land reform has both a narrow and a broader connotations. The principal measures of land reforms opted to secure the objective of land policy laid down in five-year plans, were aberration of intermediary interests, tenancy reform and ceilings on holdings (Appu, 1996). The main emphasis of land reforms was on two aspects, firstly, redistribution of land in favour of landless or marginal and small cultivators, and secondly, the tenancy reforms. On the eve of the Independence, the area under tenancy was around one-fifth of the total area and the tenant households around one-third of the total rural household.

In Madhya Pradesh also reducing the *Charnoi* land from 7.5 per cent to 2 per cent, gave a possibility to redistribute land to landless SCs & STs. But the major concern about the quality of land and feasibly to reap benefits remained unattended. Dr. Ambedkar had opined that evil of small holdings was not only fundamental but it was derived from maladjustment in our social economy. Dr. Ambedkar advocated state socialism essential for fostering economic development with justice under the State Socialism agriculture would be the State Industry and farms should be cultivated as collective farms. Sen (1962) also supported that family based peasants farm were found to be more productive. It was also evident that medium holdings (5-10 acres) were far more productive than large holdings (Nanchariah, 1995).

The distribution of *Charnoi* land to Scheduled Castes and Scheduled Tribes of Madhya Pradesh was done following the Bhopal Document and the demand of the *dalits* for land. But, unfortunately the philosophy of Dr. Ambedkar with regard to land reforms was totally ignored. There was a golden opportunity in the form of land redistribution diverted from *Charnoi* land in Madhya Pradesh where philosophy of Dr. Ambedkar could have been implemented very successfully for sustainable development of Scheduled Tribes.

Thus, it is very much evident that in the ambiguity of meaning of land reforms and ignoring the size as the important dimension in terms of quality and productivity, it has become more a political agenda just to distribute the land among landless labourers. Land is more a social status in villages particularly to large land owning communities who are mostly non-scheduled groups than a productive asset for scheduled groups mainly because the agriculture in the country is largely dependent upon Monsoon and no serious attempts have been made to ensure irrigation facilities to new-land-owners and to the marginal and small farmers as most of them belonged to STs. Therefore, it needs to be analyzed and projected that the size of forest land being proposed for distribution to tribal families is viable and sufficient to sustain their livelihood.

For social justice and development, ecoethical concerns also need to be the priority concerns (Verma, 1994, 1995). The major question in sustainable development also rests upon values and attitude of people towards socio-economic and ecological order (Verma, 1999). The existing distribution of resources and income was a continued function of the past undemocratic system of deprivation to lower and privileges to higher in the social order, which simply perpetuate inequality and injustices in the society (Verma and Sohrot, 2003). Therefore, it is desirable that tribal communities should be made the primary agents for the care and development of the forests and the exploitation of forest resources. Forest schools should be started to bring the young tribals to love, care for, and work systematically for the enrichment of the forests, which would mean in turn the betterment of their own lives and sustainable development of global society.

In conclusion, the unsustainability lies in the mismatched context of practical planning of technical know-how which often get support of and implemented for the cost-bearing class and large-asset owning communities. Scheduled tribes lack in both these aspects, hence, remains deprived and discriminated. The sustainable development of Scheduled Tribes can only be ensured if the tribal policy and development approaches are integrated with the innovations and upgradations of indigenous technologies so that benefits given by the state to Scheduled tribes are sustained both in socio-economic and ecological terms.

It is now time to set aside the politics of physical projections and target achievements. Era of economic and political empowerment is now leading the way to social empowerment. People cannot be led away and tempted by mere physical targets. They are well aware and have become socially empowered to understand their needs and making necessary changes, even adopt illegal and unsustainable, at every level if their needs are not fulfilled.

Madhya Pradesh model confirms the era of social empowerment, where the land distribution programme of a political party albeit launched with full commitment and in right spirit, could not win people's favour and failed to regain power mainly because the insensitive administrative machinery and distribution of poor quality land could not ensure sustainable livelihood options and intended benefits to the target people. Therefore, the state should adopt such an approach that not only ensure food security for people but also open economically viable as well as ecologically harmonious livelihood options for them. For this the administrative machinery need to be sensitized and reoriented towards sustainable development minimizing its role merely as regulating agency to achieve physical targets. Qualitative projections would be more important and meaningful for sustainable development.

REFERENCES

Ambedkar, B.R. (1918): "Small Holdings in India and their Remedies", *Journal of Indian Economic Society*. Reproduced in the Dr. Babasaheb Ambedkar Writings and Speeches. (ed.) Vasant Moon, Vol. I, Department of Education, Govt. of Maharashtra.

Appu, P.S. (1996): *Land Reforms in India: A Survey of Policy and Legislation and Implementation,* New Delhi: Vikas Publishing House Pvt. Ltd.

Bhatia, Bela (2005): Competing Concerns. *Economic and Political Weekly*, Vol. XL, No. 47, November 19-25, 2005, pp. 4890-4893.

Dreze, Jean and Amartya Sen (1999): *India: Economic Development and Social Opportunity*. Oxford University Press, New Delhi, 9th Edn.

Government of India: Sixth Five Year Plan, 1978-83, Chapter 13.

Joshi, Y.G. (1992): Evaluation of the New Tendu Patta Policy: an Appraisal. Research Abstracts, BANISS, 2002, p. 24.

Joshi, Y.G. (1994): Tribal Migration and Man-Power Planning in Jhabua (M.P.), Research Abstracts, BANISS, 2002, p. 72.

Joshi, Y.G. and D.K. Verma (1999): Census Data based Study on the Baiga Scheduled Tribe of M. P. Research Abstracts, BANISS, 2002, p. 85.

Joshi, Y.G. and D.K. Verma (2000): Seasonal Rural Out-migration from Chhattisgarh Region with Special Reference to the SCs & STs Communities. Research Abstracts, BANISS, 2002, p. 75.

Joshi, Y.G. and P.C. Bansal (2004): Evaluation of the Scheme of Land Allotment to SCs & STs in Madhya Pradesh. BANISS project.

Krishnaswamy, Madhuri (2005): One Step Forward, Two Steps Back. *Economic and Political Weekly*, Vol. XL, No. 47, November 19-25, 2005, pp. 4899-4901.

Madhusudan, M.D. (2005): Of Rights and Worngs: Wildlife Coinservation and the Tribal Bill. *Economic and Political Weekly*, Vol. XL, No. 47, November 19-25, 2005, pp. 4893-95.

Nanachariah, G. (1995): *Dr. Ambedkar on Small Holdings and Reorganisation of Structure of Agriculture in India* AJSDJ, Vol IV, pp. 26-37.

Rangrajan, Mahesh (2005): Fire in the Forest. *Economic and Political Weekly*, Vol. XL, No. 47, November 19-25, 2005, pp. 4888-4890.

Sen, A. (1992): *Inequality Re-examined.* Oxford University Press, New Delhi.

Sen, A. (1999): *Development as Freedom.* Oxford University Press, New Delhi.

Shah, Mihir (2005): First You Push Them in, Then You Push Them Out. *Economic and Political Weekly,* Vol. XL, No. 47, November 19-25, 2005, pp. 4895-4899.

Verma, D.K. (1993): *Inter-generational equity: environmental right of the child.* AJSDJ, Vol. III, 163-168, 1993.

Verma, D.K. (1994): *Eco-ethical approach for sustainable Development and Social Justice.* ASD J: 2:1994, p. 37-59.

Verma, D.K. (1995): Ecological sustainability in social development. In: *Social Development & Justice.* Radiant Publishers, New Delhi,1995 pp. 225-229

Verma, D.K. (1997): *Dr. B.R Ambedkar's views on Planning, Development And Conservation of Environmental Resources,* A JSDJ:5:1997, pp. 1-8.

Verma, D.K. (1998): *Role of Social Forestry Programme in the Development of Scheduled Castes & Scheduled Tribes.* AJSDJ, Vol. VI, pp. 53-69, 1998.

Verma, D.K. (1999): Sustainable Development. *Madhya Pradesh Journal of Social Sciences.* Vol 4, No.2, 1999, pp. 37-59.

Verma, D.K. (1999b): "Concept and dimensions of social environment needed for sustainable development." In book on *Social Environment for sustainable development,* published by Rawat Publishers, Jaipur.

Verma, D.K. and Sohrot (2002): Research Abstracts (Summaries and Recommendations of Research Projects, 1992-2002). BANISS Publications No.6.

Verma, D.K. and A. Sohrot (2003): The concept of Social Justice in Post-modern society : some reflections on Sustainable Development. *Prashasnika,* Volume XXX No. 2, pp. 39-59.

11 Forest Rights Act 2006

New Challenges for Development

Debasis Debnath

Introduction

Indian tribals are the indigenous populations comprising approximately 8.2 per cent of total Indian population (88.4 millions as per 2001 Census) numbering 698 ethnic communities scheduled in the list of the Government of India. As their traditional livelihoods are dependent on forests or natural resources are also known as '*Vanyajti*', '*Vanabasi*'. They are found in the different levels of socio-economic development and designated as 'isolated or primitive tribal communities', 'Semi-acculturated or shifting hill cultivators', 'acculturated or agrarian communities' and 'assimilated or urbanized' tribal groups. They are found to dwell in about 15 per cent of the country's geographical areas, concentrated in seven tribal zones, in the remote forest, hilly, undulating in accessible terrain in plateau areas, following a community way of living for maintaining community harmony. This is formed by the uniqueness of culture, distinctive customs, traditions and beliefs, which in turn develop their world views. Thus living in remote isolated and undisturbed areas the forest dwelling tribes have an integrated pattern of life in which music, dance, embellishments of body and well designed functional objects are necessary parts. Their forms are age-old but they are time tested and vital and their patterns of life, even by our modern standards are kind of ideal.

After attainment of independence the Indian tribes they were given a special status in our Indian Constitution by the article 342 under the tern "Scheduled Tribe". The criteria used are: primitive traits, distinctive culture, geographical isolation shyness of contact and backwardness. The Constitution of India contains several provisions for ensuring a better quality of life for the weaker sections of society and STs in particular based on policy of positive discrimination and affirmative action on the development and regulatory fronts. From the first plan attempts have been made to uplift the tribal communities as a part of community development programme identifying tribal development blocks, which have been given specific developmental approaches in the Third Plan. Since 1974 during the Fifth Plan for the better investment, the budget has been raised under the sub-plan programme which specific targets of the tribal groups and the specific areas where the tribal concentration are observed. The financial allocation in proportion of the population of STs in the annual plans at central and state level were done. A large number of schemes and programmes implemented. The objectives of the Tribal development are: The tribal communities must be ensured of the means to sustained livelihood, all must have sense of self-esteem and all should be freed from servitude.

On the contrary, by the large, the improvements in the socio-economic conditions of scheduled tribes measured in increased literacy rates, reduction in poverty, etc. have not been proportionate to the investments made. As compared to other sections of the Indian society, the tribal population has the lowest Human Development index (HDI). In addition, they suffer from geographical and cultural exclusion, which are not captured in the HDI. Similarly, lack of empowerment to make choices for themselves is also not accounted for. A large segment of the tribal population lives below the poverty line and suffers from a high infant mortality rate, severe malnutrition, various communicable diseases, lower literacy rates and an extremely slow pace of development. Underdevelopment coupled with lack of access to proper administrative and judicial machinery in tribal areas further increases their deprivation.

Tribal Rights, Livelihood and Governance

From the onset of the evolutionary process of the human society forest is not only their habitat, forests is their ground of the culture formation and considered as the abode of their gods and goddesses. Most of the tribals survive on collection of the forest products for fulfilling their requirement of fuel, fodder, fruit, food, fertilizer, fibre and so on. In their diversified economic system to their agriculture, animal husbandry, fishing activities forests have the significant contribution. On the basis of their dependence on the forest resources the tribals are categorized as 'primitive communities' or better in the development scale 'Primitive Tribal Groups', 'Shifting hill cultivators', 'Pastoral Nomads' etc. Forest is the common property resources in which the tribal peoples claim their customary use rights within the purview of the communal ownership. Giving the due recognition of the tribal rights the Constitution of India provides specific protection to tribal rights over their customary resources as well as their self-governing institution, particularly in Schedule V and Schedule VI areas. There are special constitutional authorities vested with the responsibility of enforcing these provisions under the oversight of the President of India. The National Forest Policy, 1988 itself has as separate section on 'Tribal people and forests' which states that: having regard to the symbiotic relationship between the tribal people and forests', a primary task of all agencies responsible for forest management, including the Forest Development Corporations should be to associate the tribal people closely in the protection, regeneration and development of forests as well as to provide gainful employment to people living in and around the forest. The section on 'rights and concessions' has focused on full protection of the rights of tribals. The Government of India is also a signatory to the convention on Biological Diversity such requires the protection of indigenous knowledge and rights of indigenous communities.

For forest growth and development the ministry of Forests and Environment. Government of India, initiated the joint forest management since 1990, as a partnership with the local communities or the primary beneficiaries, which resulted into institutionalization process in the village, livelihoods generations, equitable benefits sharing, people's empowerment and so on. The decentralization of governance has been mandated by the 73rd Constitutional Amendment, and in particular the provisions of the Extension of Panchayats of Scheduled Areas Act, 1996 (PESA), which empowers gram Sabhas in schedule 5 years to manage their community resources in accordance with their traditions and customs.

Forest Encroachment Issues

The Ministry of Environment and Forests (MoEF) issued a directive on May 3, 2002 to summarily evict "all illegal of forest lands in various states/Union territories" before September 30,2003. A set of six circulars as follows were issued on September 18,1990:

(i) FP (1) Review of encroachments on forest land
(ii) FP (2) Review of disputed claims over forest land, arising out of forest settlement

(iii) FP (3) Disputes regarding pattas/leases/grants involving forest land

(iv) FP (4) Elimination of intermediaries and payment of fair wages to the labourers on forestry works

(v) EP (5) Conversion of forest villages into revenue villages and settlement of other old habitations

(vi) EP (6) Payment of compensation for loss of life and properly due to predation/depravation by wild animals.

The latest directive of the MoEF has only referred to one of these circulars dealing with encroachment on forest land but ignores the other circulars on crucial issues such as 'Review of pattas/leases/grants involving forest land' which have a considerable on deciding what really constitutes an 'encroachment' and what does not. So circular issued on May 3, 2002 would mean that lakhs of tribals/*adivasis* and other forest department could be affected or displaced, thus threatening their very existence. The recommendations of the Central Empowerment Committee (CEC), which was constituted by the Supreme Court endorsed the view of the MoEF order, while continuing to ignore the central unresolved issues mentioned above. In consequence, the directive of the MoEF and the recommendation of CEC that encroachment on forest lands by powerful vested interests is a serious issue and must be dealt with strictly. But to label tribal/adivais communities that have traditionally and customarily cultivated lands but do not have the title deeds to prove this issue as 'encroachers' and to club them in the same category as powerful vested interests who have indeed eaten up our forests, is an unjust step to take, and in the long run detrimental to ecological conservation itself. The process outlined in the various directives should have been given first priority. The *ad-hoc* evictions would not only threaten the livelihoods of legitimate forest dwellers but lead to hostilities which could only cause harm to purpose of forest and wild-life conservation, which the MoEF order and the CEC recommendations sought to achieve. The MoEF circular of May 3, 2002 concerns a vital policy issue concerning not only the welfare of the tribal people but also governance in tribal areas, including scheduled area. It clearly attracts the provisions of Article 338(9) of the Constitution which spells out the necessity of consulting the National Commission for Scheduled Castes and Scheduled Tribes "on all major policy matters affecting Scheduled Castes and Scheduled Tribes". It appears that MoEF has not consulted the National Commission in terms of this provision. This omission is particularly serious because frame for resolution of disputes between the tribal people and the state in respect of forest land had been worked out by the Union Government at the intervention of and in association with commissioner for SC & ST in 1990, the Constitutional predecessor-in-office of the National Commission for Schedule Castes and Scheduled Tribes. It was conceded at that time by the MoEF that the disputed claims may be settled first and guidelines were issued to that effect (explained at length later in the note). No action is reported to have claims even as per admission of the Government are now likely to be treated as encroachers. It is crucial at this point the states are restrained from taking arbitrary action for eviction and a review of the action-taken by states on the suggestions made by the SC/ST Commissioner in his 29th report and the set guidelines issued by MoEF in 1990 for dealing with disputed claims is first undertaken.

Thus, there is a serious problem with the definition of 'encroachers' implied by the MoEF circular, as is illustrated in some of the following situations:

(a) There are lakhs of tribals/*adivasis* who have traditionally and customarily cultivated land before the notification of these lands as state owned forests under various laws but whose rights were not enquired into because of a fairly survey and settlement process. Hence they do not have title deeds for their lands and are today labelled 'encroachers'. Thus the circular of 2002 fails to distinguish between 'unsettled claims and 'encroachments'. In spite of this being acknowledged by the second circular [FP (2)] issued by the MoEF in 1990.

(b) In many parts of India, lands that have been under shifting cultivation for generations have been notified as forest lands. Particularly in parts of Eastern India, communities who have been cultivating these lands for generations, albeit under rotational rather than settled cultivation, are often treated as 'encroacher's as per the records, e.g. In Orissa a large population live in hilly areas and depend on shifting cultivation.

(c) Around the country there are a number of cases where *pattas*/grants/leases have been issued to people at various points of time by a proper authority of the Government (e.g. Revenue Department). But the status' of these lands is under dispute between different departments (Such as the Revenue Department and the Forest Department). Very often the lands have changed hands between various departments and the tiller of the lands has not been consulted or informed. Many such people are recorded by the forest department as 'encroachers' e.g. Certain lands declared 'protected forests in Madhya Pradesh, termed as 'Orange Areas', according to the State Government's decisions, were to be transferred to the revenue department after demarcation for issuing of *pattas* to the beneficiaries. The pattas were issued to the individuals by the Revenue Department but the transfer between the department was not completed and the land actually shows in both revenue and forest records. The issues has not been resolved as of yet.

These are some of the examples of the problems with the definition of 'encroachers' which could result in the eviction go genuine forest dwellers.

Forest Rights Act

The Ministry of Tribal Affairs, Government of India, has passed the Scheduled Tribes and other Traditional Forest Dwellers (Recognition of Forest Rights) Act, 2006, which has got the assent of the President of India on the 29th December, 2006 and was published on the 2nd January, 2007 it extends to the whole of India except the State of Jammu and Kashmir.

Amid strong oppositions from environmentalists, Dr. Bachittar Singh, Jt. Secretary, Ministry of Tribal Affairs, Government of India has appointed in exercise of the power conferred by Sub-section 3 of the Section 1 of the Scheduled Tribes and other Traditional Forest Dwellers (Recognition of Forest Rights) Act, 2006 (2 of 2007), the day of 31st December, 2007 as the date on which the provisions of the said Act came into force. The preamble of the Act is as follows:

1. Wrongful alienation
2. No titles for lands
3. Denial of ownership rights on MFP
4. Non/involvement in forest management
5. Denial of developmental benefits
6. Tribal means of livelihood not safeguarded

Main Promises

1. Ownership of the land especially Forest lands and

shifting cultivating areas actually occupied till December 2006.

2. MFP ownership.
3. Relaxation of Forest Conversation Act For Tribals.
4. Conversation of Forest Villages to Revenue Villages.
5. Ban on shifting of tribal from core areas of sanctuaries and national parks.

The Highlights of the Act

- Recognizes and vests the forest rights and occupation in forests lands in forest dwelling Scheduled Tribes and other traditional forest dwellers who have been residing in such forests for generations but whose rights could not be recorded.
- Recognizes the responsibilities of the Forest Dwelling Scheduled Tribes (FDST) and other traditional forest dwellings for sustainable use, conservation of biodiversity and maintenance of ecological balance and thereby strengthening the conservation regime of the forests while ensuring livelihood and good security of them.
- Recognizes the forest rights on ancestral lands and their habitat which were not adequately recognized in the consideration of state forests during the colonial period as well as in independent India resulting in historical injustice.
- To address the long standing insecurity of general and access rights by RDST and other traditional forest dwellers including those who were forced to relocate their dwelling due to state development interventions.
- Outlines of 13 forests rights, which include :

  (a) Right to hold or live in the forest land under the individual or common occupation by forest or self-cultivate for a livelihood by a member or members of a forest dwelling scheduled tribes.

(b) Community rights or nistar.

(c) Rights of ownership access to collect use and dispose of minor forest produce.

(d) To hold other community rights or entitlement such as fishing or grazing.

(e) Rights including community terms of habitat and habitation for primitive Tribal groups and pre-agricultural communities.

(f) Rights in or over disputed lands.

(g) Rights for conversion of *pattas* or leases or grants issued by local authority.

(h) Rights of settlement and conversion of all forest villages into revenue villages.

(i) Rights to protect or conserve or manage away community forest resources.

(j) Rights which are recognized under any state law or laws of any Autonomous district council or rights of Tribal under any traditional or customary law of the concerned tribes of any state.

(k) Right of access to bio-diversity and customary right to intellectual property and traditional knowledge related to biodiversity and cultural diversity.

(l) Any other traditional right which are not mentioned in above.

(m) Right to *in situ* rehabilition including alternative land in the causes they have been illegally evicted or displaced from forest land prior to the 13th day of December, 2005.

Almost 80 years after historic injustice was done via Indian Forest Act, 1927 taking away all the forest rights of tribals and dwellers, the Central Government took about two years in implementing the law once it was introduced in parliament. The Forest Rights Law allows Gram Sabha, the elected village body, to restore traditional land and community rights to tribals and forest dwellers, provided they have been living there for the last 25 years. The period will be calculated from December 2005. From the various studies it is found that while a number of provisions will lead to better conservation and enhanced livelihood security in certain situations, other provisions have a strong potential for damage to forests, wildlife and protected areas and increased livelihood insecurity. However, the law will not be application in the critical tribal habitats notified by the Ministry of Environment and Forest, Government of India. Or this will allow the government to relocate about 10,000 villages living in 27 tiger reserves for which the Government has provided about Rs. 4000 crore.

On the 31st December, 2007 the Gazetteer shows the rules to be implemented in the Act, are as follows:

1. Condition of actual forest stay relaxed
2. Forest rights committees to determine eligible beneficiary
3. Community forest should to be created
4. Gram Sabhas to mange community forests
5. Assistance right holder for land titles
6. Shifting cultivation and encroachment up to 2005, sought to be negotiated
7. Expert committee under Ministry of Environment of Forests to determine need and extention of core areas.
8. No displacement of tribals till enquiries are completed.

After analyzing of the Act and its implementing rules the following opportunities are:

1. Greater role and empowerment of Gram Sabha in determining claims, managing forests it has traditionally conserved, checking processes destructive of forest-dweller's habitats, and protecting traditional knowledge.
2. Site-specific and knowledge-based determination of critical wildlife habitats, and prohibition on their diversion for any other purpose.
3. Greater livelihood security for traditional forest-dwellers who have been unjustly denied tenure.
4. Displacement and relocation only by consent.

And the Challenges are Ahead

1. Identification of beneficiaries.
2. Delineation of forest areas for exercise of forest rights.
3. Survey and elements of encroachments.
4. Dissuading tribals from shifting cultivation.
5. Empowerment for management of Forests.
6. Forging links between Forests Department and Tribal Institutions to ensure proper implementation of the Act.
7. Cut-off date for eligibility of land claims as December 2005 instead of 1980.
8. Exclusion of certain development projects and activities (e.g. Construction of roads) from the purview of forest clearances.
9. Unclear relationship with existing forest/wildlife laws and institutional arrangements for enforcement.

Khargone Case

Madhya Pradesh is well known for its forest and tribal people. About 35 per cent of the total geographical area of this state occupied by forests that account for 22 per cent of the total forest area in the country. Around 23 per cent of the state population belong to the Scheduled Tribes. Khargone, the erstwhile west Nimad, is a tribal concentrated district has it good quality of forest, a major part of which has been encroached. This case study is based on an empirical study carried out in Khargone.

Location: the district Khargone is located between the latitudes 21° 12′ N and 22°35′ N and between the longitudes 74°25′ E and 76° 14′ E. The district lies on the south-western corner of the state of M.P. and is adjacent to the two states Gujarat and Maharashtra. According to the Village Directory in the census 1991 total forest area is 2,88,613.74 acres, out of total village area 2,530,541.68 acres. Most of the district is covered by woody vegetation, erstwhile managed only by the stage Forest Department. Only the scattered and unmanageable greenery remain under the revenue department. Most part of the district forest was included in the Holkar, Badwani, Dhar states. These were common property resources and consequently were easily accessible to the public for all purposes till 1892 when the forest Department in the Holkar state was organized. The forests of the Holkar state were divided into two classes, known as *Chota* (small) jungle and *Bara* (big) jungle, the former being managed by the revenue department and the latter by the Forest Department. The *chota* jungle, more or less, became part of the village access and was given for cultivation. The Khem tehsil system of management was in vogue in the bara jungle. Under this system, the purchaser of the forest produce used to cut. Collect and fetch the material to the revenue collecting check post (*naka*) where he would paid the dues and remove the produce. The best timber of more economic species was removed for a nominal fee under this system. This system was in place till 1903 when the forest department was recognized.

Forests provide the basic raw materials for various cottage and small-scale industries of the District. The forest produce is a classified into major and minor (Non-wood or timber) forest product. Timber, fuelwood and charcoal form the major forest produce of the district. The main timber yielding species are teak, *saja, bija, tinsa, haldu, shisam* and the *arjun* minor forest produce comprises bamboo, grassem, *tendu* leaves, *mahua* flowers and fruits, lac, gum, medicinal plants and others.

According to the 1991 census 35-50 per cent of the people in the Khargone district belong to the Scheduled Tribes. Mainly the tribals, viz. Bhils, Bhilalas and Barelas that together constitute over 98 per cent of the tribal population inhabit six development blocks of the district. The Gonds and Korkus also inhabit the area, in small numbers. The Barelas and the Bhilalas are the offshoots of the Bhil community. The non-tribal cultivating castes are the *patidars, kulmi, Ahir, Jat* and *Gujar,* besides the important castes like Rajput, Brahmins and Bania. They possess good quality of land and are found in better economic condition. They are skilful and laborious agriculturists. The tribals are mostly located in the forest and hilly areas, evidently possessing poor quality of land. Diversity in the social and economic conditions of tribal and non-tribal conditions is also reflected in their agricultural practices.

The following table shows the census of the Scheduled Tribes in the district and *tehsil.*

Table 11.1: Distribution of the Scheduled Tribes (1991 Census)

Sl. No.	*Name of the Tehsil*	*Tribal population*			
		Male	*Female*	*Total*	*Per cent*
1.	Badwaha	12805	12156	24961	3.538
2.	Maheshwar	13456	12543	25999	3.685
3.	Badwani	52342	51196	103538	14.677
4.	Rajpur	52802	51490	104292	14.784
5.	Kasrawad	10996	10602	21598	3.061
6.	Sendhwa	97405	96453	193858	27.481
7.	Khargone	62042	61404	123446	17.499
8.	Bhikangaon	54378	53354	107732	15.271
9.	Khargone district	356226	349198	705424	100.000

History of encroachment: The encroachment problem in Khargone is more than 50 years old. This is most prominent in the tribal like Bhagabanpura and Jhirnia in the Khargone division, Barwani and Patti in the Barwani division and Sendhwa and Mewali in the Sendhwa division. The encroachment was going on the pre-British period. The local M.P. Shri Ramchandra Bade raised the first voice in favour of encroachment on forest lands, in consequence the "Shankdhar Commission" in 1952. So by Notification No. 1104/10-f/40/50 dated 17.6.1954 from Adimjati Kalyan Vibhag of Madhya Bharat introduced the Taungya system on the forestlands. On the condition the tribal allottees would plant on One-fifth of the land allotted to the tribals. They did not grow any tree. Instead they were given forest *patta* at the rate of 8 acres per household for 99 years on lease. Till 17.7.1962 the forestlands were transferred in this manner.

Centre Forest land Transfer to Revenue Department	81	19988.177 ha.
Settle centre providing Forest *Patta*	68	17050.620 ha

In 1965 they demarcated the forestlands to be transferred to the revenue department in response to the Order No. 10598/10/65 dated 30.09.1965.

Till 31.12.1976 the land was transferred in this manner :

Type of Patta	*Total Centre*	*Total Patta Holder*	*Total Patta land*
Forest	80	4009	7004.390 ha.
Revenue	81	3472	6568.878 ha.

After that the Forest Department sent a list of encroachers to the Ministry of Environment and Forest, Government of India for the settlement of *patta* holding for agriculture on the forest lands with the deadline 24.10.1980. So far no instruction or government order has reached the forest department regarding distribution of the '*patta*'. The total number of encroachers are 9296 and the area of the land encroached is 11,852.912 ha. Since 1980, the process of encroachment has been continuous. In the Khargone division of the district the total number of the encroachment are 7837 and the area of the land encroached is 27240.00 ha.

Process of encroachment: This case study is based on the observation made in following four villages:

Table 11. 2 : The villages under study

Sl. No.	*Name of the village*	*Block/Tehsil*	*Village status*	*Total Population*	*Ethnic Group*
1.	Moghum	Gogaon/Khargone	Revenue	618	Bhilala, Barela,
2.	Kumbhi	Bhagabanpur/Khargone	Forest	490	Barela, Tadvi, Harijan, Muslim
3.	Deonaliya	Barar/Khargone	Forest	725	Barela, Mankar, Muslim, Harijan
4.	Pipal Jhopa	Bistan/khargone	Revenue	1350	Nahat, Jaiswal, Harijan, Muslim

It was found that the Barelas arc the dominating tribal group in the area. The Barela is the off soot of the Bhils and traditionally dependent on the encroached land. They are the agriculturist. They are very aggressive in nature. They have the cultural practice of polygynous marriage. Even in the single household the population growth is relatively faster. In normal case the average child strength per household is 8-10. There is a norm of establishment a separate household after marriage in the society. Hence, every yound man requires additional agricultural land for supportive his family, apart from the area he inherits from his predecessors. The only way to avail new agricultural land is encroachment. Encroachment is carried out in three stages:

(a) They girdle the tree that ultimately results into the death of the tree.

(b) They cut the trees and burn the stump so that the forest staff is unable to understand when it has been cut.

(c) Finally they till the soil to make the land cultivable.

The Cultural Process of Encroachment

The 'Nawaria Patel' System: The headman who is called the 'Patel' of their traditional political institution leads the Bhil society. In the land grabbing process they have revived this leadership when the State Government has endorsed the statutory panchayat system in the rural setting. But the services of the 'patel' are utilized for searching the new land ('*nawar*'). He tells about the condition of the land. Hence the land is not encroached in a row, rather in a scattered manner and the forest department faced problems in demarcating the forest boundary after the settlement of the forestland. For 'patta' day by day the Newaria patel never gives the ownership of the land to anybody. On the contrary, it is a custormary law that the Nawaria Patel is the owner of the land. He allows occupation by other members of the village on a tenant basis. His authority is very sound as he takes the decisions regarding land allotment and ownership.

Cause of the encroachment :

(i) *Primitive agricultural technology:* This does not meet the food requirement of the individual family. Hence they further extend the land encroachment.

(ii) *Steep land:* As the land has varying slope from gentle to steep even in 45 degree, the top soil also gets washed off during the rainy season. Due to the continuing soil erosion, the crop productivity goes down in just 2-3 years after first tilling. After this time period the land is left fallow.

(iii) *Prevalence of polygamy and child marriage* : It is a normal practice that a Bhil man has 2-3 wives. Hence the population increases at a higher rate. Besides this, the tradition of child marriage is still followed to a large extent.

(iv) *No alternative source of income :* They collect forest production in meager quantities, Chironji, Safed Musli, Mahua Mahua flowers etc. which do not give them substantial income. As they can not utilize the forest products optimally, they are much dependent on land.

(v) *Political manoeuver :* The political leaders have utilized the encroachment issue as a vote bank. For their efforts the encroachers have got either forest patta or the revenue patta. In this way the forest is getting receded.

(vi) *Loose administration :* When the villagers encroach on the forestlands the forest guards come for legal action but income inactive after getting the bribes from the encroacher. Shri Khoom Singh, a patel in the village Kumbhi told the present researcher that they had given Rs.1000 as bribe for encroaching 3-4 hectares of forest land which produced the soybean of Rs. 4000.

Emerging Conflict

Encroachment is the major issue of the organization 'Adivsai Mukti Sangathan' whose main goal was to protest against all sorts of exploitation of the tribal. Three outsiders Nikeenj, Vijay Reddi and Madhuri are the three initiators from the States of Andhra Pradesh and Tamil Nadu, who started movement against the liquor merchants, moneylenders and big farmers. The time, their fight started against the Nawaria Patel the main exploiters because they do not give the ownership right to the tillers. As the movement was not becoming successful given the common tribal's dependence and loyalties to the patel system, this movement has taken the shape of a fight against the government machinery. In the local dailies this has been reported as a movement with Naxalite ideals. The Nawaria Patel group under the influence of local political leader of ruling formed an organization, named the "Adivasi Samaj Sudhar Mukti Sena". A conflict has emerged between the two organizations and the situation turned worse when a member of the Adivasai Mukti Sangathan dies in police custody after being arrested on the complaint of the murder of a supporter of Adivasi Mukti Sena. The matter ultimately reached the Madhya Pradesh Human Commission.

Checking by JFM Activities

Joint Forest Management was initiated as a collaborative project by DEO, Deputy Rangers and Forest guard in the villagers, mainly at Papal Jhopa and Deonaliya. When the villagers were aware of the benefits that the villagers can accrue to, for example, to provide more irrigation facilities to individual land holder and more forest produces as NTFPs from the forest for the villagers. The Forest Department increased local awareness about the deteriorating condition of monsoon, the reverse growth of forest, reduced availability of the forest produce for local daily use. The other participatory approaches adopted include preparation of micro-plans though which many issues or problems could be identified. The compartments for the rehabilitation of degraded forest were selected on the basis of the probability of encroachment. Many employment opportunities in the form of a number of RDF works—contour trenches CBO (cut back operation), digging of pits etc. the VFC made trust building by providing many facilities like the installation of grinding machine which has saved the villagers time and energy for going to distant place to do the same work. The Samiti has also constructed a pond by checking water flow through the forest. By leasing this pond to a contractor a pond by checking water flow through the forest. By leasing this pond to a contractor they are getting fish at low price. The Samiti also provides loan to all the landholders for purchasing seeds and fertilizers, and soft loans for starting new petty business. In this way the JFM activities have reduced the dependency of the villagers on the land. The Samiti maintains gender equity in the distribution of jobs in the RDF work.

Conclusion

Encroachment is now a common practice of the tribals in the cultural fold in the Khargone district. But the effort have also been done by the Division Forest Officer in the Khargone and Sendhwa Divisions to sensitize and develop the awareness among local people regarding protection of the forest. Mr. Yali, DFO, Sendhwa division started the JFM activities in 1994 to protect about 100 ha in the area. Later the protected land area have been extended to 1500 ha. After observing the growth of same grasses and small plants. Later on Mr. A.S. Dabas, the then DFO of Khargone division, also took up JFM activities in his area by constituting FPCs and VFCs in 58 forest millages. In Jhirnya and Bhagabarnpur tribal blocks were cases of disputes and agitation were rampant. Under the joint forest management programme developmental works have got top priority due to their potential in the economic standard to the tribals and in providing facilities like irrigation, drinking water, health services, educational opportunities and women and child development through ICDS projects.

12 Panchayat Raj in Scheduled Areas after Implementation of PESA

Evidences from Western Tribal Belt of Madhya Pradesh

Yatindra Singh Sisodia

I

Introduction

India is truly a land of diversities; it is indeed a community of communities. One of such communities is of the tribals who have their own ways of life, customs, cultural identities, customary modes of living together as well as their customary modes of resolution of disputes. For centuries they lived in isolation, far away from the national main stream, worshipped their Gods whom they identified with their hills/mountains, lands, rivers, forests and nature. Such isolation kept them socially, economically and politically backward with its attendant handicaps of poverty, ignorance, disease, malnutrition and exploitation. The colonial rulers looked to these social groups from the point of view of maintenance of law and order, or as objects of social antiquities to be preserved in isolation. However, after independence the tribal communities received the attention of the Central and State Governments, which started undertaking measures for their socio-economic welfare and upliftment.

From the very time of Independence, the objectives of the government's policy with regard to tribes and tribal areas were directed towards the "preservation of their social customs from sudden erosion and to safeguarding their traditional vocations without their being pauperised by exploitation by the more sophisticated elements". On the suggestion of the Advisory Committee, the Drafting Committee considered the proposals at the stage of drafting and suitable provisions were included in the Draft Constitution. Historically, in the scheduled and tribal areas, individual laws were enacted applicable to particular areas. These laws prescribed simple and elastic forms of judicial and administrative procedures.

Nevertheless, when it came to integrating or associating the tribal communities with the democratic processes of the country, a major hiatus was felt. For instance, when the right to equality was granted to the citizens of free India or when the system of panchayat raj was introduced in the States of India for the sake of establishment of self-government at the grassroots level, the socio-cultural values and life styles of the tribal communities presented some insurmountable difficulties to the constitution-makers of the country. Neither it was possible to implement right to equality of opportunity in such a society nor was it possible to introduce the principle of democratic mode of decision-making in a society where decisions were arrived at by traditional methods of community consensus.

It was under these conditions of socio-economic and cultural diversities and distinctive characteristics of the tribal communities that the framers of the Constitution assigned special constitutional status to them. Therefore, the architects of the Constitution, along with the principle of non-discrimination, made some exceptions for the Scheduled Tribes, Scheduled Castes and other backward classes.

Thus, under Part X, entitled the Scheduled and Tribal Areas, it was provided that the administrative set up for the tribal people would be different from other State or Union Territory administrations. The areas, where tribal people clustered in majority, were designated as Scheduled Areas and for such Scheduled Areas, special provisions were made for their 'administration and control' under Article 244(i) of the Constitution of India.

Administration and Control of Scheduled Areas under Article 244(i)

Article 244 (i) maintains the distinctive identity of the Scheduled Areas. It requires that Governor of such a State, which has Scheduled Areas therein, shall annually, or whenever so required by the President of India, shall report to the President regarding the administration of the Scheduled Areas in that State. Also, the executive power of the Union Government extends to the giving of directions to the State about the administration of such areas. Such executive directions are not given to other States under normal conditions.

Another significant feature incorporated in the Fifth Schedule was the institution of "Tribal Advisory Council" [Article 244 (i)4] for the administration and control of the Scheduled Areas. The Constitution required that these TACs should be in each State, which has Scheduled Areas therein. A Tribal Advisory Council shall consist of not more than 20 members, of whom nearly three-fourths should be representatives of the Scheduled Tribes in the State Assembly. The primary duty/function of the TAC was to advise on such matters pertaining to the welfare and advancement of the Scheduled Tribes, as referred to the Council by the Governor. Such were the special provisions under the Fifth Schedule in the Constitution of India before 1992-93 to protect the distinctive character of the tribal communities in various States of India.

To the question of determination as to which were the Scheduled Tribes, Article 342(1) lays down that the President, after consultation with the Governor of the concerned State, shall specify the tribes and the tribal communities, or groups within them, to be deemed as Scheduled Tribes. Thus, before the enactment and enforcement of the 73rd Constitutional Amendment Act, such were the special provisions related to the administration and control of the Scheduled Areas.

II

73rd Amendment Act and PESA

The enactment of the 73rd Constitutional Amendment Act and the subsequent state-wise panchayat raj acts in India have brought to the fore the significance of grassroots democratic processes. This experience has brought with it the lesson that the success of the new panchayat raj system largely depends on the congruence of the perception and commitment of the people, their leaders and officials, about the role to be played by them in the new system. Contextually and theoretically too, the new panchayat raj system has been created as a model of self-governance (Sisodia, 2002a). The objectives of decentralisation are to execute and implement schemes and programmes to meet local needs, to mobilise people, to channelise their energies towards socio-economic reconstruction and to involve them in all activities of the communities through the new institutions. Its objectives also include reducing the work of the higher levels of government and making the people responsible to decide their destiny within the framework of the new dispensation.

The 73rd Constitutional Amendment Act, 1992 is a significant milestone in the journey of panchayati raj institutions in Madhya Pradesh. Madhya Pradesh was the first state in the country to enact and implement the panchayat raj system in the true spirit of the 73rd Amendment Act. The major gain from the Madhya Pradesh Panchayat Raj Adhiniyam, 1993, accruing to the tribal people, was in the field of reservation of seats for their representatives in all the three tiers of the panchayats. The quota of reserved seats for the Scheduled Tribes was to be in proportion to their population in the three tiers of gram panchayats, janpad panchayats and zilla panchayats.

Though the 73rd Amendment Act, provided respectable spaces to the tribal people in the working of the panchayat raj system, such legislation could not make the tribal communities the sole masters of their socio-political destinies in their homelands. The need was always felt that the institutional structures within the scheduled areas were to be in consonance with the tribal needs, ethos and tribal institutions with which these people were familiar for ages (Purohit, 2002). Also, many of such areas, which were once freely managed by the tribal people themselves, for example, the management of their forests, lands and water resources, are now out of their purview and are under the authority of external institutions/agencies. Added to such disgruntlements were the voices of the friends of the panchayat raj system as well as of the tribal people themselves who pleaded for more powers to the panchayats under scheduled areas in a way that their institutions, while enjoying decentralised status and functioning as units of self-government, could at the same time preserve and safeguard the traditions, customs and cultural identities of their people.

As a result of such demands and needs of the tribal communities a committee of parliamentarians and experts (22 members) was appointed in June 1994 by the Government of India under the chairmanship of Dilip Singh Bhuria. The purpose of the high-level committee was "to discuss and examine the issues relating to extension of the provisions of Part IX of the Constitution to the Scheduled Areas and to make recommendations on the salient features of the laws for extending the provisions of this Part of the Constitution to the Scheduled Areas". When adopted, many of the principal recommendations of the Bhuria Committee were accepted by the Union Government and the legislation was passed, to be known as *Panchayat (Extension to the Scheduled Areas) Act, 1996.*

Salient Features of Panchayats (Extension to the Scheduled Areas) Act, 1996

1. Every village shall have an elected Gram Sabha and it shall be competent to safeguard and preserve the traditions and customs of the people.
2. Gram Sabha shall approve the plans, programmes and projects for social and economic development before their implementation.
3. It would be responsible for the identification or selection of persons as beneficiaries under the poverty alleviation and other programmes.
4. Every Gram Panchayat shall obtain from Gram Sabha a certificate of utilisation of funds for the plans, programmes and projects.
5. The reservation of seats in the Scheduled Areas in every Panchayat shall be in proportion to the population of the communities in the Panchayat. The reservation for Scheduled Tribes shall not be less than one-half of the total number of seats. Further, all seats of chairpersons of Panchayats at all levels shall be reserved for the Scheduled Tribes.
6. Planning and management of minor water bodies in the Scheduled Areas shall be entrusted to Panchayats at the appropriate level.

7. Recommendations of the Gram Sabha or the Panchayats shall be mandatory in granting of licence for mining lease for minerals and concession for the exploitation of minor minerals by auction in the Scheduled Areas.
8. The state legislature shall endow Panchayats and the Gram Sabha specifically with : (i) Power to enforce prohibition or regulate or restrict the sale and consumption of any intoxicant; (ii) Ownership of minor forest produces; (iii) Power to prevent land alienation in the Scheduled Areas; (iv) Power to manage village markets; (v) Power to control money lending to Scheduled Tribes social sectors; (vi) Power to control local plans and resources for such plans, including tribal sub-plan; and (vii) The state legislation that may endow Panchayats with powers and authority, as may be necessary to enable them to function as institutions of self-government, shall contain safeguards to ensure that Panchayats at the higher level do not assume the powers and authority of any Panchayats at the lower level or of the Gram Sabha.

After the enactment of PESA in 1996, a period of one year was given to the States having V Scheduled Areas to amend their respective State Panchayat Acts to bring them in conformity with the PESA. The State of Madhya Pradesh made an amendment in December 1997.

III

Enactment of PESA in Madhya Pradesh

A cursory look at the demographic composition of Madhya Pradesh would show that the state is a rich treasure house of tribal communities. Within the State boundaries we find representation of nearly all the principal tribal groups of Central India; they inhibit all the four corners of the State. Madhya Pradesh lies in the geographical heart of India. Madhya Pradesh lies in the geographical heart of India. The state's tribal population is 12,233,474 (Census, 2001). The tribal population of state accounts for 20.3 per cent of the state's total population. The geographical area of the tribal population is 40.63 per cent. 33.6 per cent of total geographical area notified as Scheduled Area. There are 425 Scheduled Tribes in the country. The number of Scheduled Tribes in the state is 46 divided into more than 161 ethnic groups. Three Scheduled Tribes of state have the status of primitive tribes. As per 1991 census, the percentage of total literacy among STs in the Madhya Pradesh is 21.54 per cent. As regards the percentage of ST males and females, it is 32.16 and 10.73, respectively. The number of scheduled tribes in the state is 46 divided into more than 161 ethnic groups. Three scheduled tribes of state have the status of primitive tribes.

Accordingly, the Madhya Pradesh Panchayat Raj (Dwitiya Sanshodhan) Adhiniyam, 1997 was enacted by state assembly. The Adhiniyam received governor's assent on December 2, 1997 and was promulgated on December 5, 1997. While redefining the powers of Panchayat Raj Institutions, the Madhya Pradesh Panchayat Raj (Dwitiya Sanshodhan) Adhiniyam, 1997, adds Chapter XIV-A, which delineates the constitution of gram sabhas, gram panchayats, prescribes the mode of reservation of seats for them along with the powers and functions of these bodies/institutions of the scheduled areas. A perusal of the powers and functions of the panchayat raj institutions of scheduled areas and those of the general panchayat raj institutions would show that the former, particularly the gram sabhas, have their distinctive characteristics. Suffice to say at this stage that the panchayats of the scheduled areas have been assigned some special powers and functions, which are in consonance with the ethos of the tribal people/communities; such provisions bless these bodies with some preferential powers and functions. Though the panchayat raj institutions under the scheduled areas bear the same nomenclatures as those of the general areas, their mode of composition and their powers vary from panchayats of the general areas. At the foundation level is the 'gram sabha'. It is a body consisting of all persons whose names are included in the electoral rolls relating to the area of a panchayat at the village level. As the tribal people live in a scattered manner in the '*phalias*' or hamlets/group of hamlets, the Act defines a village in the scheduled areas as that "which shall ordinarily consist of a habitation or a group of habitations or a hamlet or a group of hamlets comprising a community and managing its affairs in accordance with (its) traditions and customs". Ordinarily, every village shall have a gram sabha, but if the members of the gram sabha so desired, more than one gram sabha may be constituted in the village, keeping in view the habitation pattern of the tribals under a hamlet or group of hamlets. Not less than one-third of the total number of members of the gram sabha shall constitute the quorum for a meeting, and of this number not less than one-third should be women members. The meeting of the gram sabha shall be presided over by a scheduled tribe member who will be elected for the purpose by the majority of members present in the meeting. Reservation of seats for scheduled tribes (as also for scheduled castes) in every panchayat of the scheduled areas shall be in proportion to their respective population in that panchayat area. But the reservation of STs shall not be less than half of the total number of panchayat seats. Also, all seats of sarpanch/president of panchayats at all levels in the scheduled areas are reserved for members of the Scheduled Tribes. In case there is no representation of Scheduled Tribes in a panchayat in the scheduled areas at the janpad or zilla panchayat level, the state government may nominate persons belonging to STs. However, such nomination shall not exceed one-tenth of the total number of the elected members of that panchayat.

Special Powers and Functions of Panchayats in Scheduled Areas

In addition to the powers and functions as enumerated under Section 7 of the Madhya Pradesh Panchayat Raj (Dwitiya Sanshodhan) Act, 1997, the gram sabha of a scheduled area has special powers and functions. These are: to safeguard and preserve the traditions and customs of the people, their cultural identity and community resources and the customary mode of dispute resolution; to exercise control over institutions and functionaries in all social sectors transferred to the gram panchayat through that panchayat; to manage natural resources including land, water and forests within the area of the village in accordance with its traditions in harmony with the provisions of the Constitution and with due regard to the spirit of other relevant laws in force; to advise the gram panchayat in the regulation and use of water bodies; to manage village markets and 'melas' including cattle fairs, by whatever name called, through the gram panchayat; to control local plans, resources and expenditure for such plans including tribal sub-plans, and to perform and exercise such other powers and functions as the state government may confer on or entrust them under any law for the time being in force.

This catalogue of powers of scheduled area panchayats should convince any one that they have not only been powers to manage their local affairs but also equipped with special powers for the preservation of tribal identities. The gram panchayat in scheduled areas shall work under the general superintendence, control and direction of the gram sabha.

The most significant aspect of the amendment package is the recognition of the need to safeguard and preserve the traditions and customs of the tribal people/communities, their cultural identities as well as their customary modes of social-personal relations, including the customary modes of resolution of personal/community disputes. Thus, the panchayats of scheduled areas in Madhya Pradesh will, on the one hand, have the first taste of democratic decentralisation, and on the other, will be able to protect and safeguard their cultural identity, cultural traditions and customs.

Secondly, the history of tribal societies during the past more than five decades in India would show that the people of scheduled tribes have lost their rights over land, water and forest. The resource bases of the tribal people were snatched away from them by the 'outsiders' and the tribal societies were dispossessed by laws such as Land Alienation Act, Mining Laws, Forest Act and Wildlife Act. Tribal societies, after the passing of the Madhya Pradesh Panchayat Raj (Dwitiya Sanshodhan) Act, 1997, should now feel compensated as Section 129-C (iii) empowers the gram sabha in scheduled areas "to manage natural resources, including land, water and forests within the area of the village with its traditions". This would be like regaining 'the lost horizon' for the tribal people.

IV

Grassroots Reality

Almost a decade has passed since the new system was put in practice. This part presents the field reality of the panchayat raj, particularly gram sabha. An attempt is made to shed light on the various aspects of the panchayat raj in scheduled areas.

Gram Sabha is the basic institution of decentralised

governance. It is the first modern political institution that seeks to place direct political power in the hands of the people, without the mediation of elected representatives. Gram sabha, or people's forum, has always been an integral part of the concept of a gram panchayat. Rajni Kothari visualises gram sabhas as 'watchdogs' coming between 'the politician-bureaucratic nexus'. "The only way of making this nexus responsible and accountable is to provide larger citizen involvement in new variants of old institutions like the gram sabha which can combine older forms of informal consensus-making mechanisms with the more formal, institutionalised and legal forms decreed by legislation. With the new awakening in the rural areas, these bodies have the potential of overseeing the working of elected bodies and over time, with growing confidence that they cannot be browbeaten by dominant individuals or castes, become a force to reckon with" (Kothari, 1998). The legislative empowerment of the gram sabha in India is a political development of the utmost importance, because it marks the clearest break from the most dominant political orthodoxy of the 20th century (Mander, 1999). This recent faith in the gram sabha is based on the belief that the objective conditions of the poor are directly involved in the process of formulation and implementation of decisions affecting their lives.

The vision of gram sabha in a village situation can be compared with the parliament or assembly. Gram sabha is the most powerful foundation of decentralised governance but unfortunately it could not become a vibrant and important institution at the grassroots level because of self-interest motivated local leadership and bureaucracy. Gram sabhas are mostly dominated by sarpanches and small groups of their associates.

It has been evident from the experience of panchayat raj in scheduled areas that the level of participation of people at the grassroots level has been very low and gram sabhas are almost a formal institution with no active participatory role in various assigned works. The state government transferred nearly all of the powers previously exercised by gram panchayats to the gram sabha. It has thus changed from a representative democracy at the grassroots to a vibrant direct democracy. The fact remains that despite this endeavour there is a clear gap between macro decision and grassroots reality.

It is important to recognise that this faith in the gram sabha is based on several extremely important but largely untested assumptions. It is assumed, first, that even in a village society with deep schisms of caste, class and gender, an organic community still exists and that given appropriate legal and institutional spaces, it can act cogently and responsibly as a community. A second assumption is that the collective will of the gram sabha would be a more reliable vehicle of good governance than a relatively unencumbered bureaucracy or local elected representatives.

It is certain that unless we have a vibrant gram sabha, we cannot have empowered and accountable panchayats (Nambiar, 2001). In scheduled areas of Madhya Pradesh, the village-level situation is different from the provisions in the amendment. At the state level, efforts have been made to empower the people at grassroots level but the people at large are in different and uninformed about this change. They are not even aware of such an amendment and its provisions (Sisodia, 2002 b).

It is unfortunate that both the grassroots leadership and grassroots bureaucracy have not been able to strengthen the gram sabha. The institution of gram sabha in many areas of the state is dysfunctional due to lack of leverage of local leaders to initiate meaningful participation in the sabha and their inability to persuade people to support local initiatives (Fernandes, 1999). It has been evident that meetings called were mostly without prior and adequate notice. In most places, only a formality was observed; proxy meetings were at times convened and proceedings were written even without the knowledge of those who attended. Meetings, if arranged, either proved to be abortive or unsuccessful because of thin attendance (Mander, 1999).

The grassroots experiences suggest that a majority of the panchayat representatives and villagers are not aware of the quorum required for gram sabha meetings. The required women's representation for quorum is not known to a majority of the people. The reasons shown for low attendance are mainly the engagements of people in agriculture and labour. Besides this, migration, lack of information, groupism, scattered habitation and negative point of view are other prominent reasons. It appears that the required number of people for a quorum is very high, which needs to be relooked keeping in mind the ground reality.

The panchayat raj institutions in scheduled areas are specially empowered to work as units of self-governance. But it has been observed that the level of awareness and exposure among panchayat raj representatives is very low. It is, therefore, important to initiate special training packages in scheduled areas. The provisions of the state Act should be translated into simple Hindi and local dialect and should be distributed to all panchayat functionaries in the form of pocket booklets as ready-reckoners. Posters can also be prepared and displayed on the walls of the gram panchayat buildings. It has often been seen that the panchayat representatives find it difficult to perform their duties due to the complicated rules and procedures. It is necessary that the rules and procedures be simplified; this difficulty also be eliminated with the appointment of a trainee and educated secretary at the local panchayat.

Gram sabhas are provided supreme position in the new system but the people at large are not informed about these provisions. They still accept the supremacy of gram panchayat. It is important to make them aware about such provisions. For this purpose, public awareness campaigns can be launched through NGOs. Electronic media (community television) can also be an effective medium.

Natural resource management at the grassroots level is a significant task assigned to the gram sabha. Traditionally, the tribal society had inherent rights over natural resources, but over a period of time they lost that right. The present scenario is gloomy: there is scarcity of water resources while the water level receding day by day. The process of deforestation has also been going on for long, resulting in vast patches of barren land. The need of the hour is to create an environment for better natural resource management and for this the gram sabha has an important role to perform. In this context, there is a greater need of people's involvement. Measures like better watershed management, aforestation and land utilisation can pave the way for better livelihood for the tribals. It can also help in minimising migration. The fact remains that there are few examples of such improvements in this arena. It is also evident from the field that there are so many committees dealing with different aspects at the village level, such as watershed committee, '*van*' committee, '*raksha*' committee, but the panchayat raj system in scheduled areas provides all powers to the gram sabha. Therefore, the parallel committees, where they exist need to be abolished. It will help in making the gram sabha a strong institution.

Gram sabha has been empowered to safeguard and preserve the traditions and customs of the people, their cultural identity, and customary mode of dispute resolution. In this regard, the gram sabha could do something where the traditional leadership of '*jati*' panchayat (*patel/tadavi*) is holding an important portfolio in the gram panchayat with reference to dispute resolution. It is important to consider when talking in terms of traditions and customs that the social evils be kept out of its purview. It is also advisable that traditions and customs are documented for each tribal community through panchayats. With the cooperation of the tribal leadership, a detailed list of tribal customs, traditions and rituals that need to be preserved and protected, should be prepared. This will help in its protection and promotion. Use of liquor and practice of dowry are to be discouraged. In the name of traditions and customs, the promotion of social evils should not be encouraged.

Tribal regions in Madhya Pradesh are facing chronic drought, leading to acute shortage of food resulting in starvation and compulsory migration. It is, therefore, important to prepare panchayats with training and awareness campaigns to face such calamities. Better management skills can reduce the intensity of such disasters.

It has been observed that there is no direct involvement of tribals in the execution of the tribal sub-plan despite specific provisions. The panchayat representatives and villagers at large are to be involved from planning to implementation in all development activities. Without people's participation and involvement, the targets cannot be achieved.

It seems that only an amendment in the state Act and specific provisions for a new system will not change the scenario in the scheduled areas. There is an urgent need to opt for an effective system whereby people can be informed and motivated to come forward for the implementation and execution of panchayat raj system in scheduled areas. There is an urgent need to break the culture of silence involving people in capacity building, sensitisation and orientation exercises to improve the grassroots scenario.

V

Conclusion

The above analysis clearly indicates that the panchayats are entrusted with all statutory powers and duties, but the experience of the previous years depicts a disappointing picture. Gram sabha at the grassroots levels in scheduled areas of Madhya Pradesh has witnessed low participation of stakeholders. The state government is said to have been with gram panchayats mainly because they tend to be dominated by sarpanches and small groups of their associates. Chief Minister Digvijay Singh is said to have remarked, "I did not expect panchayat raj to become sarpanch raj" (Manor, 2001). This reason has been instrumental in the introduction of the *gram swaraj* system in Madhya Pradesh from January 26, 2001. It is applicable in scheduled areas as well, provided the provisions of this amendment do not affect the spirit of the Extension Act.

Participation in gram sabha meetings has been low. Low participation can be mainly attributed to the strong factor of caste; class and gender divide the village people. Sarpanches and other influential people dominate the decision-making process. Two prominent and sharply contrasting groups lead the panchayats—one is group of traditionally influential representatives, and the other that of new entrants. The performance and efficacy of panchayat members is strongly influenced by caste and class distinctions. Gram panchayats are not adequately accountable to the gram sabha. The gram sabha is not informed of the gram panchayat's functioning. The concept of participation as an important part of panchayat raj has been rarely seen. In fact, in retrospect, it seems inevitable that persons of influence would look at larger community participation with hostility.

The vibrancy and efficacy of panchayat will remain a mirage if it does not possess the capacity to perform assigned roles and responsibilities. This question becomes more pertinent in a socio-cultural milieu where human resource development is low and society is deeply fragmented and hierarchical. Therefore, it is an urgent necessity for marginalised sections of society, which have been kept out of the process of decision-making, to be included in the mainstream through sensitisation and capacity building.

At the micro level, the gram panchayat is a people's institution and has been made a statutory body through a constitutional amendment. Panchayat raj system in scheduled areas has provided all powers and duties to the gram sabha. The resource flow to gram sabha and its ever-increasing powers and authority has generated lot of interest among people. This interest can be is translated into a more broad-based and participative leadership at the grassroots level through right measures, as suggested above. The need is to address the issue of awareness generation among the people. Training camps, awareness campaigns and audio-visual media can be of critical importance in sensitisation and capacity building of the people and their representatives.

REFERENCES

Fernandes, A. (1999): 'Reconnecting the Sabha to Gram', paper presented at the National Conference on Gram Sabha, *National Institute of Rural Development*, Hyderabad, July 28-29.

Kothari, Rajni (1998): *State against Democracy: In Search of Human Governance*, Delhi: Ajanta Publications.

Mander, Harsh (1999): 'Towards Direct Democracy: The Legal Empowerment of Gram Sabha', *Kurukshetra*, New Delhi, Vol. 48, No. 1, October.

Manor, James (2001): 'Madhya Pradesh Experiments with Direct Democracy', *Economic and Political Weekly*, March 3.

Nambiar, Malini (2001): 'Making the Gram Sabha Work', *Economic and Political Weekly*, August 18.

Purohit, B.R. (2002): 'Panchayat Raj System in Scheduled Areas of Madhya Pradesh' in G. Palanithurai (ed.), *Dynamics of New Panchayati Raj System in India*, Vol. I, New Delhi: Concept Publishing Company.

Sisodia, Yatindra Singh (2002a): 'Panchayat Raj System in Madhya Pradesh: An Appraisal' in G. Palanithurai (ed.), *Dynamics of New Panchayati Raj System in India*, Vol. II, New Delhi: Concept Publishing Company.

Sisodia, Yatindra Singh (2002b): 'Decentralised Governance in Madhya Pradesh: Experiences of the Gram Sabha in Scheduled Areas', *Economic and Political Weekly*, Mumbai, October 5.

13 Impact of Globalization, Consumer Culture and New Panchayatiraj on status of Tribes

R.S. Shrivastava

Though, Globalization and exposure to consumer culture are subjects which are being discussed worldwide in various contexts, I will discuss them in the context of the Indian Tribes. In this context, certain characteristics of the Indian tribes need to be mentioned. In terms of economies the Tribes in India have got rich natural habitats and are living in the amidst rich natural resources, both on the ground and under ground. These natural resources are great attractions for Champions and proponents of New Economies, especially, the Corporate Sector.

As a result of exposure to the outside world, their traditional culture is in transition. Modern education no doubt has opened new avenues of livelihood for them but has lessened their belief in their traditional culture.

The Constitution of India guarantees their all-round development through empowerment while conserving their culture but efforts made in these directions have rare impact on them. The facilities and services offered to them are being taken advantage of by their clever neighbourers. The measures of empowerment and decentralization of power have been discussed in the section on the Panchayatiraj in this paper.

Globalization is the end product and the process of the growing integration of economies and societies around the world. It has been one of the most hotly debated topics in international economics over the past few years. Rapid growth and poverty reduction in China, India, and other countries that were poor 20 years a go has been a positive aspect of Globalization. But Globalization has also generated significant international opposition over concerns that it has increased inequality and environmental degradation.

Interest and search for Indigenous knowledge is also said to be the outcome of globalization. The tribals in this manner have been exposed to globalization. Their minor forest produces which include medicinal herbs, shrubs, roots and fruits etc. are of great interest to the world at large for many purposes. The pharmaceutical companies comb the tribal areas for these produces as raw material for their medicines at throw away prices to the tribals. In Anthropology, Medicinal Anthropology is gaining much importance. In case of tribals it is not the societal/ social integration which is taking place due to globalization it is the economies that is being integrated.

Tribals *vs.* Globalization

When the human race was young, small, widely dispersed, and challenged by basic survival, tribalism was an adaptive device that helped people cooperate to reduce risk. With tribalism it is possible to get an in-group/out-group mentality that is a liability in the current diverse and densely populated world. When the tribes are separated with infrequent contact, everything's seems to be good. Maybe a few skirmishes when they do come in contact. When the tribes are forced to live together life gets complicated.

Globalization, not just in the economic sense but rather meaning the interconnection and interdependence of groups across national and other boundaries is the latest and so far highest level of human cultural evolution. In this general sense one might call it one-worldism except that few voices are calling for a single world government. This development values the diversity of individuals and encourages the contributions such diversity brings; it finally rings down the curtain on the view that just because someone does not belong to "my" group that person must be bad, wrong, put down, converted, or killed. We see remnants of tribalism in the Western nations in the campaigns of the anti-globalization protesters and our own religious fundamentalists (Falwell, McVeigh, and Farrakhan), so this is not just another name for the division between fundamentalist Islamists and the rest of the world.

An anthropologist might view the world this way: Behaviours persist over the long term because they have some adaptive latent effect. Just what happens when a behavior is no longer adaptive is less clear but is most likely some transient response followed by disappearance of the behaviour in the long-term. Putting a quantity to the length of long-term is difficult, as is under-standing the nature of transient response. The transient response, historically, appears to be violence.

An anthropologist views warfare as a form of rejection of the enemy's cultural values. Consider current and past wars, including terrorism, in light of this assertion and see if it holds up. The reasons why we went to war against Japan and Germany during Second World War are clear, but Vietnam is less obvious. We went to war against Iraq to move them out of Kuwait because we had a treaty with them and because the flow of oil is strategic to us. We went to war against Panama because they were enabling the Medellin Cartel to flood us with drugs.

Warfare between tribal groups in the distant past was probably an adaptive device as well. Cultures are conservative devices, the cultural systems of each group, and when taken as an indivisible whole constitute an adaptive mechanism for the group and preserve economically appropriate behaviour. When one unique culture comes into contact with another, cultural sharing could weaken the belief system and the associated economically appropriate rituals, leading eventually to the demise of the tribe. Therefore, warfare against out-groups would preserve the integrity of the cultural system, and improve the chances for survival for the individuals in the group. With widely dispersed groups this is actually a good thing; it is likely that different systems are required to adapt to differing economic environments, as different species do as well, so a little warfare following contact and then separation is a good thing. That said groups can and do borrow selectively from each other, which has occurred for thousands of years without always causing violence: the spread of agriculture, writing, spices, technology, and even ideas and religion as in the case of Christianity, Islam, and Buddhism.

Those cultures that accept diversity, in the most universal sense of the word, will survive. Those that do not accept diversity will be engaged in conflict and will not survive, or alternatively, if humanity does not have that capacity, none of us will survive. Thinking out loud, perhaps there will be conflict on such an enormous scale that population will revert to 2000 year ago levels with the whole process then to repeat until humanity is able to get past it.

If we don't learn to live together in a connected global community we will destroy ourselves. That is the next step in our evolution. We hope we can do it.

Sociology of Consumption: Outlines of Consumer Culture

The Tribals are known for their limited needs and means for survival. They are viewed as non-recipients of the unlimited boons of development due to their very limited needs. Their very limited needs check them in coming forward and receiving the benefits of development. Whereas modern consumer culture has unlimited needs and unlimited ways of fulfilling them.

What have thinkers found to be different or dangerous about the way consumption is organized in the modern world?

A Culture of Consumption

Core, social practices and cultural values, ideas, aspirations and identities are defined and oriented in relation to consumption rather than to other social dimensions such as work or citizenship, religion or military: a culture of consumption.

Dominant values of a society not only organised through consumption practices but also in some sense derive from them. Thus, contemporary society is described as materialistic, as more concerned with 'having' to the exclusion of 'being', as commodified, as hedonistic, or more positively, as a society of choice and consumer sovereignty.

The values from the realm of consumption spill over into other domains of social action:

- Consumption becomes a central focus of social life (reproduce increasingly through commodities)
- Values of consumer culture acquire a prestige that encourages their extension to other social domains, e.g. the extension of the consumer model to public service broadcasting or health provision.

The Culture of a Market Society

Modern consumption is mediated by market relations and takes the form of the consumption of commodities. The consumer's access to consumption is largely structured by the distribution of material and cultural resources (money and taste), which itself is determined in crucial ways by market relations—above all the wage relation and social class.

From a Marxist perspective, it is the wage-relation (not

industrial mass production), it is capitalist relations of production (not its technical forces) that produce the consumer.

Consumer culture is incompatible with the political regulation of consumption that suppresses the market. It does not arise in non-capitalist societies.

Universal and Impersonal Culture

Consumer culture is often identified with the idea of mass consumption. Market relations are anonymous and in principle universal.

The idea that consumer culture serves a general public also promotes a more positive idea that it embraces 'everyone'. We are all *formally* free and equal, unconstrained in our choices by legally fixed status or cultural prohibitions. Yet, it is also felt to be universal because everyone *must* be a consumer: this particular freedom is compulsory.

If there is no principle restricting who can consume what, there is no principled constraint on *what* can be consumed: all social relations, activities and objects can in principle be exchanged as commodities.

Freedom with Private Choice and Private Life

To be a consumer is to make choices: this exercise of choice is in principle unconstrained. The freedom of consumer culture is defined in a modern and liberal way: consumer choice is a private act. Two senses of meaning of this:

- In the positive sense, it occurs within a domain of the private, which is ideologically declared out of bounds to public intervention, social and political authority.
- In the negative sense, it is restricted to the household, mundane domesticity, the world of private relationships.

A critical remark is that in becoming 'free' as consumer we barter away power and freedom in the workplace or in the political arena in exchange for more private contentment.

Unlimited and never-ending consumer needs

The idea of insatiable need is bound up with notions of cultural modernization: the increased productivity of modern industry is a response and a spur to the capacity of people's desires to become increasingly sophisticated, refined, and personal, as well as people's desire to advance themselves socially and economically.

On the other hand, commercial society is systematically dependent on the insatiability of needs. Therefore, the market society fears the possibility that needs might be satisfied. To counter these fears, society develops demand management strategies and advertising, marketing and promotion.

Cultural contradictions arises

Economic modernisation underpinned by regime of rational planning and discipline and a work ethic, yet it depends upon fostering irrational desires and passions and a hedonistic ethic.

Negotiating identity and status within a post-traditional society

Modern concepts of individualism sweep away the possibility and desirability of fixed status order, characteristic of feudal times. In a post-traditional society, social identity must be constructed by individuals because it is no longer given or ascribed.

Goods can always signify social identity, but in the fluid processes of a post-traditional society, identity seems to be more a function of consumption rather than as in the feudal society where social order and identity dictate consumption patterns.

Consumer culture is crucially about the negotiation of status and identity. Regulation of these issues by tradition is replaced by negotiation and construction, and consumer goods are crucial to the way in which we make up our social appearance, our social networks, our structure of social values.

Modern Exercise of Power

Consumer culture is awash with signs, images, and publicity. This involves an aestheticisation of commodities and their environment. Consumption becomes a privileged site of autonomy, meanings, subjectivity, privacy and freedom.

Yet, all these meanings around consumption become crucial to economic competition and rational organisation, become the objects of strategic action by dominating institutions. The sense of autonomy and identity comes under threat. Hence the controversy over whether consumption is a sphere of manipulation or freedom.

New Panchayatiraj and the Tribals

The Scheduled Tribes or *adivasis* (original inhabitants) include around 400 aboriginal communities, mainly inhabiting remote and forested areas of India. They constitute 8.2 per cent of India's population. One of the characteristic features of the tribals is their very strong traditional Panchayat which govern each and every aspect of their life.

The 73rd Constitution Amendment's importance was that it aimed at achieving grassroots democracy guaranteeing adequate representation to the marginalised groups like the Scheduled Castes, the Scheduled Tribes and women. However, the 73rd Amendment was not automatically applicable to the scheduled areas (geographical area where the *adivasis* are concentrated) because of their unique characteristics and special needs. A committee under the Chairmanship of Shri Bhuria was set up to suggest the module of Panchatiraj suitable for the Scheduled Tribal Areas.

The Bhuria Committee gave a number of recommendations, important among them were that the rights of the tribals in the natural resources of their villages should be respected and their Gramsabhas should be empowered to regulate and govern them. The fifth schedule may continue but the autonomy granted in the sixth schedule should also be promulgated, slowly and gradually. The lower functionaries of Revenue, Police, and forest department and the like who are great exploiters of the tribals should work under the control of the GramPanchyats.

Keeping in view the recommendations of the Bhuria Committee, an amendment act was subsequently enacted in December 1996 titled, 'The Provisions of the Panchayat (Extension to the Scheduled Areas) Act, 1996. The scheduled areas and the tribal areas are specified in accordance with the provisions in Article 244 and fifth and sixth schedules of the Constitution of India.

After 73rd Constitutional Amendment the state governments in the Country framed Acts for the implementation of the Pancahayatiraj as required by the Constitutional amendment in their State. Madhya Pradesh was quite prompt in this direction. Madhya Pradesh Panchayatiraj Adhiniyam was framed instantaneously. Later, the Act was so revised that it guaranteed Gram Swaraj through Panchayatiraj also.

When the Central Act for the implementing Panchayati Raj into the Scheduled Tribal Areas came into force, suitable amendments in the Panchayatiraj Adhiniyam was made to make it successful in the Scheduled Tribal Areas also.

The Panchayatiraj and Gramswaraj Adhiniyam, 1993 provided:

1. Full powers regarding the Governance of the village to the *Gramsabhas*. The Gramsabhas have been called 'Swambhoo ' meaning thereby that they are self existent and quite independent in taking decisions about the Village both regulatory and developmental. The important functions to be carried out are that they can levy taxes to raise the income of the Grampanchayats for carrying out various works. Micro Plans have to be prepared keeping in view the felt needs of the people and developing the local natural resources. They can opt for Social Audit, monitor and evaluate the developmental functions going on in the Villages.
2. The Grampanchyats are supposed to carryout the decisions taken by the Gramsabhas.
3. The Janpad Panchayats and the Zila Panchayats are supposed to guide and supervise the working of the Grampanchayats, aggregate the Micro village plans and Budgets and make them finally part of the District Plan and Budget.
4. With a view to giving a representative structure to the Panchayats at different levels, provision of the Wards, election of members from different wards, Presidents (Sarpanchs) and Vice Presidents (Upsarpanchs) have been made. Representation of the reserved categories has been made in proportion of their population to the total population. One-third representation of the females has also been made.
5. Meetings at the regular monthly intervals have to be convened of the Gramsabhas so that the problems and felt needs of the villagers are deliberated upon intensively and solutions offered.
6. The meetings of the GramPanchayats have to be held regularly so that the decisions of the GramSabhas are carried out.

7. As per Schedule II functions of the 29 departments along with the personnel of those departments have to be transferred to the PRIs.

As against the above provisions it has been found that the structure of the PRIs is in accordance with the provisions made in the Adhiniyam. It is only at the functional level the PRIs are deficient:

1. The meetings of the Gramsabhas and the Grampanchayats are not held regularly. The meetings are convened either at the initiative of the departmental officers to get their schemes approved or propagated or individuals who want their vested interests to the fulfilled through the meetings of the Gramsabhas/Grampanchayats. In the meetings no serious consideration is shown about the fulfilment of the quorums especially the attendance of the female members. Sometimes, the meetings are called to fulfil the vested interests in land and other matters of the Village and suitable decisions of the Gramsabhas are taken without showing any consideration to the interest of the Villages. The same trend has been seen in the meetings of the Granpanchyats also.
2. No action has been seen to be taken in the meetings of the Gramsabhas to strengthen the financial resources of the GramPanchayats in levying taxes for which it has been empowered. Even if some taxes have been levied serious action has not been shown in collecting them.
3. Neither the departmental programmes nor the departmental personnel have been transferred to the PRIs with the result they have no control over them.
4. The Micro-Plans are not prepared in time, hardly

scrutinized or aggregated at the Janpad Panchayat levels. With the result they rarely/never formed part of the District Plan and Budget. Though, in M.P. the experiment of Zila Sarkars was supposed to be quite successful the Panchyatiraj had no role in it.

5. The funds of the DRDA and Panchayat and Social Welfare Department trickled down to the village Panchayat level; rest of the funds of various departments was spent by the respective departments only. Thus, the decentralization of powers to the PRIs remained on paper.
6. Even the District Panchayats like the Janpad Panchayats worked as "postoffices" in passing funds from their level to the Janpad Panchayats/Grampanchayats as the case may be.The Janpad Panchayat/Zila Panchayat level officers hardly monitored the implementation of the schemes at the village level.
7. Revision of the lists of families below povertyline, accessing or denying the benefits to the persons/ beneficiaries of the Indira Avas Scheme, social security pension or old age pension was referred to the Gramsabhas which obeyed the instructions from 'above' and did so in accordance with the instructions. It may be mentioned that the list of families below poverty line are made on the basis of their annual income beneficiaries under social security pension, old age pension and Indira Avas Yojana are decided on the basis of the fixed norms so there is hardly any room left for their revision based on opinions in the meetings of the Gramsabhas but it is being done so.

The Extension Act is one of the potent legislative measures of recent times, which recognizes the tribal peoples' mode of living, aspirations, their culture and traditions. However, studies to assess the implementation of the Extension Act and to examine as to what extent the 1996 Act was able to establish grassroots democracy in scheduled areas in accordance with the ethos of the tribal people reveal that nothing notable has taken place in these areas and that the condition of the tribals remain more or less what it was before.

It is a sad commentary on the political will of the state leadership that several states, e.g., Rajasthan did not amend their Acts according to the 1996 Amendment Act even after the stipulated time. A brief survey of the State Acts shows that the states have tried to fulfil the constitutional mandate half-heartedly and not in its letter and spirit. Some State Acts do not deal sufficiently with important provisions of the Extension Act like ownership of minor forest produce, prevention of alienation of land, control over natural resource, etc. This shows widespread apathy on the part of the state government towards the tribal areas and their resistance to give so much power to the tribals. On the other hand violations of tribal rights take place at regular intervals.

In December 2001 in the state of Madhya Pradesh, tribals who were relying on fishing for their livelihood in a reservoir as their sole means of subsistence were up in arms against the state government as they feared that steps were being taken to deny them the right to market their produce. In Gujarat, more blatant violations have taken place recently when the government denied reservation to tribals just 48 hours before the village council elections were announced.

Scheduled tribe men and women who get elected to office are not allowed to function in the decentralised institutions of self-government. Just like the scheduled caste, the tribals also are not treated with dignity by the panchayat bureaucracy. Elected tribal women members face violence and rape if they dare to challenge the authority of the officials or the powerful.

A tribal woman sarpanch was stripped naked while unfurling the national flag on August 15, 1998 (independence day) in a district of Rajasthan. In another case a tribal woman sarpanch in Madhya Pradesh was stripped naked in a gram sabha meeting because she was not consulting the leader of the dominant caste. Such violations of human rights are everyday occurrence in the tribal areas of India, in spite of powerful legislations for decentralised governance.

The remedial measures suggested in the context of M.P. are:

1. It is good that the meetings of the Gramsabhas are being reduced. It can be reduced to 4 every year. In the meetings well thought over giving full details on the points of the Agenda to be included in the meetings should be prepared.
   The quorums in the meetings have to be ensured especially the attendance of the female members.
   The Micro-Plans should be prepared based on the problems and felt needs of the villagers and well discussed in the Gramsabhas.
   The meetings should be called not on the basis of the initiative of the people having vested interests but really on the initiative of the villagers to discuss their problems, suggest remedial measures and monitor the implementation of the Schemes. The Panchayat Secretary can take the initiative in this regard.
2. It is also quite good to reduce the number of Committees to two, i.e. Panchja and Nirman Samiti. These two committees should be able to look after the whole work assigned to it by the Gramsabhas/Grampanchayats.
3. In stead of assigning 29 departmental functions it would be quite manageable to assign four departmental functions, viz. Education, Health, Drinking Water and

Communication. Not only the Schemes but personnel of these departments should be transferred to the PRIs. All other schemes and functions should remain with the respective departments.

4. The PRIs should be able to raise their own funds through taxation and should spend on priority on the schemes of four departments mentioned above. In addition to these, whatever, priorities are decided at the Gramsabha level should also be looked after.
5. Training can be organized to all the elected members in the basic considerations and working of the PRIs with the sole objective of making them aware of their rights and duties.

As shown above, the Tribals are forced to participate in the *Processes of Globalization* and be a party to *consumer culture*. The new *Panchayatiraj* too has not given the true rights as was intended. The status of the tribals is that they stand *'exploited'* from all of the three factors.

14 Is FRA Enough for Survival of Tribals

Evidences from Kalahandi District of Orissa

Tapas Kumar Dalapati

The Scheduled Tribes and Traditional Forest Dwellers (Recognition of Forest Rights) Act, 2006—the Forest Right Act (FRA) in short was notified for implementation from 1st of January, 2008. The notification of the Act has given rise to widespread debate between the social scientists who are advocating tribal rights to land and livelihood and wildlife conservationists who are against implementation of the same as they assume that implementation of this Act will leads to further deforestation and vanishing of wild life species. The on going debate on efficacy of FRA or its impact on wildlife is based on assumptions and calculations at the macro level. The basic objective of the Act that is giving land *pattas* to the genuine tribals and other forest dwellers for their livelihood right is side lined and not being assessed at the ground level. The present paper will highlight why FRA is important for livelihood for Kondh tribals of Orissa and critically examine the efficacy of the Act to ameliorate the livelihood conditions of the tribals. The paper is divided into three parts. The first part deals with processes of land alienation that have been marginalizing Kondh tribals of Kalahandi district in different phases of interaction with mainstream society. The second part deals with various questions whether the new Act will be able to assure a secured livelihood to tribals after its implementation through empirical evidences from two Kondh villages of Kalahandi district of Orissa and the third part concludes the article.

I

The forested tract of Kalahandi inhabited largely by the Kondh tribals was called *Kandhan* in the pre-colonial period. The Kondh tradition says that 'Kondh' were the first settlers who cleared the *Rengal* or forest and established clan based '*Desh*' territory headed by an *Umrao* who was chief of the clan. *Majhis* were Kondh village heads in the social structure of *Kandhan.* In the pre-colonial period, Kondhs had to present offers to the *Umrao* on special occasions through village headman *Majhis,* and there was no concept of revenue collection prevalent in the *Desh* during this period.

Kalahandi was a part of frontier zone of uncertain political control between different powers up to the 15th century. It is believed that, uncertainly about security encouraged an *Umrao* or group of *Umrao* to join hands with a service holder of the larger state to form an alliance. Thus, emergence of a state headed by Nagavanshi Rajputs introduced to the Kondh hinterland of Kalahandi. A Kondh myth claims that they brought a scion of Chhotanagpur royal family to install him as the ruler of Kalahandi during eleventh century. The long practice of Kondh involvement in the coronation ceremonies of various kings of Kalahandi and marriage of a Kondh woman to king of Kalahandi as first wife backs up this evidence. From 16th century onwards, a range of intermediaries between the ruler and the Kondh peasant came into political scene of Kalahandi. The royal family expanded and the practice of granting small territories to the younger branches of the ruling family with fiscal and administrative rights and fresh conquest by them resulted in political fragmentation and reorganization of the state's territory. This political fragmentation of younger branches made them independent kings in the hinterland of Kalahandi. These new independent kings tried to augment their own resources and estate. First, they needed an agricultural surplus for maintaining the state machinery. In this process, they accelerated clearings of forests by inviting non-tribal caste peasants to settle down in their kingdom.

In the state formation process, a vast tract of forest was cleared in the hinterland of Kalahandi. During 18th century onwards the local kings were invited non-tribal peasants from outside to settle on tribal land. During this period king's relatives and service holders had encroached upon lands, which the tribals had held communally. The lands of the tribal villages were granted, to the relatives of the ruler's family as *Pattayat* (the second son), *Lalu* (the third son), *Baboo* (the son of concubine/ mistress), *Rani (*the queen) as *Khorak poshak* (maintenance estate) and to Brahmins as *Brahmottar*. (Impey, 1863). The above process depicts that in the pre-colonial period, Kalahandi witnessed a state formation process and most of the tribal lands were encroached upon by land grants to non-tribals. However, in this period, land was plenty and because of the symbiotic relation between non-tribal patrimonial head and tribal masses, Kalahandi did not witness any assertion from the tribal communities.

Prior to the introduction of British rule in India Kondh territorial '*Desh*' system and post of *Umrao and Majhi* abolished in 1844. The state of Kalahandi came under the British rule in 1863 (Senapati, Kunar, 1980). This princely state was administered by two separate administrative areas the *Khalsa* area was ruled directly by the prince and *Zamindari* areas was administered through revenue intermediaries or *Zamindar*. Within this tailor-made system, the state administration played a little role in revenue collection. *Zamindars* were required to manage the tasks of revenue collection and administration efficiently for this work they were accorded substantial privileges, in terms of authority and land rights. At the village level, responsibility for revenue collection and administration delegated to the village head, or *Gountia*. This was the case in all but *Khas* (special) villages, where revenue administration was managed directly by *Zamindar.* In Kalahandi princely state, the successive rulers encouraged the inward migration of traders and skilled cultivators into Kalahandi from other areas. Ealier *Desh* managed by *Umraos* and *Majhis* were abolished and each village was assessed separately for new form of revenue collection. Villages were auctioned for a term of three years. Heavy *Nazrana* was demanded at the time of auction from the *Gountias* or the leaseholders. The old system of 'One *Umrao*, One *Desh*' or single patriarch for a circle of villages was abandoned. The new land revenue policy had an adverse effect on the Kondh *Umraos* and *Majhis*. The tribal leaseholders who were unaccustomed to the regular system of revenue payment became liable to pay for the villages. The traditional clan heads failed to collect excessive revenue required from their own clansmen. As a result, they could not compete in the triennial auction with the outsider Kulta, Sundhi and Mali caste people who were financially strong than the Kondh *Majhis* or *Umraos*. Gradually a sizeable section of tribal Majhis and *Umraos* lost their position, power and prestige in the social structure of Kalahandi due to ejection from the traditional function of regulating land relations.

In the same period establishment of royal court and maintenance of records needed experienced persons in royal court of Kalahandi. For these functions, Brahmins and Karans (writer caste of Orissa) were invited from coastal Orissa. *Malis* or gardeners were brought from Nagpur. Muslim horse traders from north India were invited for various royal services and granted rent-free lands and villages. Construction of new royal palace and new temples needed more revenue and the burden of the revenue fell upon the peasants. The new non-tribal leaseholders of Kulta, Sundhi, Mali caste had knowledge of cultivation and they exploited the peasants through the '*Da Bheti*' (gift labour) practices and became powerful in the local social structure. On the other hand, traditional tribal Kondh headmen could not develop such a system of exploitation of their own people.Therefore; the king preferred the non-tribal *Gountias* to kondh headmen. Under the new land revenue policy majority of tribal *Gountias* borrowed money from the Kultas by mortgaging their land. The Kondh in general also suffered under the new system, mortgaged their land to moneylenders and failed to recover this. In the due process, they became bonded servants of the non-tribal caste people. Their women folk became menial servants and Kondhs became labourers on what had been their own land. When Kondhs were over exploited by the new land revenue policy in the colonial period they took up arms against the *Sarkar-Raja-Gountia* nexus during 1882-83, which is known as Kondh rebellion in Kalahandi.

The Kondh uprising of 1882-83 was an eye opener to the British government. They introduced legislations like Agency Tracts Interests and Land Transfer Act (ATILT Act) 1917 to check land alienation from tribals. It provided that all land transfer by a member of hill tribes to non-tribal without permission of competent authorities was invalid. However, the Act was full of loopholes and implemented only in default. For example, the list of communities to be considered as Hill tribes in ATILT, 1917, included Malis and Gauds (currently considered OBC) as Hill tribes between 1927-1950. Even the Doms (currently considered SC) were included as Hill tribes during 1927-1943.This meant that during this period any land transfer from tribal communities like Kondhs to Gauds, Malis or Doms was valid and did not attract provisions of this Act (Kumar *et al.*, 2005:29).

In the post-independence period various progressive legislations were introduced that made bonded labour illegal and prevented alienation of land from tribals. The Government of Orissa passed Orissa Debt Bondage Abolition Regulation in 1948 based on recommendation given by Thakkar Committee for abolition of *Gothi* labour. The State government also amended the Agency Tracts and Interests and Land Transfer (ATILT) Act of 1917 to empower collection and subordinate officers to restore the tribals land, which had been taken illegally from them by non-tribal moneylenders. Additional power to restore land to tribals was provided under the Orissa Scheduled Areas Transfer of Immovable Property (OSATIP) (by Scheduled Tribes) Regulation of 1956. This prevented land transfer from a tribal person to a non-tribal without the permission of the relevant sub-divisional officer.

Legislation was passed in 1960 under the Orissa Land Reforms Act to fix ceiling on land-holdings and to enhance rights of the weaker sections of the peasantry. All these legislations were implemented to safeguard the interest of Scheduled Tribes in Orissa but the social structure dominated by non-tribal intermediaries and *Zamindars* failed the objectives of the National government. Under the Land Reforms measures, revenue intermediaries are allowed to retain some land for their self-cultivation. This process accentuated the ejection of large numbers of tribal tenants who have been cultivating non-tribal's land under different tenancy arrangements. Large quantity of land transferred to various fictitious names in the name of *Khudkast* (Self-cultivation) title ejecting the tribal and *dalits* farmers in Kalahandi. The distribution of ceiling surplus land in Kalahandi to the tribal has its marginal effects as the comparative analysis of operational holdings between 1971 and

1991 shows a declining trend of average land area operated among the households and concentration of landholding in favour of large landholders in Kalahandi (Mishra, 2001: 249). The heavy concentration of land in the hands of a few persons implies that land reform policy in the district has not been effectively implemented in respect of ceiling on land holding and the consolidation of landholding. Inequality in land ownership is Kalahandi district not based on the fact that large land owners own most of the land, but also because large land owners tends to own the best low lying *bahal* land with better irrigation and water coverage. The most important interesting fact is that the most of the productive tribal's lands have been transferred to the non-tribal through several tactics marginalizing the tribals in the socio-economic sphere.

Up to the pre-liberalization phase of Indian economy, land alienation problem in Kalahandi and its adjoining districts are caused by the non-tribals through illegal transfer of land through *Benami* transaction and illegal purchasing of tribal land through proxy name of tribals. After independence, another factor responsible for large scale land alienation of tribals is land acquisition for development projects. In Kalahandi district several development projects were undertaken to ameliorate the condition of poverty stricken people but unfortunately the most vulnerable of the tribals are displaced from their land in the name of 'National interest' and dubious claims of 'common benefit'. In the Upper Indravati Irrigation project 54610.03 hectares of private, forest and common land submerged under water and 2964.00 hectares of common land converted into tea and coffee plantation negating the tribal livelihood depending upon these common property resources. The tribal of undivided Kalahandi district were the worst sufferer of 'secondary primitivisation' ushered in by the non-tribal influx into the tribal hinterland of Kalahandi and further displaced them from their habitat without giving any compensation for their common land and very meagre amount for the sole livelihood sources,viz. land and forests.

In the post liberalisation phase the bauxite rich forested hills of Kalahandi are targeted by multinational companies for mining and aluminium production. In such a move Vedanta Aluminium Limited (VAL) entered into a memorandum of understanding with Orissa Government to set up an alumina complex, comprising a one metric ton per annum (MTPA) alumina refinery plant, a three MTPA bauxite mining facility and a 75 megawatt captive power plant at Lanjigarh. To feed its refinery, VAL signed a lease agreement with Orissa Mining Corporation Limited to jointly mine bauxite from the Niyamgiri Hill Range. In this mining project mining is to conducted over an area of 721.323 hectares out of which 672.018 hectares situated in Niyamgiri Reserve Forest of Kalahandi (south) forest division, Khambesi and Nimagiri proposed Reserve Forest and Jungle Block (protected forest) of Rayagada Forest division. For establishment of Alumina refinery near Lanjigarh about 723.343 hectares of land is required. This is being acquired forcefully in connivance of local administration, police and hired goons in the twelve villages of Bathilima and Lanjigarh panchayat of Kalahandi district. In this aluminium project, 60 families of Kapaguda and Kinari village have to be displaced and about 302 tribal families are directly affected by the mining and processing activities. Despite the problem of livelihood of 30000 forest dependent poor tribals, belonging to Lanjigargh, Trilochanpur Gram panchayat of Kalahandi district and Shihadar and Patraguda Gram panchayat of Rayagada district will face a doom due to the forthcoming mining activities in the Niyamgiri Range. To voice their discontent the tribals have formed an action group called 'Niyamgiri Surakhya Samiti' to save the mountain range as well as the socio-cultural affinities with the hill deity 'Niyam Raja', to whom the Kondh tribals have been venerating since time immemorial. In a recent development Khandualmali region adjoining Karlapat sanctuary of Kalahandi district, is planned to be mined by multinational aluminium company BHP-Hilton. To protest the mining activities in a highly forested region adjoining a tiger reserve peoples of eight gram panchayats of Thuamul Rampur block are organizing themselves under 'Khandualmali Surakhya Vahini' to resist the mining in the tribal dominated area of Kalahandi district.

II

In the previous section, a brief summary has described how Kondh tribals of Kalahandi alienated from their land and forests since the pre-colonial period. In this section, the efficacy of newly notified the Scheduled Tribes and Traditional Forest Dwellers (Recognition of Forest Rights) Act, 2006 will be analysed through empirical evidences from two Kondh dominated *dongerla* villages of Thuamul Rampur Block of Kalahandi district of Orissa.

In the Scheduled Tribes and Traditional Forest Dwellers (Recognition of Forest Rights) Act, 2006, there is a provision to give legal entitlement to forestlands that the tribals have been cultivating for long, as well as over forest rights such as grazing rights and access to minor forest produce. The Act will provide titles to forestland they have been cultivating since before December 13, 2005, up to 4 hectares (10 acres) per nuclear family. Similarly, the Act will give tribals secure entitlements to minor forest produce. Other forest rights covered by the Act includes right to *nistar* (Collection of forest products for subsistence needs), the right to conversion of 'forest villages' in to revenue villages, right to settlement of old habitations, community rights to intellectual property related to forest biodiversity and cultural diversity, and "any other traditional right customarily enjoyed by the forest dwelling scheduled tribes excluding the right to hunting." A unique feature of the Act is that the rights of tribals go with responsibilities of conserving forests and protection of wildlife. The Act also seeks to end the exploitative hold of forest department over the tribals by recognizing the Gram sabha as the authority to recognize and verify claims.

There has been intense debate about the impact of the Act on livelihood of tribals, forest dwellers and wildlife in the forested areas of our country. This debate has been clouded by several misconceptions and apprehensions. Some opponents of the bills claim that the Act intends to distribute 4 hectares (10 acres) of land to each tribal family in the country. This creates a fear that entire forests will then be destroyed. To ascertain the reality, empirical evidences from one shifting cultivation village (Mutachuan) and one relatively plain village (Badchhatarang) in Thuamul Rampur block are analysed to clarify the doubts and apprehensions. Data for the study was collected during the months April to May in 2005.

Mutachuan is a small remote village in the western end of the Thuamul Rampur plateau. The village is belongs to Kosabara Gram Panchayat of Thuamul Rampur Block of Kalahandi District. Kondh tribals dominate the village. Besides Kondhs, Dom, Gaud and few Paik families inhabited this forested village. There is less quantity of arable land available in the village. The village is surrounded by Sringari Reserved Forest in the north and west. Villagers depend upon subsistence cultivation in the available arable land and most of the agricultural yields come from the shifting cultivation undertaken on the hills of Sringari Reserved Forests. In some of the hills, forest is protected by tribals for sustainable use. One such type of forest is protected in the northern corner of the village adjacent to the sacred place Podpat, where triennially goat sacrifice is given to the village deity. Badchhatarang is one of the big Kondh villages in the tribal land of Thuamul Rampur block. Badchhatarang is the Panchayat head quarter of Badchhatarang Gram Panchayat. The topography of Badchhatarang is relatively plain in relation to Mutachuan but it is also comprises of numbers of hillocks having scanty vegetation on it. Majority of the villagers are Kondh residing with the Dom, Gaud, Paik and distillers Sundhi caste people. The village is rain fed and it has around seven streams coming up from the hillocks. Tribal use the stream water to irrigate the paddy crop in the *Jhola* or *Bil* land.

In Badchhatarang and Mutachuan only 473 acres (29.1 per cent) and 193 acres (54.3 per cent) lands are recorded as ryots land respectively. Government land covers about 70.1 per cent area of Badchhatarang and about 45.6 per cent of the Mutachuan. Average land holding pattern in the villages shows that in Badchhatarang 33 households (20.1 per cent) are landless and in Mutachuan landless households are 9 and they account for 20.9 per cent of the total households in the village. Barring the landless households, the average land holding structure of the villages are 3.4 acres and 5.2 acres for Badchhatarang and Mutachuan respectively.

Analysis of landholding classes in Badchhatarang village shows that out of the total 75 Kondh households, 13 are landless which account for 39.3 per cent of total landless households in the village. In the same group 8 Dom, 11 Gaud and one Sundhi households are there. In almost all the ethnic communities most of the households holds less than 5 acres of land. Only one household from Kondh tribe and two households of Dom caste hold more than 10 acres land in the village. In this village though, Kondh are dominant in landholding position, Dom and Sundhi caste households have been acquiring good quality *Bahal* land from tribals through lending of money in the time of Kondh's necessity. Land holding structure of Mutachuan shows that out of 30 households of Kondh community 6 are landless, which account for 66.4 per cent of the total landless households of the village. Majority of households from all ethnic communities hold less than 5 acres of land. Only one household from Kondh tribe and one Paik household own more than 5 acres of land in the village. Whereas only 3 Kondh households hold landholding of above 10 acres. In the remote village of Mutachuan Kondhs were dominant community but due to gradual interaction with non-tribal communities from the neighbouring villages, these Kondhs households are also started lease and mortgage out land to the Dom and Gaud caste people in the time of distress situation.

Encroached Land in Badchhatarang (acres)

Acre	*Kondh*	*Dom*	*Gaud*	*Luhra*	*Sundhi*	*Total*
.50			1			1(.5)
1.00	9	3	3	1	2	18(18)
1.50	5	1	3			9(13.5)
2.00		1		1		2(4)
Total	14(16.5)	5(6.5)	7(8.0)	2(3)	2(2)	30(40.5)

Note : Kondh—Scheduled Tribe
Dom—Scheduled Caste
Gaud, Luhra, Sundhi— Other Backward Castes

Analysis of encroachment of forestlands in Badchhatarang shows that out of 75 Kondh households only 14 (18.6 per cent) households encroached government land which account for 16.5 acres (1.01 per cent of the total village land)) in the village. If we take into account other forest dwelling communities who inhabit with Kondhs in Badchhatatarang, out of 89 other caste households 16 households jointly encroached 24.0 acres (1.4 per cent of the total village land) of government land in the village. This is evident from the analysis that 14 Kondhs encroached an average landholding of 1.17 acres of land in the village. Likewise, 16 other castes households encroached an average landholding of 1.5 acres in Badchhatarang village. If we take into account the total land encroached by both Scheduled Tribe and other forest dwellers they encroached 40.5 acres, which is account for merely .025 per cent of the total available village land in the Badchhatarang.

Encroached Land in Mutachuan (acre)

Acre	*Kondh*	*Dom*	*Gaud*	*Paik*	*Total*
1.00	4			1	5(5)
2.00	19	4	2	5	30(60)
2.50	2				2(5)
3.00	3				3(9)
4.00	1				1(4)
	29(60)	4(8)	2(4)	6(11)	41(83.0)

Note : Kondh—Scheduled Tribe
Dom—Scheduled Caste
Gaud, Paiki—Other Backward Castes

Analysis encroached land in the Sringari Reserve Forest by the villagers of Mutachuan through shifting cultivation shows that out of 30 Kondh household, 29(96.6 per cent) households undertake *Podu* (shifting cultivation) cultivation in 60 acres of Sringari Forest Range in Mutachuan village. If we take into account other caste households residing with Kondhs in Mutachuan, 12 other caste households encroached 23 acres of land in the Sringari Forest Range. The analysis evidently shows that 29 Kondh households encroached an average forestland of 2.06 acres. Analysis of encroached forestland by other communities shows that 12 other forest dwelling households encroached an average forestland of 1.91 acres in the Sringari Forest Range of Mutachuan village. If we compare the encroached forestland in Badchhatarang and Mutachuan it is far below the upper limit of 4 hectares (10 acres) prescribed by FRA, 2006.

Availability of Food in the Villages

	Kondh	*Dom*	*Gaud*	*Luhura*	*Paik*	*Sundhi*	*Total*
Badchhatarang							
Sufficient	6(8.0)	9(29.0)	5(11.4)	0	0	4(57.2)	22(13.4)
Average	11(19.7)	5(16.1)	9(20.5)	0	1(33.3)	2(28.6)	25(15.2)
Deficient	58(77.3)	17(54.8)	30(68.2)	4(100)	2(66.3)	1(14.3)	117(73.3)
Total	75(100)	31(100)	44(100)	4(100)	3(100)	7(100)	164(100)
Mutachuan							
Sufficient	4(13.3)	1(20.0)	0	NA	2(33.3)	NA	7(16.2)
Average	5(16.7)	2(40.0)	0	NA	2(33.3)	NA	9(20.9)
Deficient	21(70.0)	2(40.0)	2(100)	NA	2(33.3)	NA	27(62.7)
Total	30(100)	5(100)	2(100)	NA	6(100)	NA	43(100)

Note : Sufficient—Yield from agriculture provides foods for round the year and seeds for next agricultural season.
Average—Yield from agriculture provides only foods round the year.
Deficient—Yield from agriculture fails to provide food for the year around.
Figures in the parentheses show percentage to the total.

The Kondh tribals and Other Forest Dwellers have been cultivating in these forestlands in these two villages. If FRA will be implemented fairly, they will get the *patta* of the encroached forestland. If we look into the availability of food in the two villages, it is evident that despite cultivation in the encroached forestland their livelihood is not secured. In Badchhatarang only 22 households (13.4 per cent of total households) have assess to sufficient food. In Mutachuan only 7 households (16.2 per cent of total households) have assess to sufficient food in the village. The Kondh households are facing acute deficiency in food. In Badchhatarang 58 Kondh households (77.3 per cent of the total Kondh Households) and in Mutachuan 21 Kondh households

(70 per cent of the total Kondh households) facing deficient food availability, which is very alarming for the survival of tribal communities. It is evident from the empirical evidence that even if they get entitlement for the encroached forest land their livelihood will not be secured unless innovative agricultural practices are not introduced in the tribal regions.

In the scheduled areas of Thuamul Rampur majority of Kondh tribals are reeling under poverty, even the DRDA data for Thuamul Rampur shows that 88.76 (DRDA 1997) per cent of population living under the poverty line. The Kondh tribals of Thuamul Rampur use to lease and mortgage out land to the non tribal moneylenders in the time of distress conditions. When they unable to pay the debt they forced to sale the land under benami transaction as transfer of tribal land to non-tribal is punishable under OSATIP Act, 1956. Analysis of lease-mortgage-sale process shows that Kondh tribals have sold 28.5 acres and 8.5 acres to non-tribals in Badchhatarng and Mutachuan village respectively. In Badchhatarang 16 acres of Kondh land and in Mutachuan 17 acres of Kondh land mortgaged out to non-tribal moneylenders. In Badchhatarang village 19 acres and in Mutachuan 19.5 acres Kondh land was leased out to non-tribals by the Kondh tribals for meeting out consumption as well as various socio-cultural needs. The Kondh tribals lease-mortgage-sale out their *patta* land to moneylenders under distress condition and compelled to encroach government forest land for a livelihood. Kondh tribals identified themselves as sons of the '*Dharni Penu*' (earth deity) but compelled to clear forest and practice cultivation on the forest land due to emerging population pressure and 'secondary primitivisation' thrust upon by mainstream society discussed in the previous section. FRA Act, 2006 has clause on the rights and responsibilities of tribals for conserving forests and protection of wildlife in the tribal areas. But whether a starving tribal opt for conservation of forest is a great question mark for policy makers. In Mutachuan village a prosperous Kondh Dhan Singh Majhi preserved around twelve acres of forest through his personal initiative with help of other co-villagers. On the other hand other Kondh households in the same village practicing shifting cultivation to ensure a minimum survival. Therefore, it is evident that only those tribal can think over conservation who are sufficiently endowed with land resources for their minimum survival. It is evident from the above discussion that Kondhs of Badchhatarang and Mutachuan will not be benefited much from the new FRA Act, 2006. It is the duty of policy makers to introduce innovative agricultural practices and credit facilities for tribals which can save the tribals from further marginalization, otherwise only giving land *patta* to the poor tribals for encroached land will not serve the purpose of real development of the impoverished tribal masses.

III

On 1st January, 2008, the Scheduled Tribes and Traditional Forest Dwellers (Recognition of Forest Rights) Act, 2006 notified to undo the historical injustice done to the forest dwelling Scheduled Tribes. After notification of the Act instances of conflict between Forest department and forest dwelling communities reported from Burhanpur district of Madhya Pradesh and Udaypur, Sirohi, Pali districts of Rajasthan (*Frontline*, February 28, 2008). The tribals who settled on the forest land were ousted from their habitat as the Forest department people feared regularization of encroached land through the newly notified FRA Act. The tribal communities have been marginalized since pre-colonial period by the mainstream society and this marginalization has reached its zenith through the neo-liberal policies of state for widespread industrialization and displacement from the tribal areas. The recent notification of FRA is too late for ensuring well being of tribals. As the evidences from two Kondh villages of Kalahandi district shows that it will not going to help much to the already marginalized tribal communities. The need of the hour is to effectively implement the Act and build the capacity of tribals to manage their agriculture and forest with innovations with congruence of their culture and habitations. Otherwise the Act will face the fallacy of land reforms measures, which ousted majority of tribals and dalits tenant at will during its implementation. In this neo-liberal development paradigm state and market are insensitive to the real needs of the tribals it therefore, the duty of the third sector, the civil society organizations to tilt the FRA, 2006 in the favour of Scheduled Tribes and Forest Dwellers communities of India.

REFERENCES

Impey, H.B., (1863): 'Notes on the Garjat State of Patna', reprinted in Orissa *District Gaztteers of Bolangir*, 1968. Appendix-1. pp. 62-75

Mearns, Robin and Saurav Sinha (1998): *Social Exclusion and Land Administration in Orissa, India*. Washington: Wor!d Bank.

Mishra, Sunil Kumar (2001): 'Poverty and Economic Change in Kalahandi, Orissa: The Unfinished Agenda and New Challenge', *Journal of Social and Economic Development*, Bangalore.

Senapati, Nilamani, D. C. Kuanr (1980): *Orissa District Gazetteers Kalahandi*, Orissa: Department of Revenue.

Kumar, Kundan, P. R. Choudhary (2005): *A Socio-Economic and Legal Study of Scheduled Tribes Land in Orissa*, Bhubaneshwar: Vasundhara.

Frontline, (2008): "Conflict of interests", February 16-29, pp. 10-13.

15 Tribal Development in India

Achievements and Problems

Gaya Pandey

Indroduction

In our country India, the development of tribal population has been a major concern of the nation-builders, Central and State Governments, policy framers, strategy makers, voluntary agencies, non-governmental organizations, social scientists, social reformers, and social activists. We have constitutional provisions for social, economic, educational, political, administrative, health and sanitational achievements of the tribal people of our nation. Since our independence policy after policy, strategy after strategy, approaches after approaches and models after models to tribal development have been conceived. From the very beginning of the first five years plan to the present Eleventh Five Years Plan, programmes after programmes of tribal development have been formulated, and implemented. Billions and billions of rupees have been spent in the name of tribal development. But most of the programmes have either failed or could not yield result up to the expectation. In certain cases, tribal life has worsened. Even after sixty years of our independence, we have reached no nearer to the solution of the problem of tribal development. A number of evaluation reports dealing with the problem of tribal development have revealed that programmes of economic, educational, health, nutritional and sanitational development have not attained success.

However, some achievements of tribal development can be shown in the form of tribal MLAs, MPs, chief ministers, ministers, governors, beaurocrates, officers, doctors, engineers, professors, lawyers, IT engineers, management professionals, pilot, traders, multistory builders, media persons, school teachers, clerks, nurses, peon and others. But their percentage in total tribal population is very low. Now we can also see tribals living in towns, cities, metropolis and foreign countries. We also find marble made houses, double storey houses, two wheelers, four wheelers, costly and modern household appliances, colour T.V., refrigerators, land phones, cell phones, computers and internet in tribal families. Some families are availing good health services. On the basis of these achievements in tribal families, we cannot deny that development of tribal people has not taken place. But for tribal mass illiteracy, hunger, poverty, unemployment, ill health, malnutrition and unhygienic condition are still a reality. Such situations reveal clearly that something has gone wrong with tribal development policy programmes. Therefore, the call of time is to rethink over the policy and programmes of tribal development in our country.

Problems

The biggest mistake done while framing the tribal policy was putting all tribal communities together as 'Scheduled Tribes'. It was assumed that tribal population represented a homogeneity in culture and problems. That is why they were clubbed together. But empirical experiences are witness that all tribes of our countries are not at the same level of cultural development. For example, in our country we find cultural types such as gathering, hunting fishing, shifting cultivation, pastoralism, settled agriculture, artisan, urban and industrial labour in our tribal population. Each cultural type has its own cultural identity and its own problem. But they were put together under one category scheduled tribes.

The concept of primitive tribal group (P.T.G.) was evolved in favour of weakest sections of tribals. But it is again unfortunate that foragers and swiddeners have been clubbed together under primitive tribal groups. We anthropologists are well aware of the facts that the problems of foragers and swiddeners are quite different.

It is quite unfortunate that till now there is no separate programme for the development of minor tribes and Artisan tribes. Minor tribes like Banjara and Artisan tribes like Chickbaraik, Lohara, Mahali and Karmali of Jharkhand are facing the problem of extinction of their arts and crafts.

The problem of Santhal, Oraon, Munda, Ho, Mina, Bhil, Naga, Khasi and others are not same as that of Birhor, Raji, Chenchu and others.

The problems of tribes of North-east India and Rajasthan are not same as that of tribes of Jharkhand, Orissa and Chhattisgarh.

Providing reservation of seats in state assemblies and parliament has been beneficial for Munda, Oraon, Ho, Santhal, Mina and other major tribes of the country, but it is meaningless for other hundreds of minor and primitive tribal groups.

Reservation in jobs of Central Government may be beneficial for Mina, Naga, Khasi and others but it is again meaningless for hundreds of other tribes of our country.

From the above accounts, it is evident that the concept that all tribals are equally backward, equally poor, equally illiterate, equally deprived and equally disadvantaged does not hold true on the basis of empirical reality. So putting them together in future, too, will be a blunder.

Another problem related to the tribal development is the aim or goal of development. What we want to achieve as a result of development? What according to us is the end product of development? When and upon achievement of what shall we say that tribal development has been accomplished? Shall we call it as parity with the rest Indian population? If this is our parity, the question again comes which section of Indian society? Even among non-tribals, there are many sections more poor, more illiterate, more malnourished, more exploited and more oppressed than atleast agricultural tribes. This level obviously is not the target. Shall the parity be a *pucca* house. But eighty per cent of Indian families do not have *pucca* house. Is it our parity that every tribal family should have a government job. This parity is also not possible. Is it our parity for having a colour T.V., refrigerator, two wheeler, four wheeler, marble house, land phones, cell phones, computer and internet. It is also impossible for the government to provide these parities. Thus tribal development is facing the problem of aim or target.

The third vital problem tribal development is facing is the lack of tribal education policy. There is general argument that tribals should be made literate and educated in tribal regional languages. This may be good from the point of view of literacy and educational awareness. But this cannot be beneficial from the point of view of competitive examinations. All those who advocate this educational policy send their children and grand children in best English medium schools. So, there should be a clear cut tribal education policy in our country.

The fourth problem which tribal development in our country is facing is related to establishment of development projects, industries, dams, power stations, roadways, railways, aerodrome, station, hospitals, colonies, parks and others. Such type of development has created the problem of displacement and rehabilitation. Displacement has proved curse for the tribals. They were uprooted, displaced and not made shareholders. Some rupees and lands were given to uprooted families as a part of rehabilitation. But they could not adjust with changed environment. Their descendents are found living in slums and earning as labourers. There is a need for making them shareholders besides rehabilitation by land and rupees.

The fifth problem of tribal development is related to foragers and swiddeners. Attempts after attempts have been made to make them settled agriculturists. But instead of making them settled agriculturists, there is need to train them for existing in local environment through technological skill.

The sixth problem related to tribal development is problem of sustainable development. Big projects have polluted lands and water and have decreased the forest cover of the tribal habitat. In this situation sustainable development is impossible. Tribals have maintained sustainable and symbiotic relationship with land, water and forest since time immemorial. They are not destructors of land, water and forest. They are protectors of land, water and forest. Therefore, Forest Rights Act should be implemented with strong political will and commitment.

The seventh problem related to tribal development is the problem of pseudo tribalism. A number of politicians, bureaucrats, officers, voluntary organizations, non-governmental organizations, leaders, social activists and social reforms are bursting pseudo tears for the cause and development of tribal. But they lack honesty, commitment, dedication and will power. They want to satisfy their own interests rather than interests of tribals.

The eighth problem related to the tribal development in our country is lack of strong political will of the government. Government does not like to solve tribal problems. It wants to keep tribal problems alive for political benefits. Tribal problems should be handled with strong political will and commitment by the government.

Solution

The following suggestions may be taken into account while reclassifying Indian tribes and instating new perspective and strategy of tribal development :

1. There is urgent need for a change in reservation policy of tribals. Till now only major tribes have been benefited by reservation of seats in assemblies and parliament. Reservation should be provided termwise for major, minor tribes and P.T.Gs.
   In reservation of jobs, priorities should be given to such tribal candidates whose parents have not obtained the benefit of reservation till date.
   In reservation for admissions and scholarship, priority should be given to minor tribes, primitive tribes and of BPL families.
2. Such a model of tribal development should be evolved which could bring harmony between different tribals and non-tribals.
3. Participation of tribals should be ascertained in formulation, implementation, monitoring and evaluation of tribal development programme.
4. In decision making and judicial process participation of tribals should be ascertained.
5. Tribal development should be popularized as rights of tribals and not as gift of the government.
6. There is urgent need for formulation national tribal policy.
7. There is also an urgent need for formulation of national tribal education policy.
8. In tribal development special emphasis should be placed on tribal genius such as knowledge, intelligence, technology and value.

9. Besides income, education and health, social and cultural factors should be included as indicators of development.
10. No more displacement of tribals should be allowed. If it is essential, tribals should be made shareholders besides land to land rehabilitation.
11. Management and maintenance of forests should be given in the hands of tribals.
12. Dedicated and committed non-tribal officers can be allowed to handle the problem of tribal development.
13. To avoid corruption, selection of beneficiaries and distribution of assets should take place in village fair, weekly *haat* or gram sabha.
14. Tribal women should be empowered and trained in earning livelihood.
15. Development information should be made available to tribals through folk and electronic media.
16. Attempts should be made to formulate scheme and facilitate opportunity to develop skills with techno-environmental conditions of the group being developed.
17. Unemployment has been created by linking a traditional economy with market economy and degree linked employment opportunity. Every degree holder thinks in terms of government service rather than self-employment. There is a need for vocational training with little economic and technical support.

REFERENCES

Atal, Yogesh (1965): *Adivasi Bharat,* New Delhi: Raj Kamal Prakashan.

Halder A.K., & Gaya Pandey (2001): *Artisan Tribes of Bihar & Jharkhand,* Kolkata.

Pandey, Gaya (2007): *Bhartiya Janajatiya Sanskriti,* New Delhi: Concept Publishing Company.

Shukla, R.K. (1998) : *Forestry for Tribal Development,* New Delhi.

Singh, A.K., Gaya Pandey & P.K. Singh (1997): *Forestry for Tribals*, New Delhi: Classical Publishing House.

Singh, J.P., M.N. Vyas & R.S. Man (1985): *Tribal Women and Development*, Udaipur: Tribal Research Institute.

Sahay, V.S. and P.K. Singh (2001): *Indian Anthropology*, Allahabad: Allied Publishers.

Sahay, Shushma Prasad (1988): *Tribal Women Labourers: Aspects of Physical & Economic Exploitation*, New Delhi: Gyan Publishing House.

Upadhyay, V.S. and Gaya Pandey (2001): *Janajatiya Vikas*, Bhopal: Madhya Pradesh Grantha Academy.

Upadhyay, V.S. and Gaya Pandey (2001): *Vikasatmak Manav Vigyan*, Bhopal: Madhya Pradesh Grantha Academy.

Upadhyay, V.S. and Gaya Pandey (2003): *Tribal Development in India*, Ranchi: Crown Publications.

Verma, R.C. (1977): *Janajatiya Atit ke Jharakhe Seon* New Delhi: Government of India, Publications Division.

Vidyarthi, L.S. (1976): *Tribal Culture of India*, New Delhi: Concept Publishing Company.

16 Tribal Scene in India – Past and Present

An Overview Analysis of the Situation

V.K. Srivastava

Tribal Situation

Scheduled Tribes constitute an important segment of the Indian social fabric. They comprise about 8.20 per cent of the total population (Population Census 2001). These communities belong to different ethno-lingual groups and profess diverse faiths and occupy about 15 per cent of the country area in various ecological and geo-climate conditions ranging from plain to forests, hills and in-accessible areas. Tribal communities are at different stages of social, economical and educational development, while some tribal communities have adopted a mainstream way of life at the end of the spectrum.

The richness and the wide variety of cultural life are the most variable heritage of the great Indian tradition. The life is nowhere more spontaneous and vivid in its fullness than the small traditions of its tribal communities. More than seven hundred and fifteen such communities are spread over from Himalayas to Indian Ocean and from the Arabian Sea to the Eastern Frontiers. The origin and the progression in the current of history of most of these communities are shrouded in mystery, the tradition being largely oral. The tradition, myth and history intermingle in their lore indistinguishably[1]. The history of races in India has revealed that Negritos lost their foothold on major continents. Remnants of this great race are found in the Andaman Islands, Dravidians, Aryans and Indo-Mongoloids have appeared on the scene at later stages. The Mundas, Gonds, Santhals, Oraons and many other tribal communities are the oldest inhabitants of this subcontinent. The Bhils perhaps arrived much later[2]. In the Indian Subcontinent, the flows and counter-flows of numerous groups have been quite complex. Some of the migrants have been recent as the last three to four centuries. The Oraons have tradition of moving in the opposite direction from South to the North-East. The Ho and Santhal share the lore of moving from west to east[3]. The Dandakaranya (Chhattisgarh) represents unique amalgam of tribal population from the North, the South, the West and the East. *The tribal situation has been varying in all the states along the marrow like of history.* There was something in our own society analogous to what is called 'tribe'. To the best of our knowledge this term was known as *jana*. There were *janas* or communities of people like the *Savaras*, the *Kullutas*, the *Kollas*, the *Bhillas*, the *Khasas*, the *Kinnaras* and countless number of many others whom today we know as 'tribes', bearing almost the same recognizable names.

The so-called 'tribes' of India, it is well known, are the indigenous, autochthonous people of the land, in the sense that they had been long settled in different parts of the country before the Aryan-spreading peoples penetrated India to settle down first in Kabul and Indus Valleys and then within a millennium and a half, to spread out over large parts of the country along the plains and river valleys. There is linguistic and archaeological evidence to suggest that the pre-Aryan indigenous *janas* were settled originally on the plains and river valleys of the land. But they were not all in the same stage of development. They spoke a variety of languages and belonged ethically to a variety of physical types. Their religion comprised belief in and practices of what is called by anthropologists 'primitive' religion, and they seem to have lived in closed but well-knit social units each presided over by a headman or chief and controlled by a group of elders. Due to the pressure of a superior social organization with a superior techno-economy as that of the Indo-Aryan speaking peoples, these indigenous peoples, so-called 'tribes' were slowly but surely obliged to move bit, to farther and areas until they came to find their refuge in relatively more inaccessible regions of forests and hills and large mountain slopes, that is, in what the records call, *atavika rajyas*, *mahakantras* or great forest regions and *pratyanta desas* or frontier regions on the fringes of agriculturally settled, organized and more developed areas. The process went on for centuries and millennia, a very slow and speedy but varies in relentless manner[4].

The major concentration of tribal communities lies in a belt in middle India extending from Sahyadri ranges in Thana, Maharashtra and Daman on the western coast to Rajmahal Hills, on the west to the Ganges in West Bengal. It passes over the boarder regions of Maharashtra, Madhya Pradesh, Bihar and Orissa comprising the hill ranges of Satpura, Maikal, Vindhyas, Mahadeo and Chhotanagpur. This belt joins the other tribal region in the Himalayan near Darjeeling to the east of which lies the North-eastern tribal region covering the States and Union territories in that area. The north-eastern tribal region is split into the Assam valley which itself has a substantial migrant-tribal population from Chhotanagpur region who, however, are not included in the schedule of that state. On the western and of the great Central Tribal belt, the tribal concentration further continues in the direction along the Gujarat extending up to Udaipur in Rajasthan. The Aravalies from the northern boundary of tribal concentration beyond which the communities are found dispersed for some more distance.

The 'Dandakaranya' region is another major concentration

in the middle India with the largest land-mass. This region lies to the south of the Central Belt and is separated from it by the planes of Chhattisgarh. The Chhattisgarh region itself has substantial scattered tribal population as also other indigenous communities sharing numerous socio-economic characteristics with the neighbouring non-tribal communities making the dividing line unclear. The 'Dandakaranya' region extends from 'Phulbani' in Orissa in the east to 'Chandrapur' and 'Yeotmal' in Maharashtra in the West. The Durg-Raipur region in Madhya Pradesh from its zigzag northern boundary. In the south; it spills beyond Godavari valley into the plains of Khammam and further the Warangal in Andhra Pradesh. Tribal population in the southern state is largely confined to the forests and hills on the tri-junction of Kerala, Karnataka and Tamil Nadu[5].

According to B.D. Sharma (1977), the geographical area of tribal concentration briefly outlined above can be broadly divided into the following regions :

(i) Central - Southern Tribal region
(ii) Central - Northern Tribal region
(iii) Western - Tribal region
(iv) North - Eastern Tribal region
(v) Southern and-Tribal pockets

Overall tribal situation has revealed that living at desperate levels of socio-economic development, they are spread along the entire spectrum of social evaluation in India-ranging from the Palaeolithic hunters and gatherers of forest produce to the industrial workers. A perusal of the Population Census data characterized by the striking tendency of clustering and concentration in pockets which have suffered from isolation historically and are situated in area to sedentary agricultural. Such pattern of tribals setting is perhaps an indication that clustering and concentration have contributed significantly to the lack of adequate interaction between the tribal and the non-tribal communities within the population of India. After facing the age old hardship, isolation and exploitation, the tribal communities have developed their own traditional mode of living. "The genre devices of the tribes have been marginally modified by exogenous forces and have; symbolic relationship with the ecological condition and resources base of the enclaves of their concentration. The homelands of tribals are far away from the homogeneity in terms of their natural environment, they display a diversity of a high order in the modes of their living"[6].

Before India came under British Rule the equivalent indigenous word for the English term tribe was probably the '*atavika jana*' which denoted agglomeration of individuals with specific territorial, kinship and cultural pattern. It was during the colonial expansion into the non-Aryan areas where it faced the strongest opposition to annexation in the whole of the Indian subcontinent, that the tribe as a social category not crystallized. (The first official designation was "forest tribe" followed by "primitive tribe" (1930), "backward tribe" (1931), "Adiwasi" the original settlers (1948), and then "Scheduled Tribes" (1950) in today's tribes which answer to the anthropologist conception. The ideal type is rarely to be found. What we find are tribes in transition in India. We cannot have a readymade definition with which one can go into the field and locate a tribe. The greatest emphasis has to be placed on a historical perspective. The process by which tribes have been transformed is an historical process. Only by going into the antecedents of a group can we say with any confidence whether or not it should be considered as a tribe[7].

Tribals which we speak of today is the "remarkable phrase and social category called "scheduled tribes"—that be inherited from the 1935 Constitution and chose, in our wisdom, to incorporate in the Constitution of the Independent and Sovereign Republic of India.

Thus, the specification of tribes and tribal communities as "Scheduled Tribes" arose only after the Constitution came into force. The list of Scheduled Tribes prepared in 1950. The primitiveness and backwardness were the tests applied for specifying Scheduled Tribes. The main characteristics which are common to all the Scheduled Tribes considered have been (i) tribal origin, (ii) primitive way of life, (iii) habitation in remote and less easily accessible areas, and (iv) general backwardness in all respects.

In the present day Indian situation, the entire tribal population does not strictly exhibits the particularities attached to them. There are semi-tribal communities that have taken to agriculture and allied activities and/or have migrated to urban or semi-urban areas. Tribal people are also engaged in modern industries and vocations and have adopted modern cultural traits as well. Niharranjan Ray contends that through the question of the 'lower and depressed orders and untouchables of Hindu society' had started receiving attention from about 1880's, this matter was looked as a national issue only when Gandhiji's concern for the '*adivasis*' or '*adimjatis*' as much as for the untouchables and the depressed orders of Hindu society is too well known. It was mainly because of Gandhiji's efforts that the '*adivasis*' and untouchables and other depressed classes of the society were accorded a special treatment and their welfare was made a major concern of the state[8]. Therefore, the tribal situation in India has to be seen and evaluated broadly on many dimensions. The process of conceptualization and classifying of tribal social formulation taken place in due course of time, it has been found that a considerable differentiation can be perceived among the tribal peoples with reference to differential ratio of spread of cultural diffusion, education, urbanization intensity of outside contact exposure, access to productive resources, life style, and so on[9].

The arbitrary criteria adopted for scheduling the tribes on the lines of the Constitution, has damaged the tribal demography to a great extent. The first census of 1951 held after the independence of India followed the British tradition. It recorded total tribal population of 1911904. The identification of these tribal groups was made in terms of the "Scheduled Tribes" order of 1950. But, this situation changed after the recommendation of Backward Classes Commission, and in persuasion of "Modification Order" 1956, an additional population of 3,400,000 persons belonging to the category of 'Scheduled Tribes' rose to 22,511,584. The tribes thus accounting for 6.33 per cent of the total population of the country. The position, however, did not remain unchanged during 1961-71 inter-census period as several communities were 'Scheduled' in terms of the Presidential Order 1967. By 1971, the numerical strength of the Scheduled Tribes had risen to 3,80,15,162 and their share to the total population to 6.94 per cent. But in 1976, due to modification of the list of the Scheduled Tribes and with removal of the area restriction the population of Scheduled Tribes rose to 7.50 per cent in terms of the 'Presidential Order', 1976[10].

The number of Scheduled Tribe communities has been estimated between 300 to 450 drown from different cultural backgrounds[11]. The census of 1961 has recorded 354 communities based on Scheduled Castes & Scheduled Tribes list (Modification) Order, 1956. There is, however, a difference of opinion on the substantive of the question actual number of tribal communities in India—different estimates putting the figure between 427 and 450. The reason for this difference may be sought in the fact that the tribal groups, not covered by the 1956 list of 554 tribes and counting for a population of not less than 533,541 were clubbed together under the nebulous category called 'unclassified'[12]. The following two reasons may be attributed for the diversity of opinion about the numeral strength of the tribal communities in India.

No scientific definition has been evolved to define a tribal. Therefore, the scheduling policy is defective. It has been developed in an arbitrary manner under the diverse resource and condition.

Since the question of tribal identify has been thoroughly confused their number has crossed the limit of rationality. The identified tribes have not been compiled in proper hierarchical order. For example, Gonds and its sub-groups have been identified independently under various names/synonyms.

The lists of Scheduled Tribes are notified by the President

Note: A merit of this report is that it gives, for the first time, a reasonably accurate estimate of the numbers and distribution of primitive tribes, based on what was described as a complete census of people at that time. As Hutton says, no serious attempt had been made from 1891 to arrive at the figures of hill and forest tribes. The 1891 figure of 15 million was incomplete. The 1921 data of 16 million omitted not only many major tribes but also many small ones. In contrast the 1931 census enumerated all primitive tribes "Whatever, their numbers and irrespective of the percentage provision for individual tabulation of caste , this made it possible to give the accurate numbers of an identifiable tribal unit, though it was not easy to indicate the extent to which such a unit remained primitive in its habits. While we will revert to this aspect a little later, it would be appropriate to mention that the population of tribe went up steeply to 24.6 million in 1931 in India (including Ceylon and Burma), an increase of nearly 8 million since 1921, out of a population 352 million, which was 6.9 per cent of the total population. It is necessary to recall that in arriving at this figure Hutton had made all kinds of adjustments. The tribal figure for India (both British and Princely) was rounded off to 27.50 million out of a population of 352 million. Today the population of tribes, i.e. 51,628,638 (1981) has moved upto 7.76 per cent of the population, and their number raised from 142 in 1931 to 610 in 1981 (including sub-tribes). *Source* : The foreword written by K.S. Singh for the reprint of Census 1931.

of India in accordance with the provisions of Articles 342 of the constitution. The following Presidential Orders specifying the Scheduled Tribes in relation to the State/Union Territories have been issued from time to time.

The Constitution (Scheduled Tribes) Order, 1950: For all States except Haryana, Jammu & Kashmir, Punjab, Nagaland, Sikkim and Uttar Pradesh.

The Constitution (Union Territories) Scheduled Tribes Order, 1951: for Arunachal Pradesh, Lakshadweep and Mizoram.

The Constitution (Andaman and Nikobar Islands) Scheduled Tribes, 1959.

The Constitution (Dadra and Nagar Haveli) Scheduled Tribes Order, 1962.

The Constitution (Uttar Pradesh) Scheduled Tribes Order, 1967.

The Constitution (Goa, Daman and Diu) Scheduled Tribes Order, 1968.

The Constitution (Nagaland) Scheduled Tribes Order, 1970.

The Constitution (Sikkim) Scheduled Tribes Order, 1980.

The Constitution Scheduled Tribes Order (Amendment) Act, 1987 for Meghalaya.

The Constitution (Jammu & Kashmir) Scheduled Tribes Order, 1989.

The Constitution (Scheduled Tribes) Order (Amendment) Act, 1991 for Jammu & Kashmir.

The Constitution (Scheduled Tribes) Order (Second Amendment) Act, 1991 for Karnataka.

The Constitution (Scheduled Tribes) Order (Amendment) Act, 2003.

The Major Tribes

As per the Ministry of Tribal Affairs GOI Annual Report, 2000-01 there are 700 tribes (with many overlapping types in more than one State) as per notified Schedule under Article 342 of the Constitution of India in different States and Union Territories of the country with the largest number of 62 being in the State of Orissa. Some of the major tribes of different States are:

State	*Name of Tribes*
Andhra Pradesh	Bhill, Chenchu, Gond, Kondas, Lambadis, Sugalis etc.
Assam	Boro, Kachari, Mikir (Karbi), Lalung, Rabha, Dimasa, Hmar, Hajong etc.
Bihar and Jharkand	Asur, Banjara, Birhor, Korwa, Munda, Oraon, Santhal etc.
Gujarat	Bhil, Dhodia, Gond, Siddi, Bordia, etc.
Himachal Pradesh	Gaddi, Gujjar, Lahuala, Swangla, etc.
Karnataka	Bhil, Chenchu, Goud, Kuruba, Kammara, Kolis Koya, Mayaka, Toda, etc.
Kerala	Adiyam, Kammrar, Kndkappus, Malais, Palliyar, etc.
Madhya Pradesh and Chhattisgarh	Bhil, Birhor, Damar, Gond, Kharia, Majhi, Munda, Oraon, Parahi, etc.
Maharashtra	Bhil, Bhunjia, Chodhara, Dhodia, Gond, Kharia, Nayaka, Oraon, Pardhi, Rathwa etc.
Meghalaya	Garo, Khasi, Jayantia, etc.
Orissa	Birhor, Gond, Juang, Khond, Mundari, Oraon, Santhal, Tharua, etc.
Rajasthan	Bhil, Damor, Garasta, Meena, Salariya, etc.
Tamil Nadu	Irular, Kammara, Kondakapus, Kota, Mahamalasar, Palleyan, Toda, etc.
Tripura	Chakma, Garo, Khasi, Kuki, Lusai, Liang, Santhal etc.
West Bengal	Asur, Birhor, Korwa, Lepcha, Munda, Santhal etc.
Mizoram	Lusai, Kuki, Garo, Khasi, Jayantia, Mikir etc.
Arunachal Pradesh	Dafla, Khampti, Singpho etc.
Goa	Dhodi, Siddi (Nayaka)
Daman & Diu	Dhodi, Mikkada, Varti, etc.
Andaman & Nicobar Islands	Jarawa, Nicobarese, Onges, Sentinelese, Shompens, Great Andamanese
Uttar Pradesh and Uttarakhand	Bhotai, Buxa, Jansauri, Tharu, Raji
Dadar & Nagarhavali	Dhodi, Siddi (Nayaka)
Nagaland	Naga, Kukki, Mikir, Garo
Sikkim	Bhutia and Lepcha

Further, most of the major tribes are divided into several

social groups/communities and are spread over in plain areas/ regions adjoining to other States and Union Territories. For example, Kuki tribes in Assam, Meghalaya and Mizoram include 37 sub-groups; and sub-groups of Gond tribes are spread over in all the central, western, southern and central-northern tribal regions. State and Union Territory-wise notified list of such tribes including their sub-groups is given at Appendix I. However, for immediate reference the State and Union Territory-wise notified number of such tribes is given in Table 16.1 below :

Table 16.1 : State and Union Territory-wise Notified Number of Scheduled Tribes Communities in India

Sl. No.	*Name of the State/U.T.*	*No. of Scheduled Tribes Communities Notified*
1.	Andhra Pradesh	35
2.	Arnachal Pradesh	16
3.	Assam	
	(a) Districts of the Autonomous Karbi Anglong and North Kachar Hills	15
	(b) In the state of Assam including the Bodoland Territorial Areas District and excluding the Autonomous Districts of Karbi Anglong and North Kachar Hills	14
4.	Bihar	33
5.	Chhattisgarh	42
6.	Goa	8
7.	Gujarat	32
8.	Himachal Pradesh	10
9.	Jammu & Kashmir	12
10.	Jharkhand	32
11.	Karnataka	50
12.	Kerala	43
13.	Madhya Pradesh	46
14.	Maharashtra	47
15.	Manipur	33
16.	Meghalya	17
17.	Mizoram	15
18.	Nagaland	5
19.	Orissa	62
20.	Rajasthan	12
21.	Sikkim	4
22.	Tamil Nadu	36
23.	Tripura	19

(Contd...)

Table 16.1 : *(Contd...)*

24.	Uttarakhandl	4
25.	Uttar Pradesh	15
26.	West Bengal	40
27.	Andaman and Nicobar	6
28.	Dadra & Nagar Haveli	7
29.	Daman and Diu	5
30.	Lakshadweep	All the communities
	Total	*715*

Source : The Constitution (Scheduled Tribes) Order (Amendment) Act, 2003 dated 19.9.2003

Primitive Tribes

While adopting the strategy of Tribal Sub-Plan (TSP) on the eve of beginning of Fifth Five Year Plan for the overall development of the Scheduled Tribes and their area of inhabitation. Proper attention was given to the individual tribes in the new strategy of tribal development considering their prior stage of development and the lower level in the economic structure. To identify such individual tribes or sub-tribes, efforts were made to understand and recognize their native skill, economic activity, specific situation in terms of ecological equilibrium, self-confidence, socio-religious and economic exposure and their preparedness to accept development programme and the technology etc[13]. Such primitive communities are characteristically stable or very slowly growing and trying to maintain a constant relationship with the environment. In order to make the identification process rational, the following four criteria were laid down :

(i) Smallness of numbers, sequent or diminishing population;
(ii) General backwardness or isolation;
(iii) Pre-level of technology ; and
(iv) Very low level of literacy.

Almost following the above criteria, the respective TSP states identified the Primitive Tribal Groups (PTGs) in their State and recognizing them, the nodal Ministry of Government of India. Statewise notified total 75 Primitive Tribal Groups (PTGs). The Statewise populations of each PTG during the decade 1961, 1971, 1981 and 1991 and their decadal growth have been given at the Appendix No. 1. The overall Statewise analysis of decadal population data of each PTG has revealed that:

There is decadal growth variation in each PTG population growth at all India level, the population growth during the decade 61-71, 71-81, and 81-91 has been 44.86 per cent, 31.31 per cent and 15.33 per cent respectively. The overall growth for four decades (1961-91) has been 67.93 per cent.

Some of the PTGs have registered negative growth during the decades 1971-81 and same during the decade 1981-91, but overall they have registered positive growth.

Present Scenario of PTGs

These primitive tribes belong to different economic categories like hunters and food gatherers, shifting cultivators, marginal farmers, artisans etc. They have distinct culture and social organizations different from the tribal peasant neighbours.

Since independence till the present time of variety of programme and schemes have been formulated and implemented for the welfare and development of the tribes.

During the Sixth Five Year Plan Primitive tribal groups got a pointed impetus for the first time when separate funds were earmarked for the development of these primitive tribes under Special Central Assistance (SCA). Also top most priority to their welfare was to be accorded from the grants received under Article 275 (1) of the Constitution.

Separate micro-projects have been identified for each PTG in the respective State. Micro projects have undoubtedly benefited the primitive tribal groups in varying degrees. But all the families among the larger primitive tribal groups have not been brought within the purview of micro projects. Central Government funded for Centrally Sponsored Schemes (CSSs) like construction of hostels, establishment of residential schools, and construction of houses through *Indira Awas Yojana* through State Government of 50 per cent matching basis. Besides, central plans are also available for many other schemes. Allocation of funds for the development of tribal communities during different plan periods shows a gradual increase of the funds from the Fifth Plan onwards. The Seventh Plan laid emphasis on income generating family oriented schemes, but it is found that in spite of all the strategies and efforts of all these years 85 per cent of the tribal families remain below the poverty line compared to the national average of about 38 per cent.

The Government of India has liberally agreed to support the State efforts to boost up the economic development schemes for these people. Emphasis has also been laid on the programmes of social service sectors like education, health, housing etc. which could emancipate the tribals from the clutches of exploitative agencies have also been supported.

But as per the findings of different study reports of Ministry of Tribal Affairs, Planning Commission (Ch. 4.2) P. No. 462 and Working Group Constituted 9th and 10th Five Year Plans[14] there is difference between the conditions of the relatively advanced tribal groups and the PTGs. As they live in the most interior and inaccessible forests, they are subjected to extreme backwardness, when compared to the other tribals. A decline in their sustenance base and the resultant food insecurity, malnutrition and ill-health force them to live in the most fragile living conditions and some of them are even under the threat of getting extinct. Prominent examples in the context are the Bay-Islanders like the Great Andamanese, Shompens, Jarawas,

Sentinelese of the Andaman and Nicobar Islands. Even some of the mainland groups which can be cited in this context like the Bondos of Orissa, Cholanaikans of Kerala, the Abujhmarias of Chhattisgarh, and the Birhons of Jharkhand are also dwindling. As regards their progress, it is to be monitored on the continuing basis for different purpose; even for the purpose of accessing the need for continuation of a particular PTG. The working Group constituted by the Planning Commission for the Ninth Five Year Plan also observed this situation which is worth monitoring.

"The present occasion offers an opportunity to make a review of the criteria mentioned. It will be conceded that during the nearly two decades elapsing between the time the four coordinates of identification were evolved and now, events have marched ahead and changes have taken place even among the isolated groups under consideration. Though even now there are hunting and gathering groups, many have taken to cultivation. However, some of them are in the rudimentary stage of agriculture, some in shifting cultivation stage and a few may have gone even beyond. The scenario is varied. Hence, "pre-agricultural level of technology" may not be satisfied as a test, though a particular group may fall into the present slot otherwise".

"The difference between the general run of tribal groups and the primitive tribal groups under consideration stands out in bold relief on account of two dimensions. Much more than the common scheduled tribal groups, they stay in more interior pockets which are generally, even less accessible than the habitat of the common tribal groups. Secondly, the cultural gap between the primitive tribal groups and the non-tribal amenities is wider as compared to that between the common tribal societies and the non-tribal societies. Outstanding examples in this context are the bay-Islanders like the Shompen, Jarawa, Sentinelese of the Andaman and Nicobar Islands. Even some of the mainland groups can be cited in this context, e.g. the Bondos of Orissa, Cholanaikans of Kerala, the Abujhmarias of Chhattisgarh, the Birhor of Bihar."

"The scenario of the 75 identified PTGs is a lesson in diversity. Some of those groups which stand out as 'most primitive' needs special attention. But there are those who have come within the ambit of acculturation in the States of Bihar, Jharkand, Orissa, Madhya Pradesh and Chhattisgarh, the question arises whether it is possible and indeed, useful, to admit classification of these groups into a few neat categories. After deliberation, one has came to the view that the purpose of planned development would be better served if each group is studied carefully in its manifold aspects and related thereto a project report is prepared for improvement in the health, education, economic and other sectors. In fact, tribe-wise approach is required in other contexts also."

"Before proceeding further, one question which might be regarded as minor in one context but which has significant implications in understanding of these groups, having also a psychological bearing on these groups themselves, pertains to their nomenclature. The repeated use of the term 'primitive tribal groups' has given wide currency to it. But we are not happy over its usage. The phrase 'primitive' has evidently pejorative overtones. It seeks to elevate the non-tribal sections of the society and depressing these groups to base cultural levels. Do the relevant groups merit the description?"

The above observations of the Working Groups are meaningful. The State of primitiveness is to be carefully examined in case of each primitive tribes. But the Statewise study has revealed that the respective States are implementing the development schemes in routine manner and not keen to bring these notified primitive tribes in the category of other Scheduled Tribes.

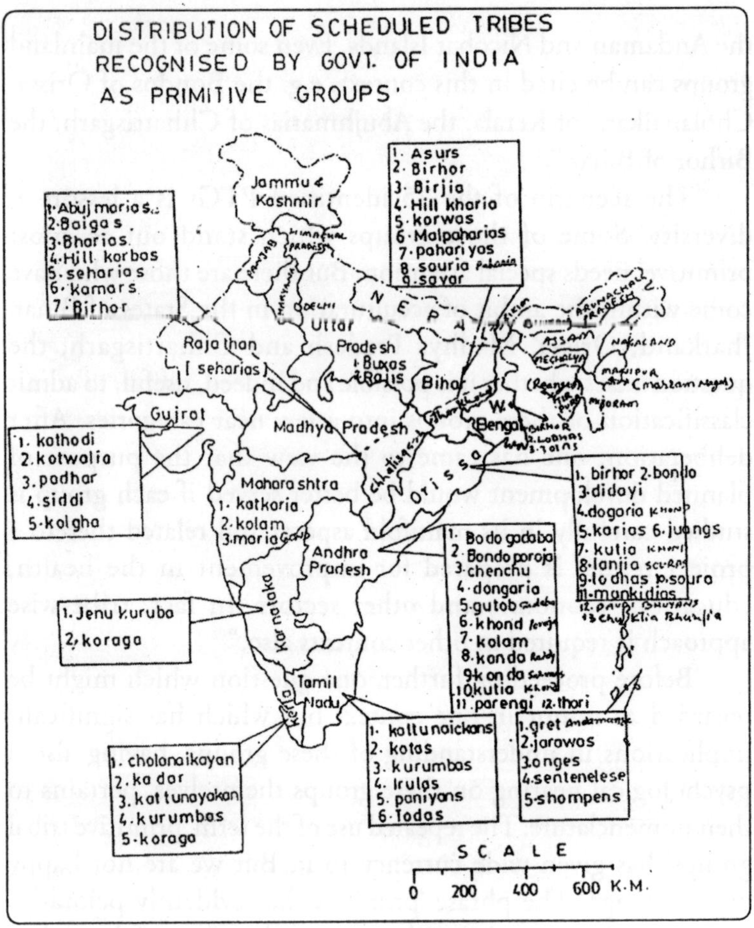

Population – Demografic Profile

Tribal being essentially ecosystem people, the country's wide ranging diversity in nature and natural resources present varied tribal population throughout India's length and breath. In general most of the population inhabits under developed areas of the country which are remote, having low density of population and lacking in adequate access to basic amenities[15]. But the analysis of Scheduled Tribes population for last four decades (1971-2001) has shown that the Scheduled Tribe population as a whole has maintained positive growth rate.

After the adoption of Tribal Sub Plan strategy on the eve of Fifth Five Year Plan, the total tribal population of India and the Scheduled Areas have been revised and re-organized in 17 States and two Union Territories, i.e. Andman and Nicobar Islands and Goa and Daman & Diu. The sub-plan strategy in the country aimed at massive development of tribal area and Scheduled Tribes through identification of administration units like blocks or 'talukas' having more than 50 per cent population, aggregating them into Integrated Tribal Development Projects (ITDPs). However, the coverage of Scheduled Tribes population has increased from 65 per cent to in Fifth Plan to 74 per cent in the Sixth Plan period, this has been an account of the fact that outside the tribal sub-plan areas of Fifth Plan period, pockets of tribal concentration not forming whole administrative units having 10,000 population with 50 per cent Scheduled Tribes population have been identified for extending the tribal development effort. Accordingly the coverage of tribal sub-plan in the various States of the country was delineated. This was done tribal sub-plan area-wise, ITDP-wise in respect of areas, total population and Scheduled Tribes population. At that time 16 states and two Union territories constituted the comity of tribal sub-plan State (Of course, State and Union Territories having more than 50 per cent Scheduled Tribes population, i.e. Arunachal Pradesh, Dadra and Nagar Haveli, Lakshadweep, Nagaland, Meghalaya and Mizoram were excluded, since their plans essentially plans for tribal development). In the Sixth Plan period one more State, i.e. Sikkim has joined the tribal sub-plan comity.

The total and Statewise Scheduled Tribe population as emerged after tribal sub-plan strategy is shown in the Table 16.2 given below:

Table 16.2 : Total and Scheduled Tribes Population

Sl. No.	State/Union Territory	Total	Population Scheduled Pre-Revised	Tribes Revised (in lakh)	Percentage of Scheduled Tribes Population to Total Population (Col. 5 to Col. 3)
1.	Andhra Pradesh	4,35,02,708	16,57,657	22.26	5.12
2.	Assam	1,46,25,152	16,06,648	16.07	10.99
3.	Bihar	5,63,53,369	49,32,767	49.33	8.75
4.	Gujarat	2,66,97,475	37,34,422	47.57	14.07
5.	Haryana	1,00,36,808	—	—	—
6.	Himachal Pradesh	34,60,434	1,41,610	1.42	4.10
7.	Jammu & Kashmir	46,16,632	—	—	—
8.	Karnataka	2,92,99,014	2,31,268	2.62	0.90
9.	Kerla	2,13,47,375	2,69,356	1.93	0.90
10.	Madhya Pradesh	4,16,54,119	83,87,403	98.41	23.56
11.	Maharashtra	5,04,235	29,54,249	38.41	7.62
12.	Manipur	10,72,753	3,34,466	3.34	31.13
13.	Meghalaya	10,11,699	8,14,230	8.14	80.51
14.	Nagaland	5,16,449	4,57,602	4.58	88.76
15.	Orissa	2,19,44,615	50,71,937	50.75	23.13
16.	Punjab	1,35,51,060	—	—	—
17.	Rajasthan	2,57,65,806	31,25,506	31.35	12.17
18.	Sikkim	2,11,853	52,056	0.52	24.53
19.	Tamil Nadu	4,11,99,168	3,11,515	4.50	1.09
20.	Uttar Pradesh	8,83,41,144	1,98,565	1.99	0.23
21.	West Bengal	4,43,12,011	25,32,969	26.03	5.87
22.	Tripura	10,56,342	4,50,544	4.51	28.98
	Union Territories				
1.	Andaman & Nicrobar Islands	1,15,133	18,102	0.18	15.65
2.	Arunachal Pradesh	4,67,511	3,69,408	3.69	79.01
3.	Chandigarh	2,57,251	—	—	—
4.	Dadra & Nagar Haveli	74,170	64,445	0.64	86.49
5.	Delhi	40,65,698	—	—	—
6.	Goa, Daman & Diu	8,57,771	7,654	0.07	0.82
7.	Lakshadweep	31,810	29,540	0.30	93.75
8.	Mizoram	3,32,390	3,13,299	3.13	94.28
9.	Pondicherry	4,71,707	—	—	—
	Grand Total	**54,81,61,662**	**3,80,67,218**	**411.48**	**7.51**

Source : 1971 Census

1971-81 decade has witnessed considerable tension, conflict and violence in tribal areas, particularly in the northeast India. It must not be forgotten that India's tribal population, estimated at 54 million has been almost equal to the total population of the United Kingdom Census Volume — [Census of India 1981, Series I, Part IIB(iii)—is wholly devoted to data on the Scheduled Tribes]. As the 1981 Population Census enumeration could not take place in Assam because of disturbed conditions, the data exclude Assam both for 1971 and 1981. The population of the Scheduled Tribes (excluding Assam) was 51.6 million in 1981 compared to 36.4 million in 1971. In terms of the proportion of India's total, the tribal population increased from 6.8 per cent in 1971 to 7.8 per cent in 1981. "This gives the impression that all is well with our Scheduled Tribes but this would be misleading" said Ashish Bose, Professor of Population Studies of Delhi's Institute of Economic Growth and President of the Indian Association for the Study of Population. The Census publication does not mention the growth rate of the tribal population but calculated from the absolute figures, it works out to about 42 per cent during 1971-81 compared to India's overall growth rate of around 25 per cent during their decade[16]. The position is clarified by Ashish Bose below:

> "Lest one jumps to any conclusion about a sudden spurt in Tribal fertility, we must hasten to point out that the 1971 and 1981 Census data are not comparable. The 1971 figures for the Scheduled Tribes were based on the Scheduled Castes and Scheduled Tribes Lists (Modification) Order, 1956 whereas the 1981 figures are based on the Scheduled Castes and Scheduled Tribes Order (Amendment) Act, 1976. This important fact is only mentioned in a small footnote to a Census table but the tragedy is that most readers do not read footnotes. When one examines the figures of individual states the complexities increase. For example, in

> Karnataka, the tribal population increased from 0.8 per cent in 1971 to 4.9 per cent in 1981. A seemingly innocent footnote in the Census Volume says : "this figure would appear to include high returns relating to certain communities with nomenclatures similar to those included in the list of Scheduled Tribes consequence on the removal of area restriction."

The growth rate figures have adjusted in the light of the 1976 Constitutional Amendment. An important factor which could cause worry is the tendency of non-tribals to describe themselves as tribals in order to take advantage of the special provisions for the tribes. Though there is no direct evidence of this in the Census tables, one can surmise that behind the inordinate increase in tribal numbers is a form of subtle and spurious "retribalization" through fraudulent returns[17].

According to the 1981 Population Census there were 650 Scheduled Tribes for which data have been published for various States and Union Territories, excluding Assam. This total of 650 does not mean that there are 650 different Scheduled Tribes in the country. Many of them have been counted more than once as they occur in different state lists. The Bhil as a Scheduled Tribe figures in Andhra Pradesh, Gujarat, Karnataka, Madhya Pradesh (including present Chhattisgarh state), Maharashtra, Rajasthan and Tripura. Bhil has been counted seven times. Likewise, Andh is a Scheduled Tribe in Andhra Pradesh, Madhya Pradesh and Maharashtra and Adiyan in Karnataka, Kerala and Tamil Nadu. Thus these have been counted 3 times each. In fact, there are about 450 communities in the list of Scheduled Tribes. Some of them are sub-tribes of larger tribes.

The population sizes of these tribes vary tremendously. There were nine tribes which did not have even a single member. On the other hand there were 21 tribes whose strength was more than 500,000. Table 16.3 given below lists descending order of their strength as revealed by the 1981 census. It is quite interesting to note that in Nagaland "Naga tribes (any)" treated as one group accounted for almost the total Scheduled Tribes population of the State (96.94%). Similarly, in Karnataka "Naikada, Nayak, Cholivala, Nayaka, Kapadia, Mota Nayaka, Nana Nayaka" together accounted for 69.04 per cent of the Scheduled Tribes population of the State. Likewise, in Meghalaya, "Khasi, Jaintia, Syntang, Pnar, War, Bhoi, Lyngangam" accounted for 58.36 per cent of the 1981 Scheduled Tribes population of the State. In West Bengal also "Santhal" accounted for 54.28 per cent of the Scheduled Tribes population of the State.

Table 16.3 : Scheduled Tribes, with 500.00 plus population arranged in Descending order of their population, 1981

Sl. No.	Name of Scheduled Tribes	States	Population	Percent of total ST Population of the State
1.	Gond Arakh....(1)	Madhya Pradesh	5,349,883	44.63
2.	Bhil, Bhilalal Barela Patelia	Madhya Pradesh	2,500,530	20.86
3.	Mina	Rajasthan	2,086,692	49.88
4.	Santhal	Bihar	2,060,730	35.46
5.	Bhil, Bhill Garasia....(2)	Gujarat	2,030,438	41.88
6.	Bhil, Bhill Garasia....(2)	Rajasthan	1,840,966	44.01
7.	Santal	West Bengal	1,666,610	54.28
8.	Naikda, Nayaka....(3)	Karnataka	1,260,158	69.04
9.	Gond Rajgond....(4)	Maharashtra	1,162,735	20.14
10.	Sugalis Lambadis	Andhra Pradesh	1,158,342	36.47
11.	Oraon	Bihar	1,048,066	18.04
12.	Bhil, Bhill Garasia....(2)	Maharashtra	993,074	17.20
13.	Khond, Kandha, Naguli Kandha Sitha Kandha	Orissa	989,342	16.73
14.	Munda	Bihar	845,887	14.56
15.	Koli Mahadev, Dongar Koli	Maharashtra	787,448	13.64
16.	Naga tribes (Any)	Nagaland	630,973	96.94
17.	Khasi, Jaintia, Synteng, Pnar, War, Bhoi, Lyngngam	Meghalays	628,104	58.36
18.	Gond, Gonda	Orissa	602,749	10.19
19.	Kawar, Kanwar, Kaur, Cherwa Rathia Tanwar Chattri	Madhya Pradesh	562,200	4.69
20.	Ho	Bihar	536,523	9.23
21.	Santhal	Orissa	530,776	8.97

(Contd...)

Table 16.3 *(Contd...)*

(1) Gond: Arakh, Arrakh, Agaria, Asur, Badi Maria, Bada Maria, Bhatola, Bhimma, Bhuta, Koilabhuta, Koliabhuti, Bihar, Bosonhorn Maria, Chota Maria, Dandami Maria, Dhuru, Dhurwa, Dhoba, Dhulia, Doria, Gaiki, Gatta, Gatti, Gaita, Gond Gowari, Hill Maria, Kandra Kalanga, Khatola, Koitar, Koya, Khirwar, Khirwara, Kucha Maria, Kuchai Maria, Kuchaki Maria, Maida, Maria, Mana, Mannewar, Moghya, Mogia, Monhya, Mudia, Muria, Nagarchi, Nagwanshi, Ojhs, Raj, Sonjhari Jhareks, Thatia, Thotya, Wade Maria, Vade Meria, Daroi.

(2) Bhil, Bhil Garasia, Dholi Bhilm Dungri Bhil, Dungri Garasia, Mewasi Bhil, Rawal Bhil, Tadvi Bhil, Bhagalia, Bhilala, Pawra, Vassva, Vassve.

(3) Naijda, Nayaka, Cholivala Nayaka, Kapadia Nayaka, Mana Nayaka, Nana Nayaka.

(4) Gond, Rajgond, Arakh, Agaria, Asur, Badi, Maria, Bada Maria, Bhatola, Bhimma, Bhuta, Koilabhuta, Koilabhuti, Bhar, Bisonhorn Maria, Chota Maria, Damani Meria, Dhures, Dhurwa, Dhoba, Dhulia, Dorla, Gaiki, Gatta, Gatti, Gond Gowari, Hill Maria, Kandra, Kalanga, Khatola, Koitar, Koya, Khirwar, Khirwara, Kucha Maria, Kuchaki Maria, Madia, Maria, Mana, Mannewar, Modghya, Mogia, Monghya, Mudia, Muria, Nagarchi Naikpod, Nagwanshi, Ojha, Raj, Sonjhari Jhareka, Thatia, Thotva, Wade Maria, Vade Maria.

On the other hand, there were 100 tribes in the country whose total strength was less than 100, and 78 tribes are such which had a population of less than 50 while 41 had a population of less than 10, including 9 tribes without any person belonging to these tribes.

As per 1991 Census the Scheduled Tribes of India are spread over 25 States/Union territories. State/UT-wise details of general and Scheduled Tribes population are given below in Table 16.4. The 26 States/Union Territories of India having Scheduled Tribes population may be divided into two categories. Those having more than 50 per cent of the total population, namely, Arunachal Pradesh, Dadra and Nagar Haveli, Lakshadweep, Meghalaya, Mizoram and Nagaland, constitute about 7.20 per cent of the total Scheduled Tribes Population of India. Those states having less than 50 per cent of the population, account for 92.80 per cent of the scheduled tribes in the country.

The second category includes three groups of States. The

first group of 10 States, namely, Andhra Pradesh, Bihar, Gujarat, Himachal Pradesh, Madhya Pradesh, Maharashtra, Manipur, Orissa, Rajasthan, and Sikkim which constitute 79.8 per cent of the total tribal population in the country. The second group within this category includes the States of Assam. West Bengal and Tripura where the Scheduled Tribe population is largely dispersed and form about 12 per cent of the dispersed tribal population of the country. The third group within this category includes 7 States/Union Territories, namely, Karnataka, Kerala, Tamil Nadu, Uttar Pradesh, Andaman and Nicobar Islands, Goa, Daman and Diu where the Scheduled Tribes population is small in absolute terms when compared to the total population in the above States and is confined to small/scattered pockets. In this group the tribals constitute about 2.7 per cent of the total tribal population of the country.

About 67.76 million persons were counted in 1991 census as belonging to Schedule Tribes in different States/Union Territories in India. Excluding Jammu & Kashmir, constitution 8.08 per cent of the total population. The percentage of Scheduled Tribes has marginally increased from 7.83 per cent in 1981 to 7.95 per cent in 1991 (While making the comparison between 1981 to 7.95 and 1991, both Assam and Jammu & Kashmir are excluded as census was not taken in Assam in 1981 and in Jammu & Kashmir in 1991). The Scheduled Tribe population as increased by 25.67 per cent during the decade 1981-1991. This growth rate is more. than the growth of the total population of the country (23.79 per cent).

In some of the States and Union Territories, the population was predominantly Scheduled Tribes. For example, in Mizoram 94.75 per cent of the total population belongs to Scheduled Tribes. The other States/Union Territories with predominantly Schedule Tribe population were : Lakshadweep (93.15 per cent), Nagaland (87.70), Meghalaya (85.53). Dadra and Nagar Haveli

Table 16.4 : Total Population, Scheduled Tribes Population and Percentage of Scheduled Tribes Population to Total Population in all the States/Union Territories (1991)

Sl. No.	*State/Union Territories*	*Total Population*	*Scheduled Tribes Population*	*Percentage Total of Population*
	INDIA	*8,46,302,688**	*67,758,380***	*8.08***
States				
1.	Andhra Pradesh	66,508,008	4,199,481	6.31
2.	Arunachal Pradesh	864,558	550,351	63.66
3.	Assam	22,414,322	2,874,441	12.82
4.	Bihar including Jharkhand	86,374,465	6,616,914	7.66
5.	Goa	1,169,793	376	0.03
6.	Gujarat	41,309,582	6,161,775	14.92
7.	Haryana	16,463,648	NIL	NIL
8.	Himachal Pradesh	5,170,877	218,349	4.22
9.	Jammu & Kashmir	7,718,700	N.A.	—
10.	Karnataka	44,977,201	1,915,691	4.26
11	Kerala	29,098,518	320,967	1.10
12.	Madhya Pradesh including Chhattisgarh	66,181,170	15,399,034	23.27
13.	Maharashtra	78,937,187	7,319,281	9.27
14.	Manipur	1,837,149	632,173	34.41
15.	Meghalaya	1,774,778	1,517,927	85.53
16.	Mizoram	689,756	653,565	94.75
17.	Nagaland	1,209,546	1,060,822	87.70
18.	Orissa	31,659,736	7,032,214	22.21
19.	Punjab	20,281,969	—	—
20.	Rajasthan	44,005,990	5,474,881	12.44
21.	Sikkim	406,457	90,901	22.36
22.	Tamil Nadu	55,858,946	574,194	1.03
23.	Tripura	2,757,205	85,345	30.95
24.	Uttar Pradesh	139,112,287	287,901	0.21
25.	West Bengal	68,077,965	3,808,760	5.5
Union Territories				
1.	Andaman & Nicobar Islands	280,661	26,770	9.54
2.	Chandigarh	642,015	—	—
3.	Dadra & Nagar Haveli	134,477	109,380	78.99
4.	Daman & Diu	104,586	11,724	11.54
5.	Delhi	9,420,644	—	—
6.	Ladshadweep	51,707	48,163	93.15
7.	Pondicherry	807,785	—	—

* The Census was not held in J&K in 1991 and hence Projected Population has been shown for J&K.

** Excluding Jammu & Kashmir where Census was not held in 1991.

Nil Indicates that no Scheduled Tribes has been notified in the referent State/U.T.

N.A. stands for not available.

(79.99) and Arunachal Pradesh (63.66). Manipur and Tripura also had substantial proportion of population as Scheduled Tribes. The respective proportions being 34.41 and 30.95 per cent, among the 15 major States. Madhya Pradesh had the largest proportion of Scheduled Tribe population (23.27 per cent) followed by Orissa (22.21), Gujarat, Assam and Rajasthan were the other three major states in which more than 10 per cent of the population belonging to Scheduled Tribes. The respective percentage has been 14.92, 12.82 and 12.44.

Of the total Scheduled Tribe population of 67.76 million counted in different States/Union Territories in India, 22.73 per cent are in Madhya Pradesh, 10.80 per cent in Maharashtra and 10.38 per cent in Orissa. Thus, roughly 44 per cent of the Scheduled Tribe populations of India live in these three States only. Going a little further, 71 per cent of the Scheduled Tribe population of India live in Six States, viz. Madhya Pradesh, Maharashtra, Rajasthan, Gujarat, Bihar and Orissa. In terms of absolute numbers, the Scheduled Tribe population was 15.4 million in Madhya Pradesh, 7.3 million in Maharashtra, 7.0 million in Orissa, 6.6 million in Bihar, 3.8 million in West Bengal, 2.9 million Assam, 1.9 million in Gujarat, 5.5 million in Rajasthan, 4.2 million in Andhra Pradesh, 1.9 million in Karnataka, 1.5 million in Meghalaya and 1.1 million in Nagaland. All other States and Union Territories together had a little over 4 million Schedule Tribe populations: there being absolutely no Scheduled tribe population recognized in Haryana, Punjab, Chandigarh, Delhi and Pondicherry.

Rural-urban distribution of Schedule tribe population: only 7.39 per cent of the Scheduled Tribes in India live in urban areas as compared to 25.73 per cent of the general population. Thus, roughly 93 per cent of the Scheduled Tribe populations are rural based. Of the 15 major States, only 3 States, viz. Karnataka, Maharashtra and Tamil Nadu had more than 10 per cent of their Scheduled Tribe population living in the urban areas: the respective percentages being 14.94, 12.47 and 12.01. The percentage of Scheduled Tribe population living in urban areas in other major States are: Andhra Pradesh (7.6), Assam (3.4), Bihar (7.0), Gujarat (8.9), Kerala (3.5), Madhya Pradesh (4.8), Orissa (5.1), Rajasthan (4.6), Uttar Pradesh (5.9), and West Bengal (5.2).

As per 2001 census, the total population of the Scheduled Tribes in India is 84,326,240, which is 8.2 percent of the India total population (1,028,610,328). The population of Scheduled Tribes has grown at the rate of 24.45 per cent during the period 1991-2001. This Scheduled Tribes population is spread over in 27 States and 4 Union Territories (UTs). Out of these in 4 States, viz. Arunachal, Nagaland, Mizoram and Meghalaya, the percentage of Scheduled Tribes population ranges between 94.5 to 64.2, and in Dadra & Nagar Haveli and Lakshadweep Union Territories, the percentage of Scheduled Tribe population lies between 62.2 and 94.5 respectively but, as a matter of fact more than half of the Scheduled Tribe population is concentrated in States of Madhya Pradesh, Maharashtra, Chhattisgarh, Orissa, Jharkhand and Gujarat.

Compared total population, Scheduled Tribe population and percentage of Scheduled Tribe population to total population in all the States/Union Territories and growth-rate as per 1991 and 2001 Population Census are given below in Table 16.5.

Regionwise Distribution of Scheduled Tribe Population

Further, efforts have been made to understand the location of regionwise habitation of Scheduled Tribe population in the country. It is found that as per population census 1991 concentration of Scheduled Tribe population is highest in the North-Eastern Region and lowest in southern region. Table 16.5

given below shows the region and state/union territory-wise distribution of scheduled tribes and its percentage against total population of the respective states and from total scheduled tribe population.

Table 16. 5 : Region-wise Distribution of Scheduled Tribes Population, Percentage of Total Population of States/UT and Percentage of Total Scheduled Tribes (1991-2001)

Sl. No.	*Name of Region/ State/UT*	*Scheduled Tribe (ST) Population*		*Percentage of Total Population of the State/UT*		*Percentage of Scheduled Tribe population*	
		1991	*2001*	*1991*	*2001*	*1991*	*2001*
1	*2*	*3*	*4*	*5*	*6*	*7*	*8*
All India		67758	84326240	8.08	8.2	100.00	100.00
Central Region		37057				54.69	
1.	Andhra Pradesh	4200	5024104	6.31	6.60	6.20	5.96
2.	Bihar	6617	758351	7.66	0.90	9.77	0.90
3.	Jharkhand		7078068		26.30		8.40
4.	Madhya Pradesh	15399	12233474	23.27	20.30	22.73	14.51
5.	Chhattisgarh	-	6616596		31.80		7.85
6.	Orissa	7032	8145081	22.21	22.10	10.38	9.66
7.	West Bengal	3809	4406794	5.59	5.50	5.62	5.23
	Total		**44271468**				**52.50**
Island Region		75				0.11	
1.	Andaman & Nicobar	27	29469	9.54	8.30	0.04	0.03
2.	Lakshadweep	48	57321	93.15	94.50	0.07	0.07
	Total		**86790**				**0.10**
North-Eastern Region		8233				12.15	
1.	Arunachal Pradesh	550	705158	63.66	64.20	0.81	0.84
2.	Assam	2874	3308570	12.82	12.40	4.24	3.92
3.	Manipur	632	741141	34.41	34.20	0.93	0.88
4.	Meghalaya	1518	1992862	85.53	85.90	2.24	2.36
5.	Mizoram	654	839310	94.75	94.50	0.97	1.00
6.	Nagaland	1061	1774026	87.80	89.10	1.57	2.10
7.	Sikkim	91	111405	22.36	20.60	0.13	0.13
8.	Tripura	853	993426	30.98	31.10	1.26	1.18
	Total		**10465898**				

(Contd...)

Table 16.5 : *(Contd...)*

North-Western Region	506				0.75	
1. Himachal Pradesh	218	244587	4.22	4	0.32	0.29
2. Uttar Pradesh	288	107963	0.21	0.1	0.43	0.13
Total		**352550**				**0.42**
South Region	2811				4.15	
1. Karnataka	1916	3463986	4.26	6.6	2.83	4.11
2. Kerala	321	364189	1.10	1.1	0.47	0.43
3. Tamil Nadu	574	651321	1.03	1	0.85	0.77
Total		**4479496**				**5.31**
Western Region	*19076*				*28.15*	
1. Dadra & Nagar Haveli	109	137225	78.99	62.20	0.16	0.16
2. Daman & Diu	12	13997	11.54	8.80	0.01	0.02
3. Goa	-	566	0.03	0.00	-	0.00
4. Gujarat	6162	7481160	14.92	10.80	9.09	8.87
5. Maharashtra	7318	8577276	9.27	8.90	10.30	10.17
6. Rajasthan	5475	7097706	12.44	12.60	3.08	8.42
Total		**23307930**				**27.64**

Source : Census of India, 1991, Union Primary Census Abstract for Scheduled Castes & Scheduled Tribes, India, Rajasthan Census Commissioner, p. 11 (Excluded 719 for Jammu & Kashmir) and Census of India Population 2001.

It needs special mention here that the data given in Table 16.5 do not give accurate position, because a considerable number of non-Scheduled Tribe communities have also been included in the list due to so many political an social reasons. However, it is clear cut indication that as per Population Census, 1991 highest percentage (54.69) of Scheduled Tribe population is spread over in the Central region of India and followed by the Western region (28.13). The North-eastern region has sizeable percentage of Scheduled Tribes population, i.e. 12.15 and in southern region, it is about 4.15 per cent. The North-western region and the Islands have average percentage of

Scheduled Tribe population, i.e. 0.75 and 0.11 respectively in the context of regional scenario.

In case the regional spread over of Schedule Tribe population is compared with the figures of Population Census, 2001, (Table 16.5) overall it is found that the percentage distribution of Scheduled Tribe population has minor variation from one region to another. Only in Central region the population percentage has declined to 2.20 and in western region nearly by 0.52. Regionwise distribution of Scheduled Tribe population and its relevant percentage according to Population Census, 2001 is given in Table 16.5.

Decadal Growth Rate of Scheduled Tribe Population

The analysis of Scheduled Tribe population for last four decades (1971-2001) has shown that the Scheduled Tribe population as a whole maintained positive growth rate as given in Table 16.5. The percentage of Scheduled Tribe population has increased.

The ST Population in the State of Karnataka has shown highest growth rate of 80.82 per cent (during the period of 1991 to 2001) followed by Nagaland (67.23%). The increased rate of population growth in prone states is the result of addition of new communities to the ST list. The lowest growth rate in respect of ST population as per 2001 census was recorded in Andaman & Nicobar (10.08%) followed by Himachal Pradesh (12.02%). Further, as given Table 16.6, the percentage of Scheduled Tribe population has increased from 6.9 per cent in 1971 to 8.2 per cent in 2001. As regards the decade growth rate, it has declined in comparison to last census. It was 31.4 per cent in 1991, was reduced to 24.45 per cent i.e. declination of 6.05 per cent. The highest decade growth was in 1981, i.e. 35.8 per cent.

Table 16.6 : Population and Decadal Growth Rate of STs (1971-2001)

(Figures in Million)

Census Year	*Population**		*Decadal Growth Rate***	
	Total	*STs*	*Total'*	*STs*
1971	548.1	38.0 (6.9)	24.8	26.3
1981	683.4	51.6 (7.6)	24.7	35.8
1991	846.3	67.8 (8.08)	23.51	31.4
2001	1028.0	84.32 (8.2)	22.6	24.45

Note :

* Includes ST population.

** Estimated population based on the trend of the decadal growth rate of STs between 1961 and 1991

Figures within parentheses indicate percentage to total.

Source : Census of India, 1991 and Census of India, 2001: Registrar-General and Census Commissioner of India, GOI, New Delhi.

Sex-Ratio

The sex-ratio is one of the deciding factors while analyzing the demographic features of the tribes. In general, the high sex-ratio may be attributed, to the sex selective migration, although the genetic factor cannot be ruled out. In 1991, the sex-ratio among STs was 972 compared to 929 among the general population. The corresponding figures in 1981 were 983 and 934 respectively. Thus, during both the Population Censuses, the sex-ratio of STs was much higher than among the general population. But, whereas there has been a slight decline in the sex-ratio of general population, there has been more visible decline in case of STs.

Further, it could be argued that the factors and process of this relatively greater decline could be analyzed after Census data relating to sex break-up by age-groups and migration among the STs and survey research information on changes in the status of tribal women were available.

As compared to the sex ratio for the overall population (933 female per 1000 male). The sex ratio among the STs is imore favourable, at 977 female according to population Census 2001,

It is clear that in comparison to 1991 Census the sex ratio is at higher side, bouth in general population, as well as among the STs. As regard the States, except Andhra Pradesh, Tamil Nadu and Uttarakhand, the sex ratio was better than general sex ratio.

Further, as regards the child sex ratio, the 1991 Census has revealed that in the age group 0-6 for the general population were 940 girls against 1000 boys for the country as a whole. In case of STs, this ratio was more favourable and stood at 985 girls against 1000 boys.

In 2001, the child sex ratio in general population further deteriorated to 919 girls to 1000 boys. Nevertheless, situation among STs through also on the decline remains comparatively better at 972 girls for 1000 boys.

In case of Dadra and Nagar Haveli, 2001 population Census has reported 1009 girls against 1000 boys among STs in the age group 0-6. In 1991, this figure was 1018 girls per 1000 boys as against 1005 girls per 1000 boys for the general population of the U.T[18].

Educational Status

At the time of 1991 Census, the literacy rate among Scheduled Tribes in States and Union Territories varied between 82.71 per cent in Mizoram and 17.16 per cent in Andhra Pradesh. The second highest literacy rate among Scheduled Tribes in 1991, after Mizoram, was recorded by Lakshadweep (80.58%) which increased by 58.31 percentage points from 22.27 per cent in 1961. On the other hand, the literacy rate in Andhra Pradesh increased by only 12.75 percentage points during 1961-1991 from 4.41 per cent in 1961. Rajasthan recorded a literacy rate, among its Scheduled Tribes population of 19.44 per cent in 1991 which was 15.47 percentage points higher than the literacy rate of 3.97 per cent obtained in 1961. The literacy rate among the Scheduled Tribe population recorded during 1961, 1971 (1981 and 1991 population Censuses).

29.6 per cent of the Scheduled Tribes population in the age

group 7 years and above in found to be literate as per the 1991 Census: the literacy rate being 40.65 for males and 18.19 for females. These Figures are much lower than the corresponding figures for the total population of India. If we were to take out the population of North-Eastern States like Nagaland, Mizoram, Meghalaya and Manipur which have a predominantly Scheduled Tribe population and very high literacy rates, the literacy rate of the Scheduled Tribe population would be much lower. That is, the literacy levels among Scheduled Tribe population in other States are extremely low. In Andhra Pradesh, the literacy rate of the Scheduled Tribe population was just 17.16 per cent. In Rajasthan, it was 19.44 per cent. In case of females, the literacy rates for the Scheduled Tribe population are extremely low, in Rajasthan (4.4), Andhra Pradesh (8.7), Orissa (10.2), Madhya Pradesh (10.7), Bihar (4.8) and Uttar Pradesh (15.0).

Although, there has been a substantial increase in the literacy rates of STs during the last three developmental decades, the gap between the literacy rates of STs and those of the general population is not only persisting, but only found to be widening. Adding to this, are the problems of intra and inter-state/district variations in the literacy rates amongst STs. The progress made by STs in comparison to the general population is shown in the Table 16.7 given below.

Table 16. 7 : Literacy Rates of STs and Total Population (1971-2001) (in per cent)

Category	*1971*	*1981*	*1991*	*2001*
Total Population*	29.45	36.23	52.21	65.38
Scheduled Tribes	11.30	16.35	29.60	47.10
Gap between STs and the Total Population	18.15	19.88	22.61	18.25

Note : * Includes ST population.

Sources : 1. Educational Development of SCs and STs, 1995, Department of Education, Ministry of Human Resource Development, GOI, New Delhi.

2. Census of India, 2001: Registrar-General and Census Commissioner of India, GOI, New Delhi.

As shown in Table 16.8, the most discouraging sign was the increasing gap between the literacy rates of STs and of the general categories between 1971 and 2001. While the literacy rate for the general population including STs stood at 65.38 per cent, the same for STs was 47.10 per cent in 2001.

Table 16. 8 : Females Literacy Rates of STs and Total Population (1971-2001)

(in per cent)

Category	*1971*	*1981*	*1991*	*2001*
Total Population*	18.69	29.85	39.29	54.16
Scheduled Tribes	4.85	8.04	18.19	34.80
Gap between STs and the Total Population	13.84	21.81	21.10	19.36

Note : * Includes ST population.

Sources: 1. Educational Development of SCs and STs, 1995, Department of Education, Ministry of Human Resource Development, GOI, New Delhi.

2. Census of India, 2001: Provisional Population Totals, Registrar-General and Census Commissioner of India, GOI, New Delhi.

Contrary to the efforts of reducing the existing gaps/ disparities between STs and the rest of the society, the data given in Table 16.8 reveals that although the female literacy rate, which is an important indicator in the field of education, amongst STs has increased substantially from 4.85 per cent in 1971 to 18.19 per cent in 1991, and 34.80 per cent in population Census, 2001 but the gap between ST females and the general population has also been widening during the same period, though with a slight decrease between 1981 and 2001.

While considerable progress has been registered in the literacy rates amongst STs their enrolment ratios when compared to the total population present a mixed picture given in Table 16.9. The pace of progress of enrolment of both ST boys and girls at the middle level between 1990-91 and 1999-2000 has been quite impressive, as compared to that of the total population. What is worth noting is that the ST girls maintained a good pace, especially at the middle level. However, the enrolment ratio of ST girls both at primary and middle levels was lower than that of the total population in both the years.

Table 16.9 : Gross Enrolment Ratios of STs and Total Population (1990-91 to 1999-2000)

Year		*1990-91*		*1999-2000*	
Classes		*I to V*	*I to VIII*	*I to V*	*I to VIII*
(1)		*(2)*	*(3)*	*(4)*	*(5)*
Total Population*	Total	100.1	62.1	94.9	58.8
	Boys	114.0	76.6	104.1	67.2
	Girls	85.5	47.8	85.2	49.7
Scheduled Tribes	Total	103.4	39.7	97.7	58.0
	Boys	126.8	51.3	112.7	70.8
	Girls	78.6	27.5	82.7	44.8
GAP	Total	(+) 3.3	(-) 22.4	(+) 2.8	(-) 0.8
	Boys	(+) 12.8	(-) 25.3	(+) 8.6	(+) 3.6
	Girls	(-) 6.9	(-) 20.3	(-) 2.5	(-) 4.9

Note : * Includes ST population.
Source : Annual Report of respective years, Department of Education, Ministry of Human Resource Development, GOI, New Delhi.

The dropout rate, which is another crucial indicator in the field of educational development has shown that the difference between the dropout rates between Scheduled Tribes population and under Scheduled Tribe population during the period 1980-81 and 1988-89 have been 17 per cent and almost at the same level for primary education, while for middle level, it has been about 14 per cent, but at the secondary level it has increased from 9 per cent to 11 per cent for Scheduled Tribes as compared to general population. It could be seen from the Table 16.10 given below :

Table 16.10 : Drop-out Rate of Scheduled Tribes Population and Non-Scheduled Tribe Population at Primary, Middle, Secondary Levels—Years 1980-81 to 1988-89

Year	*Dropout Rate (%) Scheduled-Tribe*			*Dropout Rate (%) for All Communities*		
	Primary	*Middle*	*Secondary*	*Primary*	*Middle*	*Secondary*
1980-81	75.66	86.71	91.18	58.70	72.70	82.46
1988-89	64.53	78.08	86.73	47.93	65.40	75.36

Source: Report of the working group for the development of Scheduled Tribes during the Ninth Five Year Plan (1997-2002) p. 18.

Further, there has also been a steady decline in respect of both Scheduled Tribe and general categories in the rate of dropout during years 1990-91 and 1998-99 while both the categories have been showing decreasing trend during this period (1990-91 & 1998-99), the problem still appear worst with regard to Scheduled Tribe, as they hold very high dropout of 57.36 per cent in primary classes I to V, 72.80 per cent in classes I to VIII and 82.96 per cent in I to X during 1998-99. Also, the gap between the general population and Scheduled Tribe was found to be widening from 13.07 per cent in 1990-91 to 15.52 per cent in 1998-99 at the secondary level. Table 16.11 shows the reality.

Table 16.11 : Dropout Rate amongst STs and Total Population (1990-91 and 1998-99)

(in percent)

Category	*Classes (I-V)*		*Classes (I-VIII)*		*Classes (I-X)*	
	1990-91	*1998-99*	*1990-91*	*1998-99*	*1990-91*	*1998-99*
Total	42.60	39.74	60.90	56.82	71.34	67.44
STs	62.52	57.36	78.57	72.80	85.01	82.96
GAP	19.92	17.62	17.67	15.98	13.67	15.52

Note : * Includes ST students.

Source : Educational Profile of States/UTs, Department of Education, Ministry of Human Resource Development, GOI, New Delhi.

The report of working group constituted by the Planning Commission, GOI on the eve of Ninth Five Year Plan (1997-2000) for the development of Scheduled Tribes has also expressed its regret that Sixth All the India Educational Survey has not taken and Scheduled Tribes its consideration as special category.

Present Programmes/Schemes for the Education of Scheduled Tribes

The Ministry of Welfare runs exclusive schemes meant for educational development of STs which include Post-Matric Scholarships. Assistance to State Government for construction of girls/boys hostels, Asharam Schools. Coaching Classes for competitive Examinations, Scheme of Book Banks and Fellowships, Educational Complexes for ST girls in low literacy pockets and Vocational Training in tribal areas.

The Department of Education, Ministry of HRD is also running some important programmes for development of ST education in the country which include reservation of seats in the institutions for higher education, remedial and special coaching for STs in these institutions, reservation in research scholarships of the U.G.C., preparation of textbooks for primers etc. in tribal languages through the Central Institute of Languages, Mysore, and N.C.E.R.T. It gives priority to the opening of schools, non-formal education of Operation Blackboard etc. in ST areas.

The National Policy on Education and various special schemes for promoting education among STs for the last 40-15 years have paid little dividend and so far. The educational system which is prevalent in the country at present does not take care of the special needs of the tribal population. It is imperative that an appropriate education policy and strategy for improving the literacy level of STs to bridge the gap be chalked out and other measures be taken to implement the strategy within a definite time-frame.

Economic Status

Various development programmes launched in the country for economic upliftment of the people have generally bypassed the Scheduled Tribes. The STs have always been on the fringe of the economic development plans, hardly, if ever, able to get into the mainstream. In fact, some major development projects like irrigation and multi-purpose dam projects have added to the miseries of the tribals by way of displacement from their socio-economic and cultural milieu. The process of liberalization which as being unleashed in the recent years may further marginalize the disadvantaged groups including STs unless proper safeguards are built into the process. It is in this context that issue of overall economic benefits to tribals has to be considered.

As a matter of fact the tribals unaccustomed to any other mode of economic or commercial activity, are still dependent almost wholly on agriculture and forest related activities for their livelihood. Their land holdings are not substantial and are unirrigated dry lands, and a large majority of them are only marginal farmers. Logistically too, the tribal areas are remote and very often inaccessible consequently, they remain unaffected and unexposed to the progressive and scientific concepts of farming forcing them to trust their own age old methods of cultivation and marketing. It is no wonder then that they continue to be exploited and pushed to extreme economic backwardness and dependence.

Occupational Profile

The work participation rate (total workers as percentage of total population) of the Scheduled Tribes population is 49.30 per cent which is much higher than that for the general population (37.46). This is primarily due to very high participation rates among the Scheduled Tribe women. In case of males, the work participation rate of the Scheduled Tribe population (51.55%). But the female work participation rate among the Scheduled Tribes is 43.71 per cent as against 22.25 per cent for the total population of the country. The female work participation rate is generally quite high in most of the States and Union Territories. Among the major states, the highest female work participation rate among the Scheduled tribes is found in Andhra Pradesh (50.63%) and the lowest in West Bengal (27.43%) the Schedule Tribe population is largely rural based which has a higher female work participation rate than the urban population. Secondly, the scheduled Tribe population may be engaged predominantly in such activities as forestry, which are female oriented. Thirdly, because the extremely poor literacy level of Scheduled Tribe women, the school going population would be much less thereby increasing the participation of younger girls in economic activity.

90.03 per cent of the main worker among the Scheduled Tribes are in the primary sector, 3.85 per cent in the secondary sector and 6.12 per cent in the tertiary sector. The corresponding figure of 1981 were 90.71, 4.71 and 4.72. Thus, there has been a very marginal in the primary sector, but there has been a considerable decline in the secondary sector leading to a substantial increasing in the proportion in tertiary sector. 54.41 per cent of the scheduled Tribe main worker has reported as cultivators while 32.69 per cent have reported as agricultural labourers. It is estimated that over 60,000 tribal families in 16 states practice shifting cultivation.

Scheduled Tribes landholding, according to the agricultural census 1985-86 accounted for 7.9 per cent of the total number of land holdings in the country. Average size of the land holdings of Scheduled Tribes was 2.25 hectare. In the case of marginal land holdings, the share of Scheduled Tribes was 5.6 per cent out of the total irrigated landholdings of the Scheduled Tribes, 0.49 million (6.5%) was wholly irrigated, while 1.06 million (14.24%) was partly irrigated. The area under grains for Scheduled Tribes holdings was 83.6 per cent of the total gross cropped area. Food crop accounted for 86.4 per cent.

The tribal also depend on collection and sale of minor forest produce (MFP) as an additional but important source of their income. Here again they have faced considerable difficulties in obtaining just remuneration for their earnest efforts. Their ignorance and gullibility continue to be exploited to the maximum by the private traders. The moneylender thrives in these conditions of tribal economic dependence. The tribal economy, short, is a pathetic scenario.

Agriculture is the main occupation for their subsistence, according to the 1991 Census, 42 per cent of the ST population are main workers, of these, 54.5 per cent are cultivators and 32.7 per cent agricultural labourers. Thus, more than 87 per cent of the tribal main workers are dependent on agriculture. Further, while 42.9 per cent of the operational holdings of tribal belong to the category marginal farmers less than 1 hectare, 24.1 per cent are of small farmers category with 1 to 2 hectares; and only 2.2 per cent STs have large operational holdings with more than 10 hectares. The tribals generally live in most in-hospitable terrain and practice shifting cultivation on higher slopes where dry-land cultivation plains and lower slopes where productivity and output are very low. Lack of proper irrigation facilities, decline in soil fertility, and risk and uncertainties involving damages caused wild animals, pests, cyclones, drought etc. have further deteriorated the agriculture yield. The growing tribal population and the declining agriculture productivity have become a serious threat to the subsistence base of the tribal communities, endangering their self-supporting food security system.

Indebtedness

The problem of indebtedness amongst tribals is not only an indication of their poverty but also reflects the wider economic malaise, i.e. lack of education, low purchasing/bargaining power and lack of resources for engaging in gainful activity and meeting emergent expenditure. Therefore, the problem continues to persist with increasing menace as the indebtedness pushes the tribal further into extreme conditions of poverty and forces them to dispense with their meager resource, including the small bits and pieces of land to pay off the loans at exorbitant rates of interest. The initiation of commercial vending of liquor in tribal areas has started impoverishing the tribal population, making them victims of indebtedness and exploitation. Although the States and UTs have broadly accepted the Guidelines (relating to the Excise Policy in Tribal Areas, 1975, issued by the Ministry of Social Welfare), effective follow-up action is not taken for their implementation. Under the Fifth Schedule to the Constitution, the Governors of states with Scheduled Areas were given powers for making regulations and for placing restrictions on money lending activities in the Scheduled Areas. Relevant Laws/Regulations exist in 16 TSP states/UTs to regulate the business of money-leading to give debt-relief. However, the legal measures to curb the activities of money-lenders and traders have failed to have much impact on the severity of the problem due to the ineffective enforcement machinery and lack of alternative sources of credit for meeting the tribals consumption and productive needs. Lack of a sound policy to support consumption credit to tribals has tended to make them dependent on usurious money-lenders, resulting in debt-bondage. The problem of tribal indebtedness often gets aggravated and compounded with the government subsidy-cum-loan schemes which further lead the tribals into deep indebtedness. Planning Commission Tenth Plan Report (ch. 4.2, p. 458).

Land is not only the most important productive resource base for the tribals, but also occupies an important place in their psyche as the mainstay of their social and religious practices. Over a period of time, this resource base of the tribal communities has tended to get eroded not only through fraudulent transfers, forcible eviction, mortgages, leases and encroachments. The per capita income of tribals continues to be one of the lowest and their alienation from their our load is on run. As on January 1999, the tribals were alienated from 9,17,590 access of load and only 5,57,610 acres of such land was restored as per the statistics published by the Ministry of Rural Development, GOI (2000). The statewise positive reveals that 4.65 lakh cases of alienation of tribal land covering an area of 9.17 lakh acres were registered in the states of Andhra Pradesh, Assam, Bihar, Gujarat, Himachal Pradesh, Karnataka, Madhya Pradesh, Maharashtra, Orissa, Rajasthan and Tripura in January 1999. Against this, only 2 lakh cases were disposed of in favour of 1.56 lakh tribal families covering an area of 5.31 lakh acres. Of these, the states affected by large-scale tribal land alienation include Andhra Pradesh (2.79 lakh acres), Madhya Pradesh (1.58 lakh acres), Karnataka (1.30 lakh acres), and Gujarat (1.16 lakh acres). Various studies have pointed out that the lack of political and administrative will continues to be the cause for perpetuation of the problem of land alienation amongst the tribals as reflected in the reluctance to amend legal provisions and plug the existing loopholes and swift administrative action to identify alienated land, and restoring it to the tribals with delivery of possession.

The strategy of promoting employment cum-income generating activities to alleviate poverty amongst STs has proved to be effective in raising a large number of ST families above the Poverty Line during the period between 1993-94 and 1999-2000, as quantified at Table 16.12 given below:

Table 16.12 : *Population Living Below Poverty Line (1993-94 and 1999-2000)*

(in per cent)

Category	*1993-94*		*1999-2000*		*Percentage Change*	
	Rural	*Urban*	*Rural*	*Urban*	*(Col. 2-4) Rural*	*(Col. 3-5) Urban*
(1)	(2)	(3)	(4)	(5)	(6)	(7)
Total	37.27	32.38	27.09	23.62	(-) 10.18	(-) 10.04
STs	51.94	41.14	45.86	34.75	(-) 6.08	(-) 6.39
GAP	14.67	7.48	18.77	11.13	(+) 4.10	(+) 3.65

Note : * Includes ST population.
Source : Perspective Planning Division, Planning Commission, New Delhi.

Along with the general population, the percentage of ST families living below the poverty line has also shown a declining trend between 1993-94 and 1999-2000 (Table 16.12). However, it is discouraging to note that the rate of decline in respect of STs is much lower than that of the general population. Also, the gap between the poverty rates of the general population and of the STs has increased during the same period. Further, the incidence of poverty amongst STs still continues to be very high with 45.86 and 34.75 per cent living below the poverty line in rural and urban areas, respectively when compared to the figures of 27.09 and 23.62 per cent, in respect of general population in 1999-2000. This is primarily because a large number of STs are landless with no productive assets and with no access to sustainable employment and minimum wages. The ST women suffer from the added disadvantage of being denied of both equal and minimum wages.

Social Organization

The social life of the tribals involves methods of grouping and grading people for the effective conduct of the various activities for common existence by sharing in common activities under the bonds of relationship. They have their own structure and organization. As the tribals form a small community of their own in a particular territory, their relations are direct and intimate. The structure may be seen in their social design.

In the general scheme of the social structure of the tribes of India it is observed that the tribes of north-eastern Himalayan region are known by a few generic names. The other groups of the tribes designated by a common name are the *Gonds, Bhils* and *Gadabas* of middle and western India. Tribes are also divided into sub-tribes in these two regions. Territorial groupings of sections of tribe are common in middle India. *Social class* is mostly found in North-western and Central Himalayan regions. The elements of *social class* and *hierarchy* are also common in middle and western India. Dual organization is found in Indian tribes but not as a rule. *Clanship* is a universal feature for Indian tribes with a few exceptions life *Maler* and *Parahiya* in Bihar, the *Khasa* in Central Himalayas, the *Savara* in Orissa, the *Kader, Pandaram, Malassar* and *Allar* in south India. The lineage grouping is, however, more common in middle India.

The major *matrilineal* zones of India are Meghalaya in the North-eastern Himalayas and the Kerala and Lakshadweep in south India. The tribal communities are the *Khasi* and *Garo* of Meghalaya and the *Kadar, Kanikkar, Mannan* living in Kerala and the borders of Tamil Nadu, and the original inhabitants of Lakshadweep.

Polyandry is not so much in practice in the tribes of India. The geographical distribution, though thin, of the custom of polyandry in tribal India can easily be demarcated in the Himalayan region, i.e. from Ladakh in Jammu and Kashmir in the north-west running through Lahaul and Spiti, Kangra, Chamba, Kullu, Mandi in Himachal Pradesh, Chakrata in Uttar Pradesh and Siang district in Arunachal Pradesh. This shows a clear continuity of the practice of Polyandry in the whole of the Himalayan region except in the north-eastern part. The other area of polyandry is in the south India, in the Nilgiri Hills of Tamil Nadu and upper part of Kerala. As far as polyandrous communities are concerned, mention may be made of the tribes like the *Ladakhi, ladakhi Bhot, Lahauli, Spiti, Kinnar, Khasa* and *Gallong* in the Himalayan region and *Toda, Kota, Kurumba, Uralis* in the Southern Region.

Religious Life

Broadly speaking, tribals in India are predominantly Hindu. The tribals have reported, in Censuses, altogether 59 religions in which they believe. A nine-tenth majority of the tribals are Hindu (89.39%). One-twentieth (5.53%) profess *Christianity.* Less than 1 per cent profess Buddhism, Islam, Jainism, Sikhism and Zorostriansim, 4.19 per cent of the tribals claim to have a distinct tribal religion of their own, numbering 52, and a half of these tribal religions (26) are named after the respective tribe.

The region-wise distribution suggests that Hindus are found in all the four regions excepting some parts of south India, i.e. Andaman and Nicobar Islands and Lakshadweep. Almost ninety-nine per cent of the tribals of western India, south India and middle India are Hindus, Christians are found among the scheduled tribes in Assam, Meghalaya, Nagaland, Manipur and

Mizoram in north-eastern India and constitute slightly less than 50 per cent of the tribal population (46.88%) of the region. In south India, particularly in Kerala, they are one-twentieth of the tribal population whereas in Andaman and Nicobar Islands three-fourths of the tribals (74.31%) are Christians and are scattered in the rest of the country. Buddhist tribes are concentrated in some parts of Assam, Arunachal, Tripura, West Bengal and Himachal Pradesh. Muslim tribes are found in Lakshadweep, Himachal Pradesh, West Bengal and Maharashtra.

Tribal beliefs subsume animism and polytheism. The myths and legends provide them with sanctions. They worship all types of spirits whether benevolent or malevolent. Their huts, villages, fields and forests are all full of sacred centres. The religious festivals are eagerly awaited by the tribals. The ancestral spirits claim worship from their descendents. They mediate between the tribesmen and the gods. It is also observed that the tribals have blended their beliefs and rituals with other faiths. They have adopted Hinduism from their close neighbours, associates and a role model for centuries.

Observance of different rituals, mainly on the occasion of birth, marriage and death are part of tribal life. The parents, elders and friends help him in acquiring a mate and a marriage rite is performed. The marriage songs an dances inspire him to the new conjugal life. The visits of relations on the occasion bind him in a close kinship relation. When a child is born, birth rites are essential to propitiate the gods and ancestors. When the parents reach old age and die, this, too, is taken as the spirits wish and the death rites are performed to satisfy the deceased for the benefit of the living members of the family. The mythology behind the different rites and gods and deities give tribals a psychological sanction to lead his life as required by the norms of his community.

Cultural Diversities

There are apparent cultural differences between the lifestyles of the Indian tribes, but historically, there is a basic unity in thought and philosophy, among these people, born and brought up in environment of diversity through the length and breadth of the country.

But the mythology analysis if Scheduled Tribe has revealed that these Scheduled Tribes is at different stages of social, cultural and economic development. The cultural pattern varies from tribe to tribe and region to region. Agriculture is practiced by the largest number. A few follow occupations like minining plantation, cottage industries, fishing and animal husbandary. The more backward communities, like the Onge, the Jarawa and the Andamanese of Andaman Islands, the Birhor of Bihar, the Malapandaram and the Arandan of Kerala are practically in the food gathering and hunting stage of economy. On the other hand, the communities like the Lushai and Khasi of Assam and Meghalaya are fairly advanced and have made significant progress. The Dhodia and the Dubla of Gujarat and the Minda of Rajasthan are hardly distinguishable from their neighbours in respect of agricultural practices and some other aspects.

These cultural differences maintained by the tribal communities are the key factors through which each tribal community is holding its cultural identity in his region of inhabitants. Because the harmony of nature and culture in small scale of societies is a priceless possession. Every tribal prepondence region is a land having great cultural heritage.

While revising the tribal situation, Prof. B.K. Roy Burman (RICS Project No. 13, Page No. 7, 1996) has highlighted the challenge response of tirbals in cultural sphere. Miri (1993 pp. 165-75) scabs "the contemporary scene and perceives that the march of modernity with its cognitivism (of its own peculiarly narrow variety), its utilitarianism and its distaste for identity of any deep kind has all but crushed tribal identity. While 'allegiance to tribe' is still a powerfully motivating value, there seems now to be a void". Sharma (1994, pp. 21-25) traces the source of the void in modernist "axiomatic faith in the inherently liberating power of Man's continually enhanced ability to reshape the world" and consequent shift in attention from 'freedom' to 'progress'. While Miri and Sharma have projected the massive challenge faced not only by the tribals, but by humanity as a whole, one must not ignore the value of frantic quest for quality of life eco-prudence, eco-ethics, and humanist resurgence by drawing upon the life pattern of tribal and analogous peoples. Many do not accept today Toynbee's perception of them as history's passing show. Some dimensions of the past of the tribals are tending to become common heritage of mankind as a whole.

While tribal people are passing through a tunnel of light and shadow, expectation and agony, hope and despair, in this continuous existential flux one finds that determined assertion of their place in human comity is also taking place. A significant indicator of the same is the explosion of tribal creative literature in different tribal languages. In the 50s there were less than 1000 publications, including text-books in tribal languages. Today there are at least 10,000 publications. Besides, tribal intellectuals are bringing out analytical histories of their literatures relating the same to their social history and social progresses. They are also raising their voice against the display of their culture objects in museums without relating the same to their historical-ecological and political-economic contexts. Another indicator is the growing tendency to claim their respective tribal religions as distinct spiritual calls. During the 1981 census about 5 per cent ST population returned their respective religions in this manner. There are indications which suggest that during the 1991 census the percentage had further gone up.

Other Situational Aspects

Various development programmes launched in the country for economic upliftment of the people have generally bypassed the Scheduled Tribes. The STs have always been on the fringe of the economic development plans, hardly, if ever, able to get into the mainstream. As a matter of fact the tribals unaccustomed to any other mode of economic or commercial activity, are still dependent almost wholly on agriculture and forest related activities for their livelihood. Their landholding are not substantial and are unirrigated dry lands and a large majority of them are only marginal farmers. The problem of high indebtedness amongst tribals is not only an indication of their poverty but also reflects the wider economic malaise, i.e. lack of awareness, low purchasing/bargaining power and lack of resources for engaging in gainful activity and meeting emergent expenditure.

The tribal communities continue to be vulnerable even today, not because they are poor, assestless and illiterate compared to general population, but often their distinct vulnerability arises from their inability to negotiate and cope with the consequences of their integration with the main stream economy, society, culture and political systems from all of which they were historically protected by their relative isolation.

Further, the requirements of planned development brought with them the dams, mines, industries and roads, all located on tribal lands. With these came the concomitant processes of displacement, followed by a conflict between development and protection of tribal rights and interests. Tribal institution and practice have been forced into uneasy co-existence, which have paved the way to market or formal state institutions. Not only that, the tribal have also found themselves at a great disadvantage in the face of an influx of better equipped outsiders into tribal areas. The repurcations for the already fragile socio-economic sustenance base of the tribals have been devastating ranging from the loss of livelihoods and land alienation it is a vast scale to hereditary bondage.

Emerging Issues

While analyzing the tribal situation in foregoing discussion certain issues have also emerged at different dimensions and one has to ascertain all these flaring issues, floating not only as persisting problems on the outer skirt of the living culture of the tribal society, but are also deeply rooted in their (tribals) life and have taken the shape of unresolved issue in due course of time. The following are the persisting problems as well as on resolve issue.

The Persisting Problems

Basic minimum services, viz. food, nutrition, safe drinking water, primary health care education, safe environment, productive assets at least at the level of survival and sustenance with a special focus on women, children and PTGs.

Educational development among the tribals especially through reducing drop-out rates and encouraging enrolment/ retention with a special focus on women and the girl child.

Education relevant and suitable to their milieu, local situations and functional needs besides vocationalisation of quip the tribal youth with the most wanted technical knowledge and upgradation of skills.

Forest villages, on priority basis, by ensuring basic

infrastructure and with basic minimum services for those tribals living therein.

Food and nutrition security so as to prevent deficiency diseases due to hunger, under-nutrition, starvation and malnutrition through expansion of the on-going progremmes of Supplementary Nutrition Programme, Integrated Child Development Services, Mid-Day Meal, Targeted Public Distribution Scheme and Village Grain Banks.

Review and reform of the working of the financial and other support mechanisms (NSTFDC, TDCCs, TRIFED etc.) not only to function as self-reliant institutions but also to maximize their efforts in accomplishing economic development amongst tribals in real terms.

Implementation of the Indian Penal Code, the PCR Act, 1955 and the SC/ST (Prevention of Atrocities) Act, 1989 in order to protect the rights and interests of the tribals and ensure their safety and security.

Meaningful of the Indian implementation of the special strategies of SCP and TSP both at Central and State levels and ensuring operational/optimisation of ITDPs.

The Un-resolved Issues

Effective steps to prevent the serious problem of displacement of tribals and ensuring their effective rehabilitation through a laid-down Rehabilitation Policy.

Effective steps to prevent the growing incidence of tribal land alienation and restoration of alienated land to the tribals in accordance with the provisions of the Fifth Schedule.

Effective enforcement of existing legal/protective measures along with the provisions made under the Fifth Schedule to prevent tribal indebtedness bonded labour and other exploitation.

Tribals, especially those engaged in shifting cultivation, closely and gainfully in joint forest management, social forestry, agro-forestry etc. and facilitate rightful collection and gainful disposal of major forest produce (MFP) and other produce.

The grassroots democratic institutions, viz., PRIs and Gram Sabhas as per the provisions of 73rd and 74th Amendments and PESA Act, 1996.

NOTES AND REFERENCES

1. Sharma, B. D. (1976): *The Tribal Scene of India*, Bhopal: Tribal Research & Development Institute, p. 1, (unpublished).
2. *Ibid.*
3. *Ibid.*
4. Encyclopedic Profile of Indian Tribes (1993): *Reported Anthropological Survey of India*, p. 3.
5. Sharma, B. D. (1976): *The Tribal Scene of India*, Bhopal: Tribal Research & Development Institute p. 11, (unpublished Report).
6. *Ibid.*, p.5
7. Encyclopedic Profile of Indian Tribes (1993): *Report of Anthropological Survey of India*, p. 4
8. *Ibid.*
9. Roy Burman, B. K. (1996): *Tribal Situation and Approach to Tribal Problems in India,* New Delhi: Rajiv Gandhi Institute for Contemporary Studies, pp. 1&2.
10. Sharma, B. D. (1976): *The Tribal Situation and Approach To Tribal Problems In India* p. 6, (Unpublished).
11. Sharma, B. D. (1980): *Brief Review on Tribal Development,* Ministry of Home Affairs, G.O.I., Series No. 28, p. 2.
12. Roy Burman, B.K. (1972): "Tribal Demography – A Preliminary Appraisal", K. S. Singh (ed.) *Tribal Situation in India* (K. S. Singh stated: There are about 450 communities throughout the country in the list of Scheduled Tribes. It has not been made clear which list has been referred to. However, the Census of India Vol. 1, Part V (ii), given a total of 354 tribes).
13. Sinha, Surjit & Sharma, B. D. (ed.) : *Primitive Tribe – The first step.* New Delhi: Publication of G.O.I., Ministry of Home Affairs, pp. 2 & 3.

14. The Ninth Five Year Plan (1997-2002) (1996): *Report of Working Group for the Development & Welfare of Tribes,* p. 121, May.
15. Annual Administration Report of G.O.I., Ministry of Tribal Affairs, year, 2005-06.
16. Ghose, S.K. (1987): *Law Enforcement in Tribal Areas,* New Delhi: Ashish Publishing House, p. 9.
17. *Ibid.*, p. 10.
18. Annual Administrative Report of G.O.I., Ministry of Tribal Affairs, Year 2005-06.

17 Passing Scene of Tribal Development in North Bengal

Shailendra Prasad Sinha

No doubt we are in the era of globalization which is by and large economic ideology, wherein market friendly and profit based economic order has started emerging world over. As if, since 1970s and 1980s national economic policies are fastly shifting towards international economic order. After the fall of USSR and Eastern Europe most of the countries on the globe are forced naturally to abide by dictates of the USA and a few others. Since 1990s India having no option has to go for economic liberalization and privatization. By opening the market for M.N.C.S. and others in the queue India has paved the way for globalization with a caution.

But "What about the tribals?" is a major issue of development. We are proud of having democracy since 1947 in India based on participation and accountability. Our genius lies in Civil liberties, open dialogue and feedback leading to increase in number of responsible citizens and civil societies having equal rights. As a result there has been increase in awareness and mass opinion for nation. The salient feature of our democratic government is that of a welfare state with five fundamental principles of "*PANCHSHEEL*" for tribals.

At its best we have Panchayati Raj system with the concept of democratic decentralization of power. As if, it underlies the approach of people's participation with a basic principle of governance and development measures less from top to bottom but more from bottom to top. Here beneficiary will plan and opt means of their choice to excel one's condition sustainable.

North Bengal

The state of West Bengal has 2 natural divisions. One is the Himalayan North popularly known as the "North Bengal" which comprises the districts of Darjeeling, Jalpaiguri and Cooch Bihar.

It has a good drainage system with the fast run-off by network of rivers like Tista,Torsa, Jaldhaka and Raidak. The other is the Southern part of Bengal prized with rich rice fields having vast alluvial plain carved by the big rivers – Mayurakshi of Bhagirathi, Damodar, Kansbati, Rupnarayan.

There are 18 districts in the state of West Bengal with well classified three-tiered Panchayati Raj System. At the grassroots there are 3437 Gram Panchayats under 331 Panchayat Samities at the level of Community Block and 18 Zila Parishads at the apex level of district. The Gram Panchayat acts as an agent or centre for initiation and implementation of development programmes.

Jalpaiguri

Jalpaiguri is the north-bordering district in the land of lower Himalayas with district geographical diversity full of natural beauty, rich traditional history and colourful ethnic groups. It lies between 26° 16′ and 27°00′ latitude and between 88°04′ and 89°53′ E longitude with a total North, Assam in the east, the district of Cooch Bihar and Bangladesh in south and the district of Darjeeling and Bangladesh in West. This district is naturally prized with good drainage system with a network of rivers—Tista, Mahananda, Kalajani, Raidak, Jaldhaka and Torsha flowing from north to south.This district comprises two distinct topographical regions—Sub montane regions known as "Duars" and the following plain land there of known as "Tarai". Under the permanent settlement Act-1793 land west of Tista river is permanent settled and ihabited area since long long ago known as "Tarai" area. It presents a rectangular shape. On the east as a gift of nature it is bounded by the Sankosh river originated from Brahmaputra and on the west by the Mahananda river originated from the Ganga.

Settlement history traced back to the British army when they tried several times to annex the Himalayan Kingdom of Bhutan adopting eighteen such roots/doors/paths passages but all their expedition were frustrated by the people and army of respective kingdom.

After, 2nd Bhutan expedition in 1864, all the Duars areas came under the British rule and made part of British India by way of famous "Chinchula" agreement and the Bhutias were thus over-ruled. This was the turning point when at first the Britains divided Duars in two parts—"Eastern Duars" and "Western Duars".

Eastern Duars soon undergone the Golpara district of Bengal for a shortwhile (1864-1869). Similarly, Western Duars losts its identity and merged with the district of Jalpaiguri in 1869. All these made the term "Duars" to be popularly known.

Western Duars is the land to the east of river Tista like a strip of sub-montane region foothills with patches of plain land in succession in front. The Western Duars have many rivers and streams intersecting forests of heavy grass and reed jungles with wild cardamoms. Cotton plants are also grown in addition to paddy, jute, maize etc.

The entire area is engaged in tea gardens covered by tea bushes all around. Human settlements are seen at the crossing and junction of the road.

Trade of the area mainly depend on tea, timber, tobacco in which tea and timber are exported outside. Plantation of *supari* is also being commercially viable and popular today.

Climate

This entire area lies in the close proximity of the high hills of Himalayas. Having an overall temperature maintained between 10°celsius to 30°celsius. This area remains highly humid and gets rain infrequent throughout the year from March-April to November-December followed by winter. The entire area is rich in flora n fauna. All the year hence the soil solumn remains moist and humid best suited to plantation, rice and jute cultivation. High damp and warm climate has influenced the vegetation of a wet and evergreen forest of Savanna type.

Soil

The earth cover is of the alluvial soil brought by the rivers from the high hills and deposited in the past and remains porous throughout the year with almost no water logging. This area has never been inundated except the two incidents—one in 1952 and the other in 1968. These two floods forced men to move to the uplands of the forest in Duars.

Jalpaiguri district has two sub-divisions—Sadar and Alipore duar with 13 blocks and 16 Police stations. The Aliporeduar is sub-montane region comprising the areas of Western Duars. Besides forest activity the economy of the area is mainly that of agriculture and plantation of tea. Paddy, jute, sugarcane, and tobacco are produced in plenty.

There are 38 scheduled tribes in the district which constitute 21.04 per cent of the total district population divided into 20.75 per cent male and 21.35 per cent female.

Background of Tribal Development

In majority tribals in India are forest dwellers. Their way of life have been roaming round the forest as if an ultimate source of survival. During the British era the forests were made the government property by snatching the traditional right of the tribals to live in isolation and lead life on their own fate.

However, the real measure of tribal development was taken up in democratic India. The tribal scenario was taken in its right earnest as that of the socio-economically deprived and marginalized group constituting nearly 8 per cent of the country's population. Hence the tribal development was given the top priority by adopting several models and approaches through all the 5 year plan periods.

At first villages were taken as unit wherein more than 80 per cent of Indian mass live forming a noticeable village community for all practical purposes. On 2nd October 1952 the Community Development Programme was launched. In addition to CDP another development programme National Extension Service (NES) was launched on 2nd October 1953 by more financial allocation to the raise the general standard of living of the weaker sections of the society including the tribals.

During the 2nd 5 years plan Special Multi-purpose Tribal Blocks was started for tribal integrated development. During 3rd 5 years plan period on the recommendation of Elwin and Dheber Commission it got changed to Tribal Development Blocks (TDBs). With emphasis on economic development. This continued during the 4th Plan period. During the 5th Plan the tribals were categorized in 3 categories by adopting Area Development Approach and development of P.T.G. This paved the way for Integrated Tribal Development Project (ITDP) followed by Tribal Sub-plan (TSP). Modified Area Development Approach (MADA) then cam in the 6th Plan. Gradually, it went to Integrated Area Development Programme (IADP) focusing on the area specific problems of the tribals.

This way or that way measures for tribal development continued and till date in a big way it is in operation.

In the West Bengal making provision for such Tribal

Development Block was not possible due to less concentration of the tribes in a single compact area, but an alternative arrangement was made through sub-block schemes where tribals were numerically large to constitute 50 per cent of the total population. After this the Central Government grant was increased and various projects were undertaken for the amelioration of the tribal people. Keeping in view the objectives of the five year plans some measures were taken for the betterment of the tribal people.

The present paper is based on the author's fieldwork while supervising 44 PG students of Anthropology at "Satali" Hashimara in Kalchini block and at "Narthali" in Kumargram block in the district of of Jalpaiguri in North Bengal in April and May, 2006 besides guidance and supervision to a Ph.D. scholar in Western Duars.

This paper is confined to a comparative analysis of Tribal Development between the two diverse racio-cultural stock (a) Munda and Oraon and (b) Mech of Jalpaiguri district in Western Duars. The former are the Protoaustraloid dark skin people with a migrant settlement history of nearly hundred years from Jharkhand, Ranchi, Gumla, Lohardaga and Bokaro. They are traditional settled agriculturists of Jharkahnd and settled at "Satai" in Hashimara area of Kalchini block. The "Mech" are Tibeto-Mangols white skin traditional semi-nomadic, shifting cultivators, cotton/silk grower/cloth maker trekked down from the high hills of Himalaya settled long ago in the densely forested foot hills of Himalaya and Tarai land in patches there of in "Narthali" Kamakhyaguri of Kumargram block and till three to four decades ago they continued with their age old economic pursuits but today they are settled agriculturists and wage earner not Jhum cultivators or cocoon or cotton growers/cloth makers.

Most of the tribals of Western Duars suffered a lot in the hands of money lenders who gave loans in terms of cash to enable them to meet their needs. Once entrapped always remain in debt even after numerous payements of the actual loan, which always remains unpaid, only the interest paid. The never ending interest went on increasing generations after generations. The situation however changed to a great extent after the arrival of the Scotish Missionaries in western Duars. The missionaries could well read the exploitation process and cautioned Christian tribals. They made valuable advice to their converts and alert them on all possible accounts.

Tribal Development Measures

Various efforts have been made during the plan periods for tribal development. During Five Year Plan periods considering problems of poverty, lack of roads and communication facilities, shortage of drinking water and irrigation, education and health various efforts were made to improve the lot in both Satali and Narthali group of villages along with vested land distribution among the poor people.

All the above programmes were financed by the Government through Bank and selected and Distributed by Panchayat.

The following types of loan have been distributed among the villagers :

(a) Narthali group of villages
(b) Satali group of villages

1. Sanchali Loan (for weaving cloth)
2. Tailoring loan
3. To purchase plough and bullocks
4. To purchase buffaloes with carts
5. To run tea-stall and betel leaf shop
6. To purchase milk cow
7. Paddy husking
8. Carpentary loan
9. Piggery loan
10. Banana trees plantation
11. Goattery loan
12. Fishery loan
13. To purchase Pumpset
14. To purchase Rickshaw van, etc.

Kumar Gram Block

Though the name of the block is Kumargram but all the concerned office—block office, land revenue office, forest office, police station, bank, electricity office, telephone exchange, main bus stand, market and cinema hall are located in Kamakhyaguri on the high road connecting Kumargram to aliporeduar sub-divisional headquarter.

(a) Narthali Group of Villages

It consists of Narthali, Madhya Narthali and Dakshin Narthali in the submontanc region and close proximity of dense forest of the Western Duars in Kumargram block. Maximum mech people are living along with Rajwanshi, Kayastha, Brahmins and Muslims as well.

1. Narthali

It is located at 14 km away from Kamakhyaguri urban centre. It has 1 ration shop, 1 sub-post office, 1 co-education high school upto class 10th, 3 primary schools, 2 anganbadi centres, 1 grocery shop, 1 cycle repair shop, 2 sweets shop with tea-stall besides bi-weekly market for Tuesday and Saturday, 1 church and river Jampoi passes in.

2. Madhya Narthali

It is interior most village 20 km away from Kamakhyaguri railway junction connecting NER to SER. To reach there 1 has to get down at Teliapara to take another bus to get down at Narthali stoppage 5 km from Madhya Narthali. It is a forest village. This has 3 primary schools upto class 4th ill-maintained, 1 ration shop, 2 anganbadi centres and 1 gramsthan besides a Shiva temple.

3. Dakshin Narthali

This village is only 2 km away from Kamakhyaguri centre

intersected by the railway line. Due to its close proximity the village has only 1 co-education high school upto class 10th and a church. For other needs the villagers mostly go to Kamakhyaguri urban centre.

Kalchini Block

This block is in the west of Hashimara urban centre at a distance of 6 km where only the block office is located but for all practical purposes Hashimara in the mid of Satali group of villages is a "rurban" centre where there are telephone exchange, electricity office, bank, hotels,police station, bus stop, bakery, several grocery shops, cloth shops, several sweet shops, and a daily market with one health centre. From here there is a straight road for Bhutan well connecting the people of this area from Bhutan.

(b) Satali Group of Villages

More than hundred years ago Britons established a tea-estate named Satali at Hashimara. It has several tea-gardens in thousands of acres of land dissected by roads having facility of labour quarters on the boundary of the tea-gardens. This estate has 2 big labour line with facility of bi-weekly markets. It has emerged now in a group of villages North Satali, Madhya Satali and Dakshin Satali.

1. North Satali

At a distance of 8 km from Kalchini block North Satali is a labourline village with a history of more than 100 years largely inhabited by Oraons, Mundas, with few Mahalis, Lohars, Santhals, Mohammedans, Brahmins and other caste. Labourline Quarters were allotted to the tea-garden labourers who had migrated from Jharkhand and spent several generations in the same quarters. But the legal owner of the quarter is the tea company. It has 2 primary schools, 1 kindergarden school, 1 ration shop, 1 grocery shop, 1 beetel shop, Lord Shiva temple 1 anganbadi centre. It is very near to Hasimara railway junction, forest office, military quarter and just 1km away from Central School upto class 12th.

2. *Madhya Satali*

This a long stretch of village habitation behind the most important country's strategic airbase of Indian Airforce. Mostly the villagers are Oraons, some Mundas and the mech tribes. It is at a distance of 15 km from Kalchini block. In late 1960s the villagers were given *pattas* of land which they cleared for paddy and jute cultivation. They in majority are wage-earners hence today they have sub-leased their *patta* land to the others or have gone for share-cropping. There are 2 government primary schools and 2 mission's nursery schools and middle school upto 8th with primary health care centres, 2 grocery shops, 2 ration shops, 1 weekly market etc.

3. *Dakshin Satali*

This village is also a labourline located in the south centre of Satali tea estate inhabited mostly by Oraons, Mundas, Santhals, tribal migrants of Jharkhand besides Nepalis, Bengalis and Marwaris. It is well connected from Hashimara and only at a distance of 8 km from Kalchini block. It has a big play ground, 1 biweekly market, 3 government primary schools, 2 mission schools, 1 health centre run by the tea company, 2 ration shops, 1 tea-stall, 2 grocery shops, 2 STD-booths etc.

Various loans are disbursed among the tribals are listed below in Narthali and Satali group of villages :

Madhaya Narthali & Madhya Satali

1. D.R.D.A. (District Rural Development Programme)

	Amount/ person	*Madhaya Narthali*	*Madhya Satali*
For betel and bidi shop	Rs. 500/-	3 people	4 people
For purchase of bullocks	Rs. 1200/-	5 people	6 people
Milk cow loan	Rs. 3500/-	5 people	5 people
Piggery loan	Rs. 3500/-	1 people	2 people
For purchase of loom (Sanchali)	Rs. 3000/-	2 people	Nil

2. S.C.P. (Special component Plan) Loan

S.C.P. loan financed by Central Bank of India		Madhaya Narthali—Nil	Madhya Satali —Nil

3. T.S.P. (Special Sub-Plan) Loan

	Amount/ person	*Madhaya Narthali*	*Madhya Satali*
For milk cow	Rs. 3600/-	3 people	3 people
Piggery loan	Rs. 2500/-	3 people	4 people
Sanchali (100m) loan	Rs. 3000/-	2 people	Nil
Plough bullock loan	Rs. 6000/-	3 people	2 people

4. S.E.S.R.U. loan (given by Unemployment Exchange)

	Amount/ person	*Madhaya Narthali*	*Madhya Satali*
For handloom	Rs. 2500/-	2 people	Nil
For ring well	Rs. 25000/-	1 people	Nil

Narthali and Satali

1. T.S.P. Loan

	Amount/person	*Narthali*	*Satali*
For looms	Rs. 3000/-	15 people	Nil
For tailoring shop	Rs. 10000/-	2 people	Nil

2. D.R.D.A. Loans

	Amount/person	*Narthali*	*Satali*
For bullocks	Rs. 1200/-	6 people	Nil

(Contd...)

(Contd...)

3. I.R.D.P. Loan

	Amount/person	*Narthali*	*Satali*
For bullock with cart	Rs. 7000/-	1 people	Nil
For purchasing loom (Sanchali)	Rs. 3000/-	2 people	Nil
For tea-stall	Rs. 5000/-	1 people	Nil
For husking of paddy	Rs. 20000/-	2 people	Nil

Village Dakshin Narthali and Dakshin Satali
Nil— No loan by any means through the government in Dakshin Narthali and Dakshin Sartali.

Problem and Prospect of Development

In spite of all efforts made there has been increase in widening the gap between the tribals and the non-tribals. In all probability the tribal exploitation has increased in organized way. The main problems of the two sets of studied villages are poverty, literacy, communication, health/hygiene and sanitation, politicization, cottage industry etc.

Poverty

In both the groups of villages most of the tribals are in precarious conditions. Extent of poverty all the time challenges their survival.This is the high-time for the mech who have been deserted from the forest-ultimate source of their survival.

Literacy

Undoubtedly education is becoming a craze among the tribals but it has gone adverse due to several factors against it and drop-outs have not been yet checked. In both the group of villages medium of instruction, teachers, type of school, location and distance of school play a important role. Education and economy are inseparable for the tribals due to child labour. In agricultural works, children help their parents by deserting schools. Insufficient teachers and improper way of teaching affect the extent of teaching in a good number of schools there is only one teacher to take care of 3-4 classes at a time. The provision of mid-day meal is not proper leading to increase in drop-outs. The poor tribals cannot afford traveling expense so unwillingly they leave their school going.

Faulty education policy of the West Bengal government is more responsible for drop-outs after class 8th. It is because the medium of learning after 8th class is either English or Bengali but not in Hindi and tribal language.

Communication

Madhya Narthali and Madhya Sarthali are the worst hit villages in communication connectivity. There is no direct road that is why they are forced to sell their produce at throw away price to anyone who goes to their doorstep at first. Many patients die on the way for lack of communication facility.

Health, Hygiene and Sanitation

There is a direct ecological bearing on the health, hygiene and sanitation of both group of tribals. Due to high humidity a lot of diseases specially water borne diseases are widely spread among these tribals. There is no good drinking water facility except 2-3 handpumps called "Hokdo" installed by the government. Everywhere there is lack of covered well. As compared to Munda and Oraon the mech people of Narthali villages in their blissful ignorance mention many of their failures, difficulties, illness etc. as the wrath of supernatural power. They try their level best to pacify the spirits and ghosts of the dead per their traditional prescription. They have a strong belief in their priest and shamans.

The qualified doctors rare in number are beyond the reach of these tribals. Primary health centres in all these villages are not upto the mark. As regards housing and sanitation they do not have proper idea, therefore, they often suffer from malaria, diarrhoea, amoebiosic dysentery, headache, sinusitis, cough and cold, seasonal fever etc.

Politicization

This is a very serious problem for hindering development of tribals of the studied villages. The panchayat members belong to a particular political party and play important roles and the panchayat office is the executing centre for development measures. The benefit goes only to the favourites of the panchayat members. Not a single mech is a panchayat member, therefore, the mech are more affected and out of reach of the development.

At times even if they go to the block office often they get discouraged. There is no "*gaon-budha*" system.

Tribe and the Forest

Earlier the mech people were the master of the forest but today in terms of the forest they are popper. They have been deprived and kept at bay. It is because of the wrong forest policy of the government which has snatched their natural rights. They are facing a lot of problems.

Cottage Industry

Specially the Tibeto-Mongols are the traditional experts in weaving of "endi" shawls, "doknas" (traditional female dress), bedsheets, *gamchas*, towels and fishing implements. Earlier they used to grow cotton in the forest and cocoon silk. But today the forest policy has adversely affected forcing to abandon their cottage industry.

Prospect of Development

The above problems discussed are suggestive of the needed steps to be taken urgently not only by the government but also by the social scientist and social workers. Development is no doubt an economic prospect but ought to be a qualitative aspect of human development. It needs to be an organized activity in satisfying basic needs of the tribals. It should be psychologically oriented to motivate the tribals to adopt new skills, change in attitudes and life style so that they should build up their inner strength with new set of infrastructures and accrue benefits from the new programme.

Agriculture

Undoubtedly tribal migrants from Jharkhand happen to be skilled agriculturist. Whatever the land they have they are going better in Madhya Satali. But the mech of Madhya Narthali are not far behind, they have adapted well to the agricultural way of life. Psychologically the mech are also eager equally to prosper in settled agriculture like their neighbouring Oraons and Mundas provided they get developed seeds, agricultural loans/grants and modern equipments for intensive cultivation besides expert training, irrigational water facility and so on.

Horticulture

Arecanut, banana, lemon, papaya, guava, mango, blackpepper are grown besides vegetable farming in a limited way. Due to lack of buyers they do not get good price. There is a good scope for commercial production by way of intensive horticulture.

They need proper training and marketing facilities to be arranged by the government.

Education

For the speedy development of the tribals a lot of measures is needed to improve the educational lot in this area. At first the condition of the school is to be improved. Pre and post-matric schools within the reach of the villagers urgently needed with good building, sufficient teachers and modern infrastructures. More, the medium of instruction must be in Hindi common to all in addition to English and Bengali. This will check immediately educational migration in which the well off send their children outside the state boundary.

Physical education preparatory to get job in the constabulary forces and the Indian Army is urgently required for the group of tribals.

Communication

For the speedy development of the tribals all these villages are urgently needed to be connected by good roads. At intervals regular bus services should be made to connect all these villages.

Health and Hygiene

To check the alarming situation mobile medical facilities and regular vaccination, spray of insecticides for the control of malaria should be arranged on an urgent basis. For portable water hand pumps should be provided to at least 50 per cent families of the studied villages.

Others

All the tribals are fond of rearing chicken and pig so on urgent basis mobile vetenary dispensary should be arranged to serve these tribals and their live-stocks at their doorsteps. There is a good prospect of poultry, farming, piggery, dairy, fishery and seri-culture besides forestry. It needs to train these tribals in modern way and provide good breed of livestock to improve the lot. Fishery can be developed in a amazing way since this area gets good rain throughout the year therefore check dam, model ponds will add to change the fate of the tribals as a mark of sustainable development. Bio-fertilizer can be made a boon in disguise for which cottage industry need to be promoted for at lest 25 per cent of the tribals.

Cocoon growing in a modern way after proper training in scientific processing will bring revolution which will specially strengthen the economy of mech tribals. It needs technical training and sufficient grant.

From the point of Applied and Action Anthropology for the groups of tribal people the author likes to suggest unexposed, semi-exposed and exposed villages should be considered and for that there genius and willingness to prosper be taken care of for the development in which two types of steps ought to be taken—one for the individual and the other for a small group of 2-3 families. Agriculture, horticulture, poultry, piggery, duck-farming, goaterry etc. need to be taken care of for urgent and speedy sustainable development. Education forms the back-bone of the tribal development.

REFERENCES

Dalton, Edward Tuit (1872): ***Descriptive Ethnology of Bengal,*** Kolkata: Office of the Superintendent of Government Printing, pp. 88-89.

Hunter,W.W. (1876): ***A statistical account of Bengal*** ,Vol.X *Districts of Darjeeling and Jalpaiguri and State of Cooch Bihar*, London: Trubner & Co.

Narginari, Harcharam (1985): ***In Search of Identity : The Mech,*** Kolkata: B.B. Prakashan.

Nath, R.M (1978): *The Background of Assamese Culture*, Guwahati: Jayanta Prakashan, p.15.

Mandal, Krishna (2006): *The Mech of North Bengal: A study on their society and economy*. (Ph.D. Thesis, Ranchi University unpublished).

Roy Burman, B.K. (1985): "Issues in Tribal Development", *Mainstream*, January 5-12.

Singh, K.S. (1994): "People of India National Series Volume III", *The Scheduled Tribes*, Anthropological Survey of India, Kolkata: Oxford University Press.

Sukla, T.N. (1991): *West Bengal land reforms Act 1955*, Kolkata: Kanal Law House.

Sunder, D.H.E. (1895): *Survey and settlement report of western Duars in District of Jalpaiguri 1889-95*, Kolkata: Government Publication.

Vidyarthi, L.P. (1984): *Tribal Development and its Administration*, Allahabad: Kitab Mahal.

Census of India (1961): West Bengal, Sikkim, Part V-A (II) Tables of Scheduled Tribes, Volume XVI.

Census of India (2001): Primary Census Abstract Total Population Table A-5.

18 Civil Society Initiatives to Support Tribes of Jhabua for Capital Building through Microfinance

Vishal Massey

The informal money lending system has existed in tribal areas from long period of time. In the present context, it shares a very large part of rural credit market. Despite of exorbitant rate of interest, the local moneylenders are considered pro-poor and pro-tribal because they provide readily available and timely loans.[1] Despite huge network of formal bank branches, formal banks have not been able to meet the credit needs of economically disadvantaged people and mobilize their savings.[2] The simple way to decapitate the money-lender is to bring institutional bank credit in tribal areas.[2] The existing banking policies, systems and procedures, deposit and loan products were perhaps not well suited to meet the most immediate needs of the tribe. It was felt that the tribal communities needed better access to these services and products, rather than cheap subsidized credit.[3] Bank has a problem related with mobility and its extension to tribal areas in order to provide immediate credit to the tribal communities. Further what adds to the problem is that if tribal community members come to Bank for credit purpose usually they don't have major documents for long and cumbersome procedures of Bank or sometimes Bank officials never provide loan to them with the fear of these loans becoming

Non-Performing Asset (NPA). Thus a need has been felt for alternative policies, systems and procedures, savings and loan products, other complementary services, and new delivery mechanisms, which would fulfil the requirements of the poorest and tribes, especially of the women members of such households. This has given rise to an increasing emphasis on MF for improving the access to credit to the marginalized and tribal community members. The MF revolution has changed attitudes towards helping the poor and tribal in many countries. In some countries, there have been substantial flows of credit, often to very low-income groups or households, which would normally be excluded by conventional financial institutions. Bangladesh is the starkest example of a very poor country, where currently roughly one quarter of rural households are direct beneficiaries of these programmes (Khandker, 2003).

Meaning of Micro Finance

It appears that what MF (Micro Finance) means is very well understood, but not clearly articulated. There are some definitions of MF offered in past literature. Robinson (2001) for instance says "microfinance refers to small-scale financial service—primary credit and savings—provided to people who farm, fish or herd." However, she later admits that the definitions could be narrower and more focused, depending on the typology of lending. She however maintains that it would be good to keep the definition to "refer to all types of financial services provided to low-income households and enterprises." There are some value attributes with are related with MF; First, MF is something that is done by alternative sector not the government, and or the commercial sector; Second, microfinance is something done exclusively or predominantly with the poor; Third, microfinance grows out of developmental roots. That is why, a large number of NGOs have started their own MF programmes in an attempt to develop the people in their respective areas. They have basically followed the same strategy although minor modifications exist in the models being used by different NGOs. Micro-credit has become a major tool of development. By providing loans rather than grants the micro-credit provider can become sustainable by recycling resources over and over again. In other words, micro-credit appears to deliver the "holy trinity" of outreach, impact and sustainability.

In Madhya Pradesh, ASA a not for profit organization, initiated its MF programme in Jhabua (Madhya Pradesh) districts on an experimental basis in 1998[4]. By 2008, it has developed a model that serves the interests of the predominantly tribal population (mainly Bhils and Bhilalas) very well in the area. ASA's approach to development is firmly founded upon participatory action at the community level. At the heart of the organization is the aim of developing livelihood security, which is facilitated by an intensive participatory process of natural resources development and local institutional development. Particular emphasis is placed upon the poor and women. Presently in over 1000 villages, ASA works directly for physical interventions in the Indian states of Madhya Pradesh, Chhattisgarh and Bihar. Besides, there would be about another 500 villages where ASA works indirectly by providing long term technical support to its partners such as M.P. District Poverty Initiatives Project.[5]

Jhabua is predominantly a tribal district with 86 per cent of nearly 13.94 lakhs population belonging to Bhil tribe. Jhabua with an area of 6793 square kilometres is the western-most district of Madhya Pradesh. It is about 320 kilometres from the state capital Bhopal. The area lies between 22.5° and 23.8° north of equator. The climate in this area varies from dry sub-humid to moist sub-humid. The rainfall is unimodal and is both spatial and temporally, variable. The annual rainfall in Jhabua is about

70-80 centimetres. Droughts occur once in every 3-4 years while years with high rainfall are also common in the area. Land holdings in the area are generally small, averaging between two to three hectares. The proportion of small and marginal farmers (with landholding less than two hectares) in Jhabua is fifty per cent, while very small holdings of about half hectare also constitute sizeable proportion of holdings. Most households own a pair of cattle. Bullocks are considered as a status symbol in the tribal society although they have very little economic value especially in drought years. Bhil women generally get married after they reach puberty and have an average of four to five children by the time they reach thirty-five years. Large-scale seasonal migration of the male workforce further increases hardships of a woman as they not only have to perform the daily chores but are also responsible for on farm activities. However, if compared with status of other women, Bhil women have a greater decision-making power. Yet the women are excluded from property rights. The tribes in this area practice the system of reverse dowry and hence it is the bridegroom who has to shell out an amount of about fifty-seventy thousand rupees for marriage. This is one of the major reasons for the indebtedness of the tribal as they end up in the trap of moneylenders, once they take loans to meet these sorts of unproductive expenditures. Apart from the family involved in the marriage, other relatives also contribute some money in the marriage. The tribal have a custom by the name of *Nyotra,* wherein they need to double the gift amount that they had received from the person. This cooperation proves to be very beneficial to them in times of marriages when around 25-30,000 rupees are obtained from this system of *Nyotra.* Migration is an important feature of this region. Around 60-70 per cent of the families migrate for around six to seven months in a year. They migrate in two stretches, the first being from the month of

November (just after *Deepawali*) to February (just before *Holi*). Thereafter, they enjoy themselves in the festival season and then again leave for work from the end of March to May. They return to work on their fields just before monsoon. Families, which had a good crop in the preceding year or own better located and irrigated land stay in the village while others migrate again. The migrants work as wage labourers and their wages vary from fifty to hundred rupees a day. The subsistence agriculture resulting from the harsh agro-climatic conditions and the rocky terrain is the primary cause for the households to borrow for consumption and productive investments. Rutherford (2000:4) has rightly argued that poor households need relatively large amounts for life cycle needs like marriages, festivals, and old age, emergencies like illness, death of breadwinner etc. This was evident in the field observations as the loans were primarily taken for agriculture, household consumption, social and religious purposes like marriages etc. and also for emergencies like illness etc. Loans taken for the purpose of consumption, agriculture and social events are seasonal in nature. The monsoon season (June-August) when land preparation, sowing and weeding are at a peak, are the times of greatest shortage. At this time, the price of staples is almost double the selling price at harvest. The social expenditure, which is at the peak during March till onset of monsoon, contributes largely to the total households borrowings. The tribal especially the Bhils spend huge amounts on drinking and eating during the festival season. If the family has accumulated large debts, then more members of the households go on migration than in a normal year. The income earned during the period of migration goes into the servicing the debt incurred while going for migration while the part left goes into drinking etc. in the festival season. This leaves them with no other option but to go to moneylenders again to finance the next year's requirement. The assets possessed by a farmer in the form of animals, silver jewelry etc. play an important role in obtaining loans from money lenders or in arranging marriages. Other animals like goats and hens are also part of investment strategy, which are sold in local markets to meet unexpected occasions.

Rationale of the MF Programme in Jhabua

The gap between the supply of credit from formal sources and the demand from the rural based tribal communities is widening in tribal areas. The harsh terrains, uncertain agriculture are some factors that contribute to an increased requirement for credit in order to meet the basic human needs. The reach of the formal or institutional credit sources is insufficient, inflexible and uncertain. The formal sector failed to realize the mismatch between the hierarchies of credit needs and credit availability, resulting in 'adverse usage' of credit. Credit need starts with consumption purposes, which are only being met through informal sources at high costs. Higher needs come into play only when the lower needs are satisfied. However, credit is usually available for higher needs like establishing new enterprises. Money being fungible, loans taken for diversification is used for lower level needs first. This often results in adverse usage and hence lower repayment rates. Therefore, the local informal credit sources (moneylenders) have grown to control the livelihood cycle of this largely agricultural based community. Although, they charge exorbitant interest (60-150%) rates, but provide timely credit to the needy without any hassles. Once the tribes get into the debt trap they are left with no other option but to migrate as the local livelihood systems are not productive enough to generate sufficient income to liberate them from the debt trap. The money earned from migration goes into the repayment of earlier loans and very little is left to cater to even the basic needs. This scenario has fueled the debate on the type of institutional structures that can provide easy and cheap credit to the poor. The transaction costs of savings can be as high as 10 per cent for poor rural households. Self Help Groups (SHGs) of rural poor are perhaps the most potential organizations to this end. They not only reduce the transaction cost of saving for the poor, free them from the clutches of moneylenders but also empower the members to take on the world more confidently. ASA also saw them as a solution to the problem and therefore, formed SHGs and linked them to the banks for credit services. This intervention can be considered as a shift in approach from development to empowerment, wherein they plan their withdrawal strategy from service delivery projects and think of their own sustainability by providing financial services. As per the studies undertaken on behalf of ASA by various scholars, it has been found that the banks have not been forthcoming in extending credit to the SHGs. The NABARD guidelines for the banks insist that the first loaning amount should be twice the savings amount, second must be thrice, and third should be four times. The extent to which this guideline is followed is questionable given the constraints under which the bank managers are supposed to work. Instead of the usual 1:4 ratio that should exist between the groups' savings and the credit extended, the banks have merely extended the credit at ratio of 1:2. The bank managers plead that the high risk of default leaves them with no other option but to be cautious in their approach towards SHG loaning. The delays in getting the loans have led to the tribes being still dependent on the moneylenders.[6] Consequently, ASA felt that there is a need for a Micro Finance Institution (MFI) that would extend credit to the SHGs in a timely manner at affordable rates. In this context, ASA established MFI under Section 25, India Company Act in year 2006-07.[7]

Present MF Scenario

The basic foundation of ASA's programme lies with the operation of SHGs of rural poor. In ASA's case, each SHG is formed with the representation of 10-15 households, the membership being restricted to one person per household, to ensure equal power distribution. Almost 65-70 per cent of the households in a village are eventually covered under SHGs and a village would have an average of 4-5 SHGs. 75 per cent of these SHGs are exclusively women SHGs. The primary function of the SHGs is savings and credit. By the time an SHG becomes three years old, it tries to meet at least 50-60 per cent of total annual credit. ASA makes two critical value additions into the programme, which is largely managed by the local communities. First, local individuals, trained as team members, are responsible for the routine management tasks of SHGs, including conducting meetings, book-keeping, bank linkage and training of SHGs. Second, in order to bridge the gap between banks and SHGs so as to increase the total funds available for loaning, ASA has been promoting SHG federations. The SHGs of all operational villages in a block are federated at the block level. By the third year of operation, a block level federation of SHGs typically provides service to approximately 350-400 SHGs. The federation is a democratic organization represented by each SHG through membership. The general body elects the executive committees and office bearers for a term of two years.[8] The federation is registered under the Societies Registration Act of the State. The District Rural Development Agency (DRDA) Jhabua has made available a seed corpus to one of the federations of Rs.10.00 lakhs to secure the loans provided to its SHGs. The entire money is profitably invested, since there is no default in repayment of loan by the SHGs. ASA also has been acting as an MFI and has lent Rs.75.00 lakhs directly to approximately 150 SHGs (1900 members).[9] ASA has also provides micro-insurance facilities to its SHGs. As on date, general insurance has been provided to 667 beneficiaries belonging to 54 SHGs, who have availed a loan through HDFC Bank. Micro insurance will be a continuous process and will be provided to all micro-credit beneficiaries. Unfortunately, two deaths have been reported, but due to insurance cover, the families received an insurance payout within 3 days. The process is on to buy insurance policy for all SHG members, irrespective to status of their borrowership.[10]

Table 18.1 : Progress of Microfinance in Jhabua

Particulars	*Unit*	*March 2003*	*March 2004*	*March 2005*	*March 2006*	*March 2007*	*February 2008*
SHGs	No.	189	244	366	519	719	928
Women SHGs	No.	123	209	311	398	531	661
Members	No.	2141	2452	4248	5912	8601	10393
Saving (lac)	Rs.	8.47	11.03	23.78	32.00	77.70	97.80
Loans Outstanding (lac)	Rs.	23.89	28.14	56.56	84.32	192.48	203.01
Loan SHG	No.	25	67	92	83	567	652
Repayment rate	—	100%	100%	100%	100%	100%	100%
Portfolio at risk	%	Nil	Nil	Nil	Nil	Nil	Nil

Source: Internal Reports of Manager Micro Finanace Programme—ASA.

The whole world agrees on what is the best way to eliminate poverty; it is to be achieved by creating employment. But economists recognize only one kind of employment—waged employment. In their book there is nothing called "self-employment". Actually microfinance supports in generation of self-employment. The loan amount which tribes take through MF is mainly (65%) consumed for agriculture related activities. ASA has observed that due to infusion of MF programme in Jhabua, the time period of migration of tribes for jobs in unorganized sector has reduced significantly. It has reduced from 6-8 months to 4-6 months, whereas the National Rural Employment Gaurantee Programme (NREGP) was not initiated in Jhabua. Somewhere, it is also to be seen that tribes are paying off their debts taken by moneylenders through loan taken by MF. As a result, the moneylenders have dramatically decreased their rate of interest in Jhabua. Nonetheless, it is only a crack of dawn of MF in Jhabua and small efforts that have been made as few drops in the ocean of credit need in Jhabua. But it has impacted on various aspects of development of tribal areas like their deeper involvement in agriculture and their self-employment, escape from the shackles of money lenders. It is very hard to say that a poor tribal becomes a wealthy tribal by the infusion of MF (a lot depends on the entrepreneurship skill of an individual), however, it plays a vital role in protecting the tribal's need for capital building.[11]

However, few deaths from micro credit have also reported in the country. Surendra Sharma reported in *Times of India,* 16 September 2006, that more than 60 self-help group (SHG) members in Andhra Pradesh in SHG-saturated districts of Krishna, East Godavari, Guntur and Prakasam had committed suicide, this shows the negative face of MFI in India, whereas few people believe that MF is a pure technical topic rather it is "Micro Banking", no room for charity, which is almost irrelevant to compare with the actual soul of micro finance. The pillars of micro finance have grown on the base of capacity building of poor, needy and vulnerable section of the society. Government is also turned up with many projects and programmes based on micro finance, "Swarnjayanti Gram Swarozgar Yojana" (SGSY) is one of them, which provides support to many civil society organizations to format and nurture the self help groups and link them with banks. But due ambiguity in crystal clear differentiation in credit and production line followed with lack of proper monitoring framework the impact of this scheme is not highly significant, whereas many civil society organizations have came up with acceptably successful models on micro finance their own exercises. There is a need to strengthen these kind of models in others tribal dominated areas as well, so that they may also be benefited by these efforts. Not even that Government should also come up with a clear cut guidelines and policy for Micro Finance and institution so that it can actually be tool of poverty reduction in India.

NOTES

1-5. Singh, *Average Annual Credit needs of households of different Socio-economic classes in Rannaour Block of Jhabua District* (Bhopal: Indian Institute of Forest Management, 2002). p. 1.

6. Mohummad Yunus, *Banker to the poor—the story of the Gramin Bank,* (New Delhi: Penguin Book India Publication, 2007), p. 82.

7. Astad Pastaki, *Promoting Microfinance in the Tribal district of Jhabua (MP) & Dahod (Gujarat),* an evaluation study, (Bhopal: Action for Social Advancement, 2002).

8. Source: *http://www.jhabua.nic.in/factfile.htm*

9. Fisher, Thomas and Sriram, M.S., *Micro-finance and social and economic security,* (New Delhi: Vistaar Publications, 2002).

10. Mohummad Yunus, *Banker to the poor- the story of the Gramin Bank,* (New Delhi: Penguin Book India Publication, 2007) p. 233.

11. Sapana Dubey, *Impact of Microfinance Programme on the migration trends of Tribal people,* (Bhopal: Action for Social Advancement, 2006) p. 3.

REFERENCES

Dubey, Sapana, (2006): *Impact of Microfinance Programme on the migration trends of Tribal people,* Bhopal: Action for Social Advancement.

Fisher, Thomas and Sriram, M.S.(2002): *Micro-finance and social and economic security,* New Delhi: Vistaar Publications.

Khandker, S. (2003): "Micro finance and Poverty: Evidence Using Panel Data from Bangladesh," *World Bank Policy Research Paper 2945,* Washington: World Bank.

Pastaki, A. (2002): *Promoting Microfinance in the Tribal district of Jhabua (MP) & Dohad (Gujarat)—An evaluation Study*. Bhopal: Action for Social Advancement.

Robinson, Marguerite (2001): *The Microfinance Revolution: Sustainable Finance for the Poor.* Washington DC: The World Bank.

Sharma, S. (2006): "Death by Micro-credit", *Times of India,* 16th September.

Singh. S, (2002): *Average Annual Credit needs of households of different Socio-economic classes in Rannaour Block of Jhabua District,* Bhopal: Indian Institute of Forest Management.

Tucker Michael and Miles Gerard : "Financial Performance of Microfinance Institutions: A comparison to performance of Regional Commercial Banks by Geographic Regions.", *Journal of Microfinance,* Volume 6, No. 1, pp. 41-79.

Yunus, Mohummad (2007): *Bankers of the poor—The story of the Gramin Bank,* New Delhi: Penguin Book of India Publication.

19 Evaluation of Kasturba Gandhi Balika Vidyalaya

Status of Residential Facilities and Community Mobilization in Jhabua District of Madhya Pradesh

Asha Shukla, Jaya Phookan and *Tripti Singhai*

Introduction

Education of girls and women in general has been a high priority with Government of India and many initiatives have been taken in this regard. In the new millennium, India has consolidated its earlier educational reforms with increased resources and stronger policy commitments for achieving elementary education for all children, particularly girls.

Efforts are being made to generate a community demand for girl's education and enabling conditions for community and women participation, to create the push factors necessary to guarantee girl's education. Motivation and mobilization of parents and community at large, enhancing the role of women and mothers in school related activities and participation in school committees, and strengthening the linkages between the school, teachers and communities are some of the ways in which the enabling conditions are created.

In India 20 per cent of children aged between 6 to 14 years, the majority of whom are girls, are still not in the school (*source :* UNICEF website).UNICEF (2005) stated that the girls' education is one of its priorities. UNICEF is working with governments and range of partners to achieve robust and sustainable gains in gender parity in primary and secondary education. To tackle this problem, the Government of India amended the Constitution in 2003 to make elementary education a 'Fundamental Right'.

There are several functional schemes planned in order to lay emphasis on girl's education. The National Programme of Education for Girls at elementary level (NPEGEL) is one such scheme which is being implemented in 61 educationally backward blocks of 21 districts. The programme, launched in September 2003, provides additional components of education of girls at the elementary stage, specially from disadvantaged communities, such as the development of a model upper-primary school in each cluster. It offers material incentives such as stationery, and introduces additional interventions like awards, remedial teaching, and bridge courses (Krishna Kumar and Latika Gupta: 2008).

Sarva Siksha Abhiyan (SSA) is aimed at ensuring that by 2010, all children will be receiving eight years of basic education of acceptable quality, regardless of sex, caste, creed, family income or location. The SSA programme has involved increased investments in classroom construction, teacher recruitment and development, but it has also involved innovative project such as 'Education Camps for Girls' (Balika Sikshan Shivirs).

Sarva Siksha Abhiyan(SSA) was launched in 2000-01 across the country as a centrally sponsored scheme with the primary objectives of Universalization of Elementary Education through the provision of community owned school system. The SSA is a historic stride towards achieving the long cherished goal of Universalisation of Elementary Education (UEE) through a time-bound integrated approach, in partnership with the states it aims to change the face of elementary education in the country by providing useful and quality elementary education to all children in the age group of 6-14 years by 2010.

Rajshekhar (2005) stated that the education of illiterate had been one of the major national concerns of the government of India since Independence. The need for a literate population was recognized as a crucial input for nation building. To address these issues and as per its commitment to the common minimum programme, the Central Government is giving priority for literacy programme. Apart from giving thrust to elementary education programme like Sarva Siksha Abhiyan, the government has approved a new scheme called Kasturba Gandhi Balika Vidyalaya. The scheme is implemented in 20 states, Andhra Pradesh has taken the lead in getting sanction for setting up of 94 schools followed by Jharkahnd (74) and Madhya Pradesh (70) schools.

Save the Children (2006) newsletter says that understanding the barrier to girls' education in particular is the key to launching our innovative approaches. Educating girls and women results in:

- Healthier, better educated children and grandchildren
- Fewer maternal deaths
- Delayed marriage and better parenting skills
- Improved literacy and numeracy skills leading to greater economic opportunities
- More skills and knowledge enhancing women's self-esteem and well-being of families.

Innovations and specific strategies targeting girls and ensuring their enrolment and retention in schools have been extremely important for achieving gender parity. The Central and State governments have already recognized this as a thrust area and have initiated a number of initiatives such as providing free text books, gender sensitization of teachers, community mobilization and formation of MTAs, providing separate toilets, engendered curriculum, pre-school education etc.

KGBV Scheme

One exception in the scenario of girls' education is the Kasturba Gandhi Balika Vidyalaya (KGBV) scheme which is running under the SSA and accounts for about 7 per cent of its total outlay. The basic idea under pinning the scheme is to give a second chance fro mainstreaming rural girls belonging to deprived social backgrounds who could not study up to or beyond class V. The second opportunity consists of the facility to stay in the hostel while studying for the upper primary stage of elementary education, namely classes VI to VIII. The KGBV scheme draws it legitimacy from the thrust in national policy documents and international discourses on the 'gender gap'. Following this thrust, the scheme has been implemented in educationally backward blocks with wider gender gap. The social categories covered are the Scheduled Castes (SC), Scheduled Tribes (ST), other backward classes (OBC), religious minorities, and below poverty line (BPL) households. The scheme offers three models, the first consisting of a hostel-cum-school for 100 girls, the second providing the same for 50 girls, and the third offering only a 50-seat hostel attached to an existing upper primary school. As all the girls are primary school "drop-outs", they are above ten years of age and mostly in their teens. Enrolment requires mobilization among families of the designated eligible groups (Krishna Kumar and Latika Gupta, 2008).

Current figures indicate that more than 1,00,000 girls are studying in some 2,000 KGBVs across the country. Once enrolled at a KGBV, the girls go through a bridge course which attempts to cover the knowledge and skills required for negotiating the class VI curriculum. Although there is a considerable variety in the length and content of the bridge course offered in different parts of the country, most of them include components that have been neglected in the curricula of most states packaged under labels like "Life skills", such components offer empowerment strategies, such as personal development, communication capacity and health related activities (*ibid.*).

The scheme has been coordinated with the existing scheme of Department of Elementary Education and Literacy, viz. SSA, National Programme for Education of Girls at Elementary Level and Mahila Samakhya (MS). The design of the scheme means that only educationally backward blocks (EBBs) can be covered under the scheme. KGBV is a unique scheme which provides free and quality education to the girls belonging to SC, ST, OBC or minority communities and female children hailing from families below poverty line of backward blocks, with the residential facilities at elementary level. So far 70 KGBVs have started functioning in Madhya Pradesh State. According to State Government Declaration, April, 2005—the seventy blocks where the KGBV are being established have rural female literacy rate below the national average (54.2) and gender gap in literacy is more than the national average there. A sum of 70 crore rupees has been sanctioned for these schools during this year.

Scope/coverage of the scheme

The scheme is applicable only in those EBBs where, as per census data of 2001, the rural female literacy is below the national average and gender gap in literacy is more than the national average. Among these blocks, KGBVs can be opened in areas with:

- Concentration of tribal population with low female

literacy or a large number of girls still remain out of school
- Areas with low female literacy
- Areas with large number of small, scattered habitations that do not qualify for a school
- The criteria for eligible the EBB is same as in the NPEGEL scheme of SSA.

Target Beneficiaries

- Out of school girls who are unable to complete upper primary education in difficult areas.
- Adolescent girls who are unable to go to regular school (upper primary level).
- Younger girls of migratory population in difficult areas/ scattered habitation that do not qualify for upper primary school.
- Priority of 75 per cent enrolment to girls from SC/ST/ OBC and minority communities and 25 per cent to girls from BPL.

Objectives of KGBV

The objectives of Kasturba Gandhi Balika Vidyalaya (KGBV) are:

- Ensure access to elementary education to the disadvantaged group of society
- Provide quality education of accepted national standard
- Bring in female children with non-stream of education
- Achieve the goal of UEE
- Impart life- skilled based education needed for women's self-reliance and respect
- To make school environment of girls, child friendly

Strategies

- Initially, the prepared KGBVs shall be opened in a phased manner in rented or other government building
- Such residential schools will be set up in those backward blocks that do not have residential schools for elementary education of girls under any scheme of Ministry of Social Justice and Empowerment and Ministry of Tribal Affairs.
- This shall be ensured by the District level authority.

Components of KGBV scheme

- Setting up of residential schools where there are a minimum of 50 girls predominantly from the SC, ST and minorities communities available to the study in the school at the elementary level. Females of families under poverty line can also be considered for admission in KGBV.
- Provide necessary infrastructure for these schools.
- Prepare and procure necessary teaching-learning material and aids for the school.
- Put in place appropriate systems to provide necessary academic support for evaluation and monitoring.
- Motivate and prepare girls and their families to send them to residential schools.
- The emphasis shall be on slightly older girls who are out of school and are unable to complete primary education.
- At the upper primary level, the emphasis will be in girls, especially adolescent girls who are unable to join regular schools.
- In view of the targeted nature of the scheme, 75 per cent girls from SC, ST, OBC or minorities communities

would be accorded priority for enrolment in KGBVs and only thereafter, 25 per cent girls from below poverty line will be considered.

- Established NGOs and other non-profit making bodies will be involved in running of the schools, wherever possible. These residential schools can also be adopted by the corporate groups.

Implementation, Monitoring, Evaluation and Training

- The scheme has been implemented by the State Government through Mahila Samakhya (MS) Society and through SSA society.
- Funds will be released as per SSA pattern to the state SSA societies/MS societies.
- Monitoring and evaluation at the state and district level will be undertaken by the MS state resource centres. In non-MS states, through the committee created for the NPEGEL in the SSA society.
- Training of teachers and stage of residential schools will be coordinated by the District Institutes of Education Training (DIET), Block Resource Centres (BRCs) and Mahila Samakhya (MS) resource groups.
- Community led monitoring shall be encouraged to ensure enrolment, retention, regularity, punctuality and promoting female children to 10th level as well.

Present Study

Jhabua District

Present study was carried out in Jhabua District of Madhya Pradesh. Jhabua is predominantly a tribal district which is one of the most backward districts of the state. The literacy rate according to 2001 census is 36.87 per cent with female literacy rate with only 4 per cent. It is a sparsely populated area with the total population of 13.94 lakhs according to 2001 census.

Table 19.1 : Demographic Status of Jhabua district

Sl. No.	*Demographic parameters*	*Exhibiting data*	*Percentage*
1.	Geographical	6782 sq.km	—
2.	Total literacy rate	—	37.80
3.	Total population	1394563	—
4.	Male population	702055	50.34
5.	Female population	692508	49.66
6.	Children population (6-14yrs)	395169	—
7.	Population of boys	213125	53.93
8.	Population of girls	182044	46.07

Sample Selection

In order to conduct the present study on Kasturba Gandhi Balika Vidyalaya in Madhya Pradesh, the researcher took the Jhabua district as a purposive sample where all the three KGBV were studied comprehensively. This study covered all the three blocks of Jhabua district where this scheme has been implemented:

1. Kardawad, Badi, Jhabua Block.
2. Kardawad, Petlawad Block.
3. Bedawa, Thandla Block

Development of Tools

In order to develop tools for conduction of the main study pre-survey was carried out in KGBV of Kamtirangpur village of Hoshangabad District. Two workshops were organized for discussion and development of tools. As a part of Pilot study, the investigators visited the target residential schools. For this purpose KGBV centre running in village Kardawad Badi in

Jhabua Block was selected. The third workshop was organized for finalization of tools. Tools and techniques like Questionnaires, Interview schedules, Case study, Reliability and validity of tools were used for data collection.

Data Collection

Data was collected in two Phases: In the I phase, the investigators visited the target group and questionnaires were administered on all the KGBVs. Besides the administration of these scales the critical observations of the team were also made to receive much other information. In the second phase, the investigators again visited the including sample hostels in the study and interview schedules were administered on all the target groups especially on girls who are residing there and community case study form were filled up by the three girls enrolled in KGBV hostel but non resident girl. Data was analysed on the form of content analysis.

Research Questions

Residential Profile of KGBV

- Did the building selected for KGBV, suit to the enrolled girls for studies, living purpose and allied activities?
- Did the building facilities possess necessary facilities—electric light, proper air, alternative light arrangements, kitchen, store rooms, toilets, bathrooms, playground etc.?

Community Mobilization

- How did the community get the information about the KGBVs and its purpose?
- Are the nodal agencies responsible for mobilizing playing their role effectively?

- Participation of community.

Discussion

Table 19.2 shows the details of present KGBV centres established in the village Kardawad Badi, Kardawad and Bedwa of Jhabua, Petlawad and Thandla Block which were 8 km, 72 km and 68km away from the Jhabua Headquarter respectively. All the three KGBV are running since 1 July 2005.

The two KGBV (Kardawad and Bedawa) centre running in the building allotted by the State Government and one KGBV (Kardawad Badi) centre is running in the building rented by the government. The cenres have started 75 residential seats for girls and number of girls enrolled at the KGBV centre was also 75.

Table 19.3 shows that all the three KGBV centres have two big rooms of maximum seating capacity of about 30 girls and out of three, two have reported one small room and and one has reported two small rooms. Still it is true that both these rooms do not cover with the sufficient space for girls. Each centre has kitchens with 2 toilets and two bathrooms, which is not sufficient as per number of the enrolled girls. All have reported playground.

Electric supply was also a great problem there. As a result mostly all the centres use candle and chimni as an alternative measure. On the whole condition of building was not found satisfactory and space was not found sufficient for such a bigger group of girls.

Krishana Kumar and Latika Gupta (2008) while evaluating the performance of KGBV in Uttar Pradesh noticed that the crowded dormitories in which the girls sleep are similarly converted into classroom during the day. The rather depressing reality of the KGBV scheme is not unusual. Most schemes aimed

Table 19. 2 : Showing General Information of the KGBVs at Jhabua District

Sl. No.	*Name of the centre*	*Distance form head-quarters*	*Name of the block*	*Name of the village*	*Govern-ment*	*Rented*	*Donated*	*Date of Functioning*	*No. of seats enrolled*	*No. of children enrolled*
1.	KGBV-Kardawad Badi	Approx. 8 km	Jhabua	Kardawad Badi		Rented		1 July 05	75	75
2.	KGBV Kardawad Petlawad	72 km	Petlawad	Kardawad Petlawad	Govt. Buldg.			1 July 05	75	75
3.	KGBV Bedawa	68 km	Thandla	Bedawa	Govt. Buldg.			1 July 05	75	75

Table 19.3 : Showing Infrastructural facilities in KGBV

Sl. No.	*Name of the centre*			*Toilets*	*Bath-rooms*	*Kit-chen*	*Play-ground*	*Electri-city*	*Alternative measures*			*Condition of Building*
		Big	*Small*						*E light*	*Candle*	*Chimney*	
	KGBV-Kardawad Badi	2	2	1	1	Yes	inadequate	Yes Supply uncertain	–	Candle	Chimney	Unsatis-factory
	KGBV Kardawad Petlawad	2	1	2	2	Yes	adequate	Yes Supply uncertain	E light	Candle	Chimney	Unsatis-factory
	KGBV Bedawa	2	1	2	2	Yes	adequate	Yes Supply uncertain	E light	Candle	Chimney	Unsatis-factory

at children belonging to the poor section of society have a minimalistic orientation. Their design reflects such a drastic lack of estimation of the basic necessities of life that they seem no better than acts of organized charity. The recipients are assumed to be satisfied with whatever is given. The compromises inherent in the design of the KGBV scheme are sharp indeed. Hygiene and good health, for example, constitute a focus for the scheme, but many KGBVs manage with three/five toilets for 80/100 young girls. The scheme's planning lacks any professional understanding of girls as human beings and as learners (Krishna Kumar and Latika Gupta, 2008).

Table 19.4 indicates that attendance of girl students was deviated in all the three centres in 3 visits by the researchers. The reasons for absenteeism of the girls are many: Poverty and household responsibilities force them to leave the school. Secondly, because of migration of whole family in other states for jobs increases absenteesim. They take the girls with them or they inclined to get married at a very early age.

Table 19.3 : Showing Attendance Details

Sl. No.	*Seats allocated*	*Attendence as per records*	*No.of Visits*		
			Ist visit	*IInd visit*	*IIIrd visit*
1*	75	75	48(64%)	48(64%)	45(60%)
2*	75	75	65(86.66%)	65(86.66%)	69(92%)
3*	75	75	61(81.33%)	61(81.33%)	69(92%)

1*— *Kardawad Badi* (KGBV), 2*—*Kardawad Petlawad* (KGBV), 3*—*Bedawa* (KGBV)

An educational opportunity cannot be limited to bringing girls to a school and keeping them there. The aim of education in democracy is to enable all children to realise their right to participate in governance as sensitive and responsible citizens who are also capable of shaping their personal destiny. This is a difficult aim to achieve for all children who come from dalit, tribal, minority and other groups among the poor. For girls belonging to these groups, every battle is twofold. They not only have to face the community's general deprivation, they also have to fight the negative and suppressive forces which every girl faces in our society (Krishna Kumar and Latika Gupta: 2008).

In order to make cent per cent attendance in these residential centres motivation camps should be organized to aware their parents and their guardians, so that they may know the value of education of these girls. Secondly, the teaching and hostel management staff should be trained with teaching and administrative skills, so that proper education and facilities may be provided to the target group. Further, the psychological environment of the centre should be very cordial, cooperative and enjoyful with proper understanding between pears and teachers, so it will motivate these girls to continue their study in the centre.

Table 19.4 shows that motivation camp was organized for 3 days and targeted 75 girls students were selected in each hostel. In KGBV at Kardawad Badi, out of 75 girls, 94.66 per cent were ST, 4 per cent were SC and 1.33 per cent was of OBC category out of which 4 per cent belonged to the category of handicapped.

Table 19.4 : Information about Motivation Camp

Sl. No.	*Number of organized motivation camp*	*Duration of motivation camps*	*No. of girls selected after motivation camps As per record (06)*	*Category status*			*Handicapped*
				ST	*SC*	*OBC*	
1*	1	3	75	71(94.66%)	3(4%)	1(1.33%)	3(4%)
2*	1	3	75	74(98.66%)	1(1.33%)	–	4(5.33%)
3*	1	3	75	75(100%)	–	–	6(8%)

1*—*Kardawad Badi* (KGBV), 2*—*Kardawad Petlawad* (KGBV), 3*—*Bedawa* (KGBV).

KGBV at Kardawad village, out of 75 girls 98.66 per cent were ST, 1.33 per cent were SC out of which 5.33 per cent belonged to physically disabled category.

KGBV at Bedawa village belonged to 100 per cent girls from ST category out of which 8 per cent were physically challenged.

It was found that motivation camps were very successful in motivating the girls and parents for residential education so that they may receive formal and informal education at all times.

Table 19.5 shows better coordination and parental representation in the residential programme of education. Parent-Teacher Association was formed on the basis of top 10 to 15 meritorious students. Their parents were selected for this PTA. In all the associations, meeting held once in a month where educational, financial facilities and other distributed material were evaluated for proper use of the girls. But parents participation was minimal in terms of educational input.

Table 19.5 : Information about Parent Teacher Association

Sl. No.	*No. of PTA members*	*Organized meetings of PTA*	*PTA meeting*				*The account open for the hostel*	*Type of account*
			Educational	*Financial*	*Distributional*	*Facilities*		
1*	15	monthly	–	Yes	Yes	Yes	Rural Bank, Jhabua	Joint
2*	10	monthly	Yes	Yes	Yes	Yes	SBI Indore, Petlawad	Joint
3*	15	monthly	–	Yes	Yes	Yes	Rural Bank, Thandla	Joint

1*—*Kardawad Badi* (KGBV), 2*—*Kardawad Petlawad* (KGBV). 3*—*Bedawa* (KGBV).

Table 19.6 shows that the information regarding this programme is given by *panch/sarpanch* of the village as 80 per cent of the villagers were informed about the programme by *Sarpanch* and remaining 20 per cent were informed by the teachers of these schools rating to this scheme. But it is suggested that the community should have the knowledge of this type of programme by door to door communication from various community members, so that they may also convince them about the advantages of this programme for the better development of girls. It is also noticed by communicating with the parents of other girls who are not taking this type of education programme. They reported that although they wish to motivate their daughters to take such type of education but due to the financial constraints in the family they involve their daughters in home activities as well as other livelihood related activities.

Table 19.6 : Information about Parent Community View

Sl.	*Contact with the community*			*Causes of Not sending girl child to school*			
No.	*Panch/ Sarpanch*	*Officers*	*Teachers*	*Poverty*	*Household work*	*Agricultural work*	*Lack of awareness*
1.	50%	NIL	50%	NIL	90%	10%	NIL
2.	70%	10%	20%	NIL	50%	20%	30%
3.	80%	20%	NIL	NIL	80%	NIL	20%

1*—*Kardawad Badi* (KGBV), 2*—*Kardawad Petlawad* (KGBV), 3*—*Bedawa* (KGBV).

Some Observations

- Condition of building was not satisfactory and total space was not sufficient for such a bigger group of girls.
- Drinking water facilities were not found adequate as per norms.
- Although kitchen was well equipped but electric supply was a great problem.
- It was found that proper health facilities were provided in all the three hostels. Facilities like first aid, accessibility to primary health centres was found in all the centres.

- Regular monthly health checkups were done by the nurses and medical staff but medical check up cards were not prepared in any of the KGBV as per norms of KGBV scheme.
- PTA are not showing major concern for educational development of KGBVs.
- State and district authorities are not giving sincere emphasis for motivational camps to mobilize communities.
- Cleanliness was found in all the hostels at satisfactory level because girls were also cooperating in the cleanliness work.
- The security arrangements were also proper and girl's parents and the other members of the community felt high satisfaction in respect of security.
- Early marriage remains one of the major reason for girls drop-out
- Girls are employed in a variety of work that is crucial in poor families as it has a bearing on family livelihood. Apart from the conventional responsibility of sibling care, household chores are the other reasons for leaving the school.
- Many communities still do not consider it appropriate to send girls to school. They easily withdraw their daughter from the schools due to distance, security reasons and cultural customs.
- Girl children helping parents in their work is a social norm in many tribal communities. The involvement of children in livelihood activities, cattle razing, collection of forest production etc. makes it difficult for them to attend the school.
- Poverty and unawareness are the greatest obstacles in the way of education in the tribal areas.
- Migration in search of employment is another reason.

Conclusion

The KGBV is a innovative concept through which attempt has been made to provide second chance for mainstreaming rural girls belonging to marginalized and deprived social backgrounds who could not study up to or beyond class V. The second chance gives them an opportunity to stay in the hostel while studying for the upper primary stage of elementary education. There are certain guidelines and norms which are to be followed for residential arrangements to cater to the needs of the girls staying in the hostel. And in the absence of proper infrastructural facilities and comfortable environment for education, the scheme would not be able to achieve its objectives. It is evident from the study carried out in KGBV of Jhabua District that in all the three KGBVs, condition of building was not satisfactory and total space was not sufficient for such a bigger group of girls. Construction of the building was not according to the norms of the KGBV, therefore, separate building as per norms of the KGBV scheme should be constructed so that proper facilities may be available for girls. Toilets, sanitation facilities were not satisfactory as per norms. Therefore it is recommended that proper building facilities should be provided to these schools so that the girls may have the good education climate. It was found that motivation camps were organized for the sensitization of parents and girls were selected for KGBVs as per norms. But for their sustainability in the KGBV, regular motivation camps should be organized. People's participation, therefore, is recognized as a basic component for improving elementary education programme in terms of both quantitative and qualitative monitoring at the local community, state level and national level. The families of non-school going girls should be motivated to send them to school. For this, mass contact programme and motivation camp should be organized. Parent teacher association (PTAs) which have been formed should be more participative both from parents and teacher's side. At primary level attention should be focused on girls (10+) who are unable to complete primary education.

The KGBV is a timely initiative to address the problems arising out of systemic anomalies and cultural barriers impeding girls' education and development. More efforts should be made both at the level of planning and implementation to make the scheme a successful endeavour.

REFERENCES

Kumar, Krishna and Latika Gupta (2008): "What is Missing in Girls' Empowerment?" *Economic and Political Weekly*, Vol. XLIII No. 26 and 27.

Newsletter (2006). Save the Children, Girls Education, USA, pp. 1 & 2.

Govt. of India (2002-05). *Sarva Shiksha Abhiyan: A Programme for Universal Elementary Education Framework for Implementation*, Department of School Education and Literacy, pp. 1 & 7.

Evaluation of Kasturba Gandhi Balika Vidyalaya in Jhabua District, Madhya Pradesh: A Research Study by Women' Studies Centre, Barkatullah University, Bhopal in the year 2007.

Rajsekhar, V. (2005): Kasturba Gandhi Balika Vidyalaya: A Ray of Hope for Educationally Backward Girls, Government of India, Press release, Friday, May 20, pp. 1& 2.

State Govt. Declaration (2005): 70 Kasturba Gandhi Balika Vidyalayas in Backward Areas of Madhya Pradesh from this session. April 30, Saturday, Bhopal.

UNICEF (2005): Girls Education Campaign by 2005: accelerating progress in girls education, UNICEF NEWS, pp. 1 & 2.

Benefits of Girls Education, pp. 1 & 2.

http://sage.acd.org_/ *practice / benefits.html*

Education-Girls Education. pp. 1 & 3.

http://web.worldbank.org/*WBSITE/ EXTERNAL/TOPICS/ EXTEDUCATION/US content.*

Kasturba Gandhi Balika Vidyalaya: A Ray of hope for educationally backward girls. V. Rajshekhar, Friday, May 20, 2005.

PIB—Press Information Bureau
http//pib.nic.in / release/ release.asp?relict = 9407
NPEGEL. http://www.opepa.in / *npegel.asp?glink = GL010 & plink = PL102*
SSA. http://www.opepa.in / *ssa_new.asp?glink = GL010 & plink = PL101 & se/plink = PL101.*
Sarva Shiksha Abhiyan – Progamme for Universal for Elementary Education in India, pp 1 & 4, Oct. – Dec. 2000 (Janshala).
http://www.un.org.in / *JANSHALA / Oct.- Dec. 2000 / sarva.htm*
Save the Children: Girls Education, pp. 1 & 2.
http://www.savethechildren.*org/education/girls.asp*
UNICEF India—Education, pp. 1 of 3. Girls form tribal villages going access to higher education. http://www.unicef.org/india education_1028.htm

Index